THE
UNITED NATIONS
CONSPIRACY

THE
UNITED NATIONS
CONSPIRACY

by Robert W. Lee

WESTERN ISLANDS

PUBLISHERS

BOSTON   LOS ANGELES

Published by
Western Islands
395 Concord Avenue
Belmont, Massachusetts 02178

Printed in the United States of America
ISBN: 0-88279-236-9

To
Mom and Dad
Karen
Mike, Gary, Reed, Bruce, Larry
— and Snooks

CONTENTS

A Note Of Interest

An idler, looking up at the narrow side of the Secretariat Building from Forty-second Street, spoke cynically to his companion.

"You know why they built it that way?" he asked. "Like a matchbox sitting on one end? They did it so, when they get ready, they can strike a match down the side and the whole thing'll go up in smoke."

UN: Today and Tomorrow by Eleanor Roosevelt and William DeWitt (New York: Harper & Brothers, 1953), p. 35.

Foreword

The United Nations is in serious trouble. The American people have finally begun to recognize the world organization for what it is — a pro-Communist force designed to enslave us in World Government — rather than the peacekeeping entity its advocates have claimed it to be.

In 1959, the Gallup Poll reported that eighty-seven percent of the American people thought that the UN was doing a good job.[1] Four years later, polls were claiming eighty percent support.[2] But on UN Day, October 24, 1970, Thomas Vail, a member of the President's Commission for the Observance of the 25th Anniversary of the United Nations, told an audience in Des Moines, Iowa, "Public faith in the U.N. peacekeeping ability has declined from eighty percent to fifty percent."[3] In 1971 Dr. Gallup reported a drop to thirty-five percent,[4] and in 1973 U.S. Ambassador to the UN John Scali referred to a poll indicating that only thirty-four percent of the American people thought the UN was doing an effective job.[5] By January, 1976 the Gallup Poll revealed that support for the UN had fallen to an all-time low of thirty-three percent, with an actual majority of those polled (fifty-one percent) specifically asserting that the UN was doing a "poor job."[6] And, on November 19, 1980, Dr. Gallup released the results of yet another poll which revealed: "The public's rating of the United Nations' performance has declined to a 35-year low. Currently, only three Americans in 10 (31 percent) feel the U.N. is doing a 'good job' in trying to solve the problems it has had to face, while 53 percent feel it is doing a 'poor job.'" Dr. Gallup then notes that his poll "has measured the public's attitudes toward the U.N. since its formation in 1945, using questions appropriate to the international situation at the time. At no point since then has satisfaction with the overall performance of the world organization been as low as it is today."[7]

This mounting antagonism toward the UN has been reflected in many other ways as well. For example, visitors to UN headquarters in New York City numbered over one million in 1967,

x The United Nations Conspiracy

but dropped to 765,000 in 1972, and plunged an additional thirteen percent in 1973.[8] In 1975, an unidentified member of the US mission to the UN lamented, ". . . there are even some Congressmen calling for us to quit the U.N. altogether . . . believe me, those of us involved with, and concerned about, the organization are pretty damned worried."[9] In March of that year, Senator Charles Percy (R.-Illinois) reported, "Criticism of the United Nations has probably never been greater than it is now in the United States,"[10] while his Democrat colleague, Senator Dick Clark of Iowa, stated two months later, "It is becoming fashionable to be against the U.N."[11] In November, 1975, Senator Gale McGee (D.-Wyoming) reinforced these statements by asserting, "I have never seen the anti-U.N. sentiment within the Congress so strong in my 17 years as a U.S. Senator."[12] And in May, 1976, Assistant Secretary of State for International Organization Affairs Samuel W. Lewis told an audience in Milwaukee, "The polls show that public regard for the UN has recently reached a new low. . . . And more Americans are writing to us, calling for the U.S. to leave the UN if it does not 'mend its ways'."[13]

During 1977 alone, at least fifteen separate bills and Resolutions were introduced in the House and Senate to limit or reduce U.S. contributions to the UN; and yet another demanded the impeachment of UN Ambassador Andrew Young.[14] Meanwhile the news media are increasingly critical of the UN, with many of those who have defended the world body taking a second look, and others who have grudgingly tolerated it concluding that the time has come for the United States to get out.

These withdrawal symptoms are encouraging, for they apparently mean we are moving ever closer to the day when we will get the UN monkey off our back. As an editorial in the *Arizona Republic* put it:

When the United Nations once was generally considered a respectable forum for maintaining some semblance of world harmony, the John Birch Society virtually was alone in its billboard demands to "Get US out of The U.N."

Time and events seem to prove the Birch Society may simply
have been ahead of its time.
 The U.N. has lost its sacred cow standing. Members of
Congress, the man on the street and the media have been showing
increased belligerence to the U.N.[15]

Time is always on the side of truth. Today the UN is
increasingly regarded not as a sacred cow, but rather as a troika
composed of a white elephant, a Trojan horse, and a Judas goat.
 White elephants were the rare albino pachyderms that tradi-
tionally belonged to Siamese kings, who would then present
them to courtiers they didn't like. Since white elephants were
not allowed to work, could not be disposed of without offending
the king, and had enormous appetites, they would eventually
reduce the courtier to ruin. The United Nations, a "gift" to our
country from its founders, has had roughly the same destructive impact. The decline of our national honor, influence, and
independence since 1945 has resulted in large part from the
manner in which our foreign policy (and much of our domestic
policy) has been molded to meet United Nations specifications.
 The Trojan horse was presented as an offering of peace and
good will to the people of Troy; in fact, it was loaded with
Athenian warriors bent on Troy's destruction. The main difference between the Trojan horse and the UN is that the Trojans
didn't know that the horse contained their enemies; the UN, on
the other hand, was wheeled into New York City with the full
knowledge of our leaders that its key posts were controlled by
Communists and other anti-Americans, and that diplomatic
immunity would give our enemies a protected base for their
operations within our borders. As the late FBI Director J. Edgar
Hoover warned in 1971:

 Red Chinese intelligence in the United States, as compared
 with Soviet Russia's, has a major handicap in that Peking is
 not . . . a member of the United Nations. This deprives the Red
 Chinese of a legal base from which to operate spies. A high
 percentage of Soviet espionage, for example, is carried out by

Soviet diplomats assigned to . . . the USSR's Mission to the
United Nations in New York.[16]

Of course, the "problem" of Red Chinese recognition by the
UN was solved later that same year when President Richard
Nixon and Secretary of State Henry Kissinger successfully
maneuvered Red China into the world body.

Judas goats are animals trained to lead other animals peace-
fully to slaughter. Their job is to keep the victims deluded about
their actual situation until it is too late to do anything about it.
Similarly, propagandists for the UN have consistently misled
the American people regarding the true nature of the world
body. They imply that it is carrying us along the road to peace
when, as we shall see, it is taking us down the garden path
toward a Marxist-oriented World Government. Such deception
has become so salient a feature of the United Nations operation
that it is doubtful the organization could survive without it. In
fact, it is largely because Americans are finally catching on to
the subterfuge that the UN is in such hot water today.

The following chapters are intended to hasten the exposure
of this deceit.

THE
UNITED NATIONS
CONSPIRACY

*World War I witnessed physical destruction, bloodletting,
and social disorganization on a scale seldom equaled in human
society to that time. It furnished a powerful stimulus to an
often complacent Victorian world for eliminating war and
creating machinery for nonviolent adjustment of disagreements
in the world community. Out of the "war to end wars" and to
"make the world safe for democracy" came intensive and
widespread study of methods for setting up a viable
international organization. From numerous sources, both official
and private, suggestions and proposals were made which finally
coalesced into the Covenant of the League of Nations . . . .*
— Cecil V. Crabb, Jr.[1]

Chapter 1

Setting The Stage

Colonel Edward Mandell House was President Woodrow
Wilson's closest and most influential adviser. A powerful be-
hind-the-scenes manipulator, House had enormous influence in
shaping Wilson's domestic and foreign policies to support economic collectivism and political internationalism. As noted by
one biographer:

> For all his might, Wilson could not stand alone. In every
> fruitful enterprise he borrowed the Colonel's brain. I shall not
> impute feet of clay to the idol. I concede they are living flesh.
> But they are not his own. Woodrow Wilson stalks through history
> on the feet of Edward Mandell House.[2]

Colonel House wrote the first draft of the League of Nations
covenant[3] and, in September, 1917, convinced President Wilson
to commission a group of "intellectuals" to devise terms for
peace and draft a program for a world government.[4] The group,
later known as The Inquiry, consisted of some highly talented
individuals, many of whose names later became household

4 The United Nations Conspiracy

words as prominent journalists, top government officials, and influential academicians. For instance:

> Sidney Mezes, House's brother-in-law and president of the City College of New York, was named director. James T. Shotwell was in charge of historical geography and then of the library. There was [sic] Christian A. Herter, later to become Secretary of State, and Norman Thomas, a Marxian Socialist. And the secretary was a gentleman named Walter Lippmann . . . .
> And then there were a couple of brothers, enterprising chaps — Allen Welsh Dulles [later Director of the Central Intelligence Agency] and John Foster Dulles [later Secretary of State].[5]

President Wilson drew heavily upon the work of The Inquiry in formulating his famous Fourteen Points program which was presented to Congress on January 18, 1918, as a peace strategy to save the world.[6] The group incorporated various peace proposals and the League of Nations covenant into the document, which the United States rejected first on November 19, 1919, and again on March 20, 1920.[7]

American Internationalists expected the frustration and disruption generated by World War I to condition the American people so the United States could be enticed into the League of Nations as an alleged means of avoiding future wars.

However, by the spring of 1919 it had already become clear that the League would face serious, possibly fatal, opposition in the United States Senate. Colonel House and a few of his followers therefore began laying groundwork for a long-range effort to condition Americans to accept eventual United States membership in a supranational organization steeped in their particular brand of collectivist internationalism. If World War I couldn't do it then perhaps some later conflict could, for as Alexander Hamilton had recognized decades earlier:

> Safety from external danger is the most powerful director of national conduct. Even the ardent love of liberty will after a time, give way to its dictates. The violent destruction of life and property incident to war, the continual effort and alarm atten-

dant on a state of continual danger, will compel nations the most attached to liberty to resort for repose and security to institutions which have a tendency to destroy their civil and political rights. To be more safe, they at length become willing to run the risk of being less free.[8]

On May 30, 1919, Colonel House and his associates met with some like-minded Englishmen at the Majestic Hotel in Paris. The British participants subsequently established the Royal Institute for International Affairs (RIIA), while the Americans returned to the United States and founded the American Institute for International Affairs (AIIA). (See Appendix A.) The AIIA subsequently merged with the Council on Foreign Relations (CFR), a languishing discussion group which had been formed in New York during the war. The merger was formally incorporated in New York City on July 29, 1921. According to Hamilton Fish Armstrong, who served for fifty years (until October, 1972) as managing editor and editor of the CFR's influential quarterly, *Foreign Affairs*, "Besides taking the Council's name, they gained the financial backing of its public-spirited membership. They also acquired a locus, something vital if they were to continue functioning collectively and not as individuals dispersed in academic and other centers."[9]

Since that time, the CFR has greatly influenced American foreign and domestic policies to fit the designs for world government envisioned by its founders, and has conditioned the American people to accept the changes as both wise and necessary.

This is not to imply, of course, that *all* members of the CFR support the dangerous internationalism promoted by the organization as a whole. To the contrary, some members have themselves attempted to expose and clarify the group's *modus operandi* and goals. Admiral Chester Ward, for instance, a CFR member and former Judge Advocate of the United States Navy, has pointed out:

. . . the vast influence attributed to CFR is not exercised

through or by the Council on Foreign Relations as an organization.
. . . CFR, as such, does not write the platforms of both political
parties or select their respective presidential candidates, or control U.S. defense and foreign policies. But CFR members, as
individuals, acting in concert with other individual CFR members, do.[10]

The Admiral continues:

> Once the ruling members of CFR have decided that the U.S.
> Government should adopt a particular policy, the very substantial
> research facilities of CFR are put to work to develop arguments,
> intellectual and emotional, to support the new policy, and to
> confound and discredit, intellectually and politically, any opposi-
> tion. The most articulate theoreticians and ideologists prepare
> related articles, aided by the research, to sell the new policy and to
> make it appear inevitable and irresistible. By following the
> evolution of this propaganda in the most prestigious scholarly
> journal in the world, *Foreign Affairs,* anyone can determine years
> in advance what the future defense and foreign policies of the
> United States will be. If a certain proposition is repeated often
> enough in that journal, then the U.S. Administration in power —
> be it Republican or Democratic — begins to act as if that
> proposition or assumption were an established fact.[11]

Americans in recent years have been asking the question:
"Why do policies detrimental to our nation continue regardless
of which Party is in power?" An important clue to the answer
can be found in a careful study of the Council on Foreign
Relations.* As Thomas Jefferson once observed: "Single acts
of tyranny may be ascribed to the accidental opinion of a day;
but a series of oppressions, begun at a distinguished period, and
pursued unalterably through every change of ministers, too
plainly prove a deliberate, systematical plan of reducing us to
slavery."[12]

---

*See Appendix B for the complete CFR membership roster as of June 30, 1980.
An excellent source of background information on the CFR is *The CFR Packet,*
available for two dollars from American Opinion, Belmont, Massachusetts
02178.

World War II was launched by the German invasion of Poland on September 1, 1939. Even before the end of that year, influential Americans were planning for the post-war years. A CFR publication describes how the organization achieved its early influence on governmental affairs:

> Within a week [*of the war's start*], Hamilton Fish Armstrong, Editor of *Foreign Affairs*, and Walter H. Mallory, Executive Director of the Council, paid a visit to the Department of State to offer such aid on the part of the Council as might be useful and appropriate in view of the war.
> The Department was already greatly overworked as a result of the crisis. . . . The Council representatives suggested that, pending the time when the Department itself would be able to assemble a staff and begin research and analysis on the proper scale, the Council might undertake work in certain fields, without, of course, any formal assignment of responsibility on the one side or restriction of independent action on the other. . . .
> The Department officers welcomed the Council's suggestion and encouraged the Council to formulate a more detailed plan. This was done in consultation with Department officials. The Rockefeller Foundation was then approached for a grant of funds to put the plan into operation. When assurances had been received that the necessary funds would be available, the personnel of the groups were selected and on December 8, 1939, an organization meeting was held in Washington . . . .[13]

Following that meeting, the State Department established a Committee on Post-War Problems, assisted by a research staff that in February, 1941, was organized into a Division of Special Research. After the Japanese attack on Pearl Harbor, the research facilities were expanded and the overall project was reorganized into an Advisory Committee on Post-War Foreign Policies. Serving on the Committee were a number of influential CFR members, including Hamilton Fish Armstrong, Sumner Welles, Isaiah Bowman, Norman H. Davis, James T. Shotwell, Myron C. Taylor, and Leo Pasvolsky. The Russian-born Pasvolsky became the Committee's Director of Research.[14] (When

8   *The United Nations Conspiracy*

Pasvolsky died in 1953, *Time* magazine described him as "archi-
tect of the United Nations charter . . . ."[15])

On August 14, 1941, President Roosevelt and British Prime
Minister Winston Churchill signed the Atlantic Charter, claiming the need for "establishment of a wider and permanent
system of general security." The Charter makes no mention of
an international organization:

> Mr. Churchill, as we have since learned, had proposed to
> include this; but President Roosevelt was unwilling. He told Mr.
> Sumner Welles [*Undersecretary of State*] that he thought
> "nothing could be more futile than the reconstruction of a body
> such as the Assembly of the League of Nations."[16]

On January 1, 1942, the nations at war with the Axis powers
formed a wartime coalition by signing a Declaration by United
Nations pledging their adherence to the principles of the Atlantic Charter. The pieces were rapidly falling into place.

On September 21, 1943, the House of Representatives passed
the Fulbright Resolution (House Concurrent Resolution 25)
favoring "the creation of appropriate international machinery
with power adequate to establish and to maintain a just and
lasting peace, among the nations of the world" and "participation by the United States therein through its constitutional
processes." A few weeks later, in November, the Senate approved the Connally Resolution (Senate Resolution 192) that
recognized, among other things, "the necessity of there being
established at the earliest practicable date a general international organization; based on the principle of the sovereign
equality of all peace-loving states, and open to membership by
all such states, large and small, for the maintenance of international peace and security."

A month earlier, President Roosevelt had traveled to Moscow
for a meeting (October 13–30) with the Foreign Ministers of the
United Kingdom and the Soviet Union. The resulting Moscow
Declaration, to which China also became a party, committed the
four nations to close cooperation after the war and to the

establishment of an international organization to keep the peace.

The Moscow Declaration was confirmed and strengthened at subsequent high-level Conferences in Cairo (November 22–26, 1943) and Teheran (November 28–December 1, 1943). In mid-1944, draft proposals submitted by the four governments became the basis for the Dumbarton Oaks discussions (August 21–October 7, 1944) from which the basic structure of the UN emerged. The Dumbarton Oaks Conference, however, failed to reach a decision on two key points: the extent of the veto power to be exercised in the Security Council, and the number of seats each government was to have in the General Assembly. Those matters were resolved at the notorious Yalta Conference (February 4–11, 1945). Each of the major powers was given a Security Council veto, while the Soviet Union — and *only* the Soviet Union — was given two extra votes in the General Assembly! The story of those extra votes is both interesting and revealing.

Former Secretary of State Dean Acheson (CFR) met with FDR for the last time shortly before the President's inauguration for an unprecedented fourth term in January, 1945. Acheson relates:

> Leo Pasvolsky, Alger Hiss, and I went with [*Secretary of State*] Stettinius to brief the President for the forthcoming meeting at Yalta on Russian claims to multiple votes in the General Assembly of the proposed United Nations. . . . I reported that the Russian position would cause trouble on the Hill. He would deal with it, he said, by claiming a vote for each of the forty-eight states and work it out from there.[17]

The Russians were demanding additional votes and separate UN memberships for the Ukraine and Byelorussia, which were actually intergral parts of the Soviet Union. When the request was formally made at Yalta on February 7, Roosevelt agreed to go along, but he told Stalin in a February 10 communication:

> I am somewhat concerned lest it be pointed out that the United

States will have only one vote in the Assembly. It may be necessary for me, therefore, if I am to insure wholehearted acceptance by the Congress and people of the United States of our participation in the World Organization, to ask for additional votes in the Assembly in order to give parity to the United States.

I would like to know, before I face this problem, that you perceive no objection and would support a proposal along this line if it is necessary for me to make it at the forthcoming conference.[18]

Stalin replied the next day, agreeing that "since the number of votes for the Soviet Union is increased to three . . . the number of votes for the USA should also be increased. . . . If it is necessary I am prepared officially to support this proposal."[19]

President Roosevelt, in other words, had three votes for the United States in hand, if he wanted them. But what did he do? Secretary of State Byrnes had left Yalta for Washington prior to conclusion of the Conference. Awaiting his return was a telegram from Presidential adviser Harry Hopkins confirming Stalin's willingness to give the United States three votes, but also noting: "In view of the fact that nothing on this whole subject appears in the communiqué [*issued following the Conference*], the President is extremely anxious no aspect of this question be discussed even privately."[20] Even when the President finally told the United States delegation to the San Francisco Conference about the scheme, he did so "in strictest confidence. . . ."[21] The curtain of secrecy prevented the American people from learning about the situation. As a result, the feared protest failed to materialize, and "Later Roosevelt decided not to ask for the three votes for the United States."[22] So, while the Soviets got their three votes, we got one — plus an early example of the "America Last" attitude which has so consistently afflicted our home-grown UN clique.

On April 6, 1945, the Harold Pratt House in New York City was formally opened as headquarters for the Council on Foreign Relations. Secretary of State Stettinius (CFR) addressed a general meeting of the UN Council on that date and asserted: "I come to bear witness, as has every Secretary of State during the past quarter of a century, to the great services and influence of this organization. . . ."[23] And when the San Francisco Conference convened on April 25 of that year to finalize and approve the UN Charter, more than forty members of the United States delegation had been, were, or would later become members of the CFR (see Appendix C). This indicates the success with which that organization had promoted its aims and strategically placed its members and fellow travelers to carry them out.

Chapter 2

Men At The Top

The Secretary-General is the UN's chief executive officer and its primary spokesman on matters of purpose and policy. Articles and statements from influential American Internationalists have regularly praised the leadership of those who have held the post. For example, UN Ambassador Adlai Stevenson once effused: "I can only say that we have been fortunate indeed in the quality of the men we have chosen [*as Secretary-General*]."[1] Another UN supporter claimed: "Future historians of the United Nations will undoubtedly refer to successive Secretaries-General . . . as among the outstanding personalities who have represented most powerfully and effectively in the public mind the UN idea and who have made major contributions to its development in practice."[2]

Who are these men whose lives have had such a prodigious influence on the United Nations? Let's see.

Alger Hiss

The first man to fill the important post of UN Secretary-General was a CFR member who had been active at the San

Francisco Conference — and whose name is today a household
word synonymous with subversion and betrayal. As *Time* magazine announced in its issue for April 16, 1945:

> The Secretary-General for the San Francisco Conference was
> named at Yalta but announced only last week — lanky, Harvard
> trained Alger Hiss, one of the State Department's brighter young
> men. . . . At San Francisco, he and his Secretariat of 300 (most-
> ly Americans) will have the drudging, thankless clerk's job of
> copying, translating and publishing, running the thousands of
> paperclip and pencil chores of an international meeting. But
> Alger Hiss will be an important figure there. As secretary-general,
> managing the agenda, he will have a lot to say behind the scenes
> about who gets the breaks.

Life magazine's "Picture of the Week" for July 16, 1945,
portrayed a triumphant Hiss with the Charter at his feet, and
was captioned: "At the conclusion of the San Francisco Conference the Charter of the United Nations was bundled off to a
waiting plane. . . . Chief custodian was Conference Secretary-
General Alger Hiss, shown here with the Charter at end of the
cross-country trip."

Hiss, who had served as a key adviser to President Roosevelt
at the Yalta Conference, had been influencing United States
foreign policy for many years. According to Dean Acheson:

> From the time I came into the [State] Department in 1941 to
> sometime in April or May 1946 . . . Alger Hiss had worked first
> for Dr. Stanley Hornbeck in the Far Eastern Division and later
> for Dr. Leo Pasvolsky in a division preparing for and participat-
> ing in the Dumbarton Oaks and San Francisco conferences on the
> United Nations and the Chapultepec conference in Mexico, and
> still later in the winter of 1945–46 he participated in the organiza-
> tional meeting of the United Nations in London. . . . In April or
> May 1946 he was put in charge of a division having charge of our
> relations with the United Nations. He reported to Secretary
> Byrnes, or to me in the Secretary's absence, until he left the
> Department for the Carnegie Endowment around the end of the
> year.[3]

Hiss was eventually exposed as a Soviet spy, convicted for perjuring himself before a federal Grand Jury while being questioned about his Communist activities (the statute of limitations for espionage had run out), and served forty-four months in a federal penitentiary.

Many of Hiss's influential friends rallied to his defense both prior to, and after, his conviction. For example, Mrs. Eleanor Roosevelt told readers of her newspaper column for August 16, 1948:

> Smearing good people like Lauchlin Currie [*former administrative assistant to President Roosevelt*], Alger Hiss and others is, I think, unforgiveable. . . . Anyone knowing Mr. Currie or Mr. Hiss, who are the two people whom I happen to know fairly well, would not need any denial on their part to know they are not Communists. Their records prove it.[4]

Parenthetically, FBI Director J. Edgar Hoover had informed President Truman on November 8, 1945, that Lauchlin Currie was one of a number of federal employees who "have been furnishing data and information to persons outside the Federal Government, who are in turn transmitting this information to agents of the Soviet Government."[5] In 1951, Currie was identified before the Senate Internal Security Subcommittee as a member of a Communist cell by Elizabeth Bentley and Whittaker Chambers (both of whom had testified similarly, from first-hand experience, against Hiss) and former Communist Party functionary Louis Budenz. Budenz, for example, testified

> that Currie played a prominent role in the Communist Party's plans in 1942 to smear patriotic officials in the State Department. Budenz said that Earl Browder, then the boss of the Communist Party in the U.S.A. told him that Currie had helped to work out the propaganda used in the Communist press against the patriots.[6]

Following Hiss's conviction on January 21, 1950, Secretary of State Dean Acheson told a news conference on January 25: "I should like to make it clear to you that whatever the outcome of any appeal which Mr. Hiss or his lawyers may take in this case I do not intend to turn my back on Alger Hiss."[7]

In the wake of the Hiss scandal, many UN propagandists attempted to downplay Hiss's highly significant role in launching the UN. One, for example, claimed that "Hiss was a minor figure in San Francisco in 1945,"[8] while another haughtily (and falsely) asserted: "As a staff member of the State Department, he did *not* work on the original draft" of the UN Charter. Forgotten, or purposely ignored, was the following colloquy between Hiss himself and Representative (later Senator) Karl Mundt (R.-South Dakota) during Congressional hearings in 1948:

> Mr. Mundt: What I was trying to get to is whether you participated in the creation of the draft [*of the Charter*].
> Mr. Hiss: I did participate in the creation of the draft that was sent by President Roosevelt to Churchill and Stalin, which was the draft actually adopted at San Francisco.[10]

Alger Hiss, the man who gave the post of Secretary-General an inauspicious beginning, was released from prison on November 27, 1954.*

Trygve Lie

Norwegian Socialist Trygve Lie succeeded Alger Hiss, becoming the UN's first elected Secretary-General after ratification of the UN Charter on October 24, 1945. CFR member Thomas J. Hamilton, who was also head of the UN Bureau of the *New York Times*, noted in *Foreign Affairs* that Lie had been brought up "to see evils in both Communism and capitalism," and excused the Norwegian's reluctance to "commit himself irrevocably to the anti-Communist side" on grounds that Norway was vulnerable to Soviet reprisals.[11] If this was true, then Secretary-General Lie's decisions were partly influenced by Soviet extortion.

---

*For excellent first- and second-hand accounts of the Hiss case, see (respectively) Whittaker Chambers, *Witness* (New York: Random House, 1952), Ralph de Toledano, *Seeds of Treason* (Boston, Western Islands, 1965 [1950]), and Allen Weinstein, *Perjury: The Hiss-Chambers Case* (New York: Knopf, 1978).

The record indicates, however, that Lie's pro-Communist activities were simply an extension of his own Leftist commitment. He had been a high-ranking member of Norway's Social Democratic Labor Party, which was an offshoot of the early Communist International.[12] And when Leon Trotsky, chief rival of Soviet dictator Joseph Stalin, was exiled in Norway,

> Trygve Lie was the minister of justice of that country. Acting in accordance with the wishes of Stalin, Lie confronted Trotsky with an ultimatum of choosing between either ceasing all criticism of the Communist regime in Moscow or going to jail. Trotsky continued to write exposés of the ruthlessness of Stalin and his henchmen. Lie, consequently, had him thrown in prison and later deported him to Mexico.[13]

Trotsky was assassinated in Mexico, apparently by one of those Stalin henchmen, on August 21, 1940.

The socialist League for Industrial Democracy (LID), which in the early Sixties spawned the violent Students for a Democratic Society (SDS), honored Lie at its annual conference in 1947. "In his introductory remarks, Bryn J. Hovde, L.I.D. vice-president and former president of the New School for Social Research, gloried 'in the fact that one of our kind is Secretary-General of the United Nations.' "[14]

Prior to selecting a Secretary-General, the newly formed United Nations had had the task of choosing a President for its General Assembly. Trygve Lie had been a candidate for the post, but had withdrawn. On the morning of January 10, 1946, the day the Assembly President was to be elected, the Soviet Ambassador sought him out to say that the USSR and its Eastern European satellites wanted to nominate him. According to Trygve Lie:

> Mr. [Andrei] Gromyko [Soviet UN Ambassador] strode to the rostrum and declared:
> "Weighing the candidates which have recently been mentioned in connection with the election of the President . . . the Soviet Delegation has come to the conclusion that the most appropriate

candidature would be that of the Foreign Minister of Norway,
Mr. Trygve Lie.". . .
Wincenty Rzymowsky of Poland then rose in dutiful support
of the nomination, and spoke of Norway and of me in generous
terms. He was followed by Dmitri Z. Manuilsky, the "Old
Bolshevik" from pre-Stalin days who was then Foreign Minister
of the Ukrainian S.S.R., and was to be one of the United
Nations' more dramatic personages in its first years.[15]

Nevertheless, Lie was narrowly defeated by Belgian Socialist
Paul-Henri Spaak, a setback which left him available for the
much more influential post of Secretary-General. In the subsequent campaign for the higher office, the Soviets again assumed the role of virtual campaign manager for Lie. "The
Soviet Union strongly supported Trygve Lie as the first Secretary-General of the United Nations. Andrei Gromyko nomi-
nated Lie for the position. . . ."[16]
Following his confirmation, Lie fully justified the confidence the Communists had placed in him. As noted in *Foreign
Affairs*: "Prior to his intervention on [sic] Korea Mr. Lie had
supported Soviet moves in the 'cold war,' and criticized those of
the United States, more often than he had supported the United
States."[17]
For example, in April, 1946, Lie sided with the Soviets on an
issue involving Iran. Iran had filed a complaint against the
Soviet Union for its failure to remove Red troops from Iranian
territory as agreed to earlier. Then, Iran suddenly withdrew the
complaint and joined with the Soviets in urging that the matter
be removed from the agenda of the Security Council. "This was
opposed by the United States and a majority of the Council,
who felt that the withdrawal of the Iranian complaint had been
extorted by Soviet pressure. Mr. Lie supported the Soviet
Union. . . ."[18]
Again, in early 1950 Lie started a campaign for the Soviet
goal of having Communist China admitted to the UN. "Formerly he had drawn back when he met serious opposition. On China
he did not draw back, although his moves aroused increasing

disapproval in the United States and some of the other democracies, approval in others, and hosannas of praise from Communist organs throughout the world."[19]

On another occasion, Lie threatened to resign his position because he disagreed with the American position regarding the partition of Palestine.

> . . . I went to see Mr. Gromyko. . . . I announced the feeling that I should resign in protest at the American shift of position, and I have never found Ambassador Gromyko more friendly. His melancholy features lit up with sympathy. But he seemed half alarmed at my idea. "Speaking for myself," he said, "I hope you will not resign, and I advise you against it. . . . In any case, I would be grateful if you would take no action before I have time to consult my government."[20]

Lie waited, and on "Tuesday, Mr. Gromyko took me aside. He had cabled Moscow, he reported, and Moscow's reply was: 'No, definitely not.' "[21]

Lie stayed.

Thomas Hamilton claimed in *Foreign Affairs* that, since there is no Charter provision for removing a Secretary-General prior to the expiration of his term, there is "force in the argument that a more able or courageous spokesman [*than Lie*] might have split the organization apart."[22] One certainly has to wonder about an organization which is threatened by leaders who might exhibit excessive amounts of ability and courage. And it is a revealing commentary on Trygve Lie that friends of the UN actually defended his pro-Communist commitment by contending that he was a man of limited ability and courage, which they cited as being an asset to the world body!

On October 1, 1949, "[*Soviet Foreign Minister Andrei*] Vyshinsky told Lie at a dinner party in New York that he was the only man the Soviet Union would support. In January 1950 the Soviet Government informed the Norwegian Government of its intention to support Mr. Lie for another term, and this was announced in Moscow on May 15, 1950."[23]

Open Soviet ardor for Mr. Lie cooled following UN intervention in Korea, but, as we shall see later, Soviet "opposition" to
UN action in Korea was roughly equivalent to Br'er Rabbit's
"opposition" to being tossed into the brier patch.

Dag Hammarskjöld

Trygve Lie retired at the conclusion of his second term as UN
Secretary-General on April 10, 1953 and was succeeded by
Sweden's Dag Hammarskjöld. Yet another Socialist imbued
with an exaggerated, humanistic view of his ability to "save the
world," Hammarskjöld once wrote to a girlfriend, "I think I was
12 years old when I had a very strong feeling that I am a new
Jesus."[24] Well-informed Swedes at home deemed him "an
extreme left-winger in politics."[25] In another letter to a friend in
the mid-1950's Hammarskjöld confided, "It is a little bit humili-
ating when I have to say that Chou En-lai to me appears as the
most superior brain I have so far met in the field of foreign
politics. As I said to one of the Americans: 'Chou is so much
more dangerous than you imagine because he is so much better a
man than you have ever admitted.' "[26] This despite the fact that
Chou En-lai, in association with Mao Tse-tung, administered
in China what the *Guinness Book of World Records* describes as
"The greatest massacre in human history,"[27] slaughtering (according to a study commissioned by a Senate subcommittee)
between 34,300,000 and 63,784,000 human beings.[28] While Hammarskjöld was in charge of UN affairs in the Swedish Foreign
Office in 1951, his government refused to support a UN
resolution mildly condemning Red China as an aggressor for its
subjugation of Tibet.[29]

Like Trygve Lie, Dag Hammarskjöld had no trouble with the
Soviet Union until it was too late for such contrived Russian
"opposition" to do him much harm. For example, the Soviets
backed his actions in the Suez crisis of 1956 and,

on October 31, 1956, the Soviet representative made an even
stronger statement in support of Hammarskjold when he said:

"May I begin by saying that the Soviet delegation has confidence in the Secretary-General of the United Nations and lends him its support." This attitude prevailed when Mr. Hammarskjold was re-elected Secretary-General on September 26, 1957.[30]

Hammarskjöld was primarily responsible for the early planning and direction of the UN's war against the anti-Communist Congolese province of Katanga in the early 1960s. The UN moved to crush Katangan independence by conducting a vicious military operation that included the bombing of hospitals, attacks on ambulances, and general violence so extreme that the forty-six civilian doctors in the Katangan capital of Elizabethville, who had to care for the dead and wounded, sent telegrams to world leaders imploring them to intervene "to stop the terrorist bombardment of hospitals and civilian populations by the United Nations." The telegram was later incorporated in a lengthy report issued by the doctors which, accompanied by pictorial examples of UN atrocities, documented the horror the UN was inflicting in the name of "peace."[31] Today, thanks in large part to the UN operation in Katanga, the former Belgian Congo (now called Zaïre) is ruled by the Communists — as are its mineral wealth and vast supplies of nuclear raw materials.

Secretary-General Hammarskjöld was also responsible for the persecution of Danish UN diplomat Povl Bang-Jensen after Bang-Jensen refused to turn over to Hammarskjöld a list of Hungarian refugees who had testified in confidence to a special UN committee that investigated the 1956 anti-Communist uprising in Hungary. The refugees feared reprisals against relatives in Hungary if their names were revealed and Bang-Jensen, as assistant secretary of the UN committee, had promised to keep the names confidential. When he attempted to keep his word, Hammarskjöld had him suspended and subjected to an incredible campaign of harassment and character assassination. Bang-Jensen's appeal for reinstatement was pending when he was found dead of a bullet wound in a New York City park on November 24, 1959. His death was quickly labeled a suicide, but a subsequent investigation by the Senate Internal Security

Subcommittee raised the real possibility that he had been the victim of a Soviet MVD assassination. After cataloguing numerous flaws in the suicide theory, the Subcommittee concluded:

> If Bang-Jensen did not commit suicide, he was the victim of political murder dressed up as suicide. While the Kremlin maintains a terror apparatus for the purpose of liquidating enemies and suspects, it must have serious motivation before it issues instructions for murder. It is the opinion of this report that such motivation probably did exist in the case of Povl Bang-Jensen.[32]

Following his death, information was revealed that Bang-Jensen had been in contact with a Soviet national at the UN who wanted to defect and expose Soviet penetration of both the UN Secretariat and American intelligence.

> This shocking information was then dispatched to Allen Dulles [*CFR*], head of our Central Intelligence Agency, who, instead of moving resolutely to acquire the full details from this vital source of information, let Bang-Jensen and the Soviet defector cool their heels for seven long and agonizing months before even expressing any interest. By this time the defector had been sent back to Russia. The CIA never did ask Bang-Jensen for details.[33]

The Senate Subcommittee reported:

> During the course of 1958 it had become known to at least several people that Bang-Jensen had been approached in November 1956 by a would-be Soviet defector who wished to convey information concerning Soviet control of key persons in the U.N. Secretariat and Soviet infiltration of American intelligence. Bang-Jensen had information — but the reports were vague and no one knew precisely how much he had or how much he had conveyed. Worried by this uncertainty, the MVD may very well had [*sic.*] decided to take Bang-Jensen in for the purpose of finding out what contacts he had had, how much he knew, and how much he had already told the American authorities. If Bang-

Jensen was taken into custody for such an interrogation, his liquidation would have been the inevitable sequel.[34]

Whether Povl Bang-Jensen committed suicide or was murdered by the MVD to protect their agents in the UN and elsewhere, it seems clear that his demise was directly related to the frustrating attempt to maintain his integrity and anti-Communist position within a pro-Communist UN hierarchy. Had he gone back on his word to the Hungarian Freedom Fighters as demanded by Secretary-General Hammarskjöld, and simply ignored the would-be Soviet defector, he would likely be alive today.

U Thant

Dag Hammarskjöld died in a plane crash in Northern Rhodesia on September 18, 1961. Prior to that incident, much publicity had been given to an alleged Soviet attempt to undermine the office of Secretary-General with demands for a *troika* arrangement which would replace that office with a triumvirate of representatives from Communist, Western, and "neutral" nations. That this was simply a ploy intended to generate sympathy and support for the UN in non-Communist countries was confirmed when the Soviets passed up the opportunity to veto candidates to succeed Hammarskjöld and to press for their *troika*. Instead, they turned off the *troika* talk like a water faucet and rallied behind Burmese Marxist U Thant's campaign for the office of Secretary-General.

When the Secretariat election came, Thant won more easily than expected. "Every time a serious crisis threatens world peace," said Anastas Mikoyan, Russian first deputy premier and firm *troika* advocate, "we shall turn to Secretary-General Thant, who has won confidence and support."[35]

Thant was appointed Acting Secretary-General on November 3, 1961.

24 The United Nations Conspiracy

This appointment ended the major Soviet effort to establish the "troika." It may be important to note that Soviet protests about important decisions between the death of Hammarskjöld and the appointment of U Thant were relatively perfunctory.[36]

In November, 1962, Thant was appointed Permanent Secretary-General. On July 27, 1966, an Associated Press dispatch datelined Moscow reported:

U Thant has been assured the support of the Soviet Union for another term as Secretary General of the United Nations. . . .
The sources said Premier Alexei N. Kosygin told Thant during a long talk yesterday that the Soviet government wants him to accept reelection when his current 5-year term expires Nov. 3.
. . . Soviet support for another term had been reported from the United Nations as early as last April.[37]

Thant did, indeed, accept another five-year term, eventually retiring on December 31, 1971.

The Soviets were pleased with Thant because his Marxism and anti-Americanism dominated his decade of service. Thant was a protégé of U Nu, the Burmese Prime Minister who on May 1, 1948, asserted during a speech: "If we now look back to history, we find that Stalin followed the right path."[38] During that same speech, U Nu advocated strengthening ties with the Soviet Union, confiscating all capitalist enterprises in Burma, abolishing private ownership of land, and forming a league to propagate Marxist doctrine.

After the Japanese occupation in 1942, U Nu invited Thant to Rangoon to become secretary of Burma's Educational Reorganizing Committee, and to plan a new system of education in Burma. Thant accepted, and wrote a report which was published and put to use after the war.

That was the beginning of Thant's public career. The next step came in 1948, when U Nu asked him to become press officer of the Anti-Fascist People's Freedom League, the political party that developed out of the wartime resistance movement. When U Nu became Prime Minister, U Thant was named his aide, with a bewildering range of appointments, from Deputy Director of

Information to the catch-all title of Secretary to the Prime
Minister. From 1952 on, U Thant traveled the world with U Nu,
served in the Burma delegation at the United Nations, and
became head of the delegation in 1957.[39]

In 1966, Thant confided to correspondents that he had
written anonymous editorials for a Burmese newspaper for a
decade prior to his 1957 appointment as United Nations delegate.[40] Such clandestine press manipulation by a key government official was a revealing insight into Thant's philosophy
about press freedom and the proper role of government.

During his years as Secretary-General, Thant constantly
feigned concern about "racism" in the world, frequently using
it as an excuse to undermine anti-Communists, but was always
careful to ignore "racism" in Communist countries. After
concluding the UN's bloody war against black-ruled, anti-Communist Katanga, he turned his attention to the white-ruled,
anti-Communist regimes in South Africa and Rhodesia. Under
Thant's leadership, Rhodesia became (on December 16, 1966)
the target of the first economic sanctions ever voted by the
United Nations.

In contrast to his staunch anti-Rhodesia position, in early
1969 Thant called for an end to the economic boycott of
Communist Cuba, falsely asserting: "I am always for the
termination of the isolation or segregation of any member of
the international community. I am always for the revival of
contacts and communications and exposure, as I have said."[41]

In his annual report to the United Nations released in
September, 1966, Thant claimed: "The most conspicuous and
anachronistic mass violation of human rights and fundamental
freedoms is that which continues to be enforced against the
nonwhite majority of the people of South Africa."[42] This was
utter nonsense, since the worst violations of human rights and
fundamental freedoms had been and were occurring in the
Soviet Union, Red China, Cuba, and other countries held captive
by Communists, and the victims were a majority comprising *all*
races, creeds, and colors. No word was ever spoken of the

millions held in concentration camps by Communist regimes. Instead, Thant followed the Red line and vented his wrath against anti-Communist Rhodesia and South Africa.

During the Vietnam War, Mr. Thant continually used his prestige and influence to undermine the United States and propagandize for the Communists. News reports consistently documented the extent to which Thant ignored Communist aggression and blamed the war on the United States. For instance:

UNITED NATIONS, N.Y. Nov. 11 [*1966*] — Secretary General U Thant today cited an unconditional cessation of American bombing in North Vietnam as the first key to peace.[43]

UNITED NATIONS, N.Y., April 1 [*1967*] — The United States should unilaterally declare a cease-fire in Vietnam as the first step toward peace, U.N. Secretary General U Thant said today.[44]

UNITED NATIONS, N.Y., July 30 [*1967*] — U.N. Secretary General U Thant said tonight that the conflict in Vietnam cannot be ended until the United States recognizes that it is "a war of national independence" rather than a war of Communist aggression.[45]

Thant continued to compare "the position of North Vietnam to that of the American colonies in the Revolutionary War,"[46] proving simply that history was not his strong point. Indeed, his claim reminded some observers of Thant's May 26, 1964, attack on the United States for dropping the atomic bomb on non-white Japan, but not on white Germany. He had asserted, "As you know, Nazi Germany was also at war with the allies."[47] Nazi Germany had surrendered on May 7, 1945 — three months before the A-bomb was dropped on Hiroshima (August 6th) and Nagasaki (August 9th).

On April 7, 1970, the Associated Press ran the following revealing dispatch, datelined the United Nations:

Secretary General U Thant praised Vladimir I. Lenin, founder of the Soviet Union, as a political leader whose ideals were reflected in the U.N. charter.

Thant released Monday the text of a statement sent to a symposium on Lenin at Tampere, Finland, sponsored by the U.N. Educational, Scientific and Cultural Organization.

"Lenin was a man with a mind of great clarity and incisiveness, and his ideas have had a profound influence on the course of contemporary history," Thant's statement said.

"(Lenin's) ideals of peace and peaceful coexistence among states have won widespread international acceptance and they are in line with the aims of the U.N. Charter."[48]

Considering the extent of Thant's admiration for Lenin, it should come as no surprise to learn that he chose as his personal assistant a Communist who was also an officer of the Soviet KGB, the modern-day successor to the original terrorist police organization (Cheka) established under Lenin in December, 1917.

Former Secretary General U Thant for years had a personal adviser named Viktor Mechislavovich Lessiovsky, who, unbeknown to him [sic], was a KGB officer. U Thant states that he first met Lessiovsky in the early 1950s when he was Burmese Minister of Information and the Russian was stationed at the Soviet embassy in Rangoon. The two became so well acquainted that U Thant gave Lessiovsky's baby daughter a Burmese name.[49]

It is UN custom that the Secretary-General's staff include a citizen from each of the major powers. Lessiovsky was the only Russian Thant knew in the Secretariat, so he appointed him as Personal Assistant. "U Thant notes that he had no reason to be wary because no one had ever warned him that Lessiovsky was a KGB officer."[50] To the contrary, Lessiovsky's former service in the Soviet embassy in Rangoon was indeed a reason to be wary, since Soviet embassies are notorious nesting grounds for KGB agents. The simple truth, we suspect, is that Thant simply didn't care about his friend's KGB background.*

---

*"A Soviet 'diplomat,' named by the *New York Times* as a veteran espionage agent, will be retained by the United Nations as director of external relations for the Office of Public Information. The $27,000-a-year contract of Vladimar P. Pavlichenko, identified as a veteran officer of the dread KGB, was due to expire earlier this month. It was extended for two years by Secretary-General U Thant." (*Human Events*, October 30, 1971, p. 2.)

Kurt Waldheim

U Thant retired on December 31, 1971. Ten days earlier, Kurt Waldheim of Austria had been selected by the Security Council as his successor. The *New York Times* reported, "One of Mr. Waldheim's greatest assets in his successful campaign was that he was the preferred candidate of the Soviet Union from an early stage. . . ."[51] Even so, Red China (which had been admitted to the world body on October 25, 1971) could have vetoed the nomination, but chose instead to abstain. As the *Times* put it, Communist "China's abstention made Mr. Waldheim's election possible."

A few months earlier, Waldheim had received forty-seven percent of the vote as the presidential candidate of the Catholic People's Party of Austria. He ran so inoffensive a campaign that, after being defeated by the Socialists, the winners returned him to the United Nations as *their* representative and backed his candidacy for Secretary-General.[52]

Waldheim's native Austria was the first free country to fall victim to Adolf Hitler's aggression. An article in the Boston *Pilot* for January 1, 1972, reported: "Never having engaged in politics, he [*Waldheim*] survived the Nazi occupation of Austria without stigma. As a soldier in World War II, he was wounded in 1942. . . ."

Let's see. If the year is 1942, and you are wounded as an Austrian soldier, then you are fighting for a regime that has captured your country — you are, in fact, marching with Hitler's legions! As foreign affairs expert Hilaire du Berrier has noted, Waldheim served as "an infantry lieutenant with the swastika on his collar."[53] Kurt Waldheim, as usual, was simply going along to get along.

In 1968, the Soviet Union invaded Austria's neighbor, Czechoslovakia. Rather than condemn the Communists, Mr. Waldheim again proved accommodating. As the Boston *Pilot* article noted, "Dr. Waldheim is also gratefully remembered in Moscow for helping to soothe tensions in Austria during the Soviet's August 1968 invation [*sic*] of neighboring Czechoslovakia."

During a speech to the Chicago Council on Foreign Relations (a separate entity from the national CFR referred to earlier) on April 23, 1975, Waldheim asserted:

> It was a little more than thirty years ago that Wendell Willkie wrote his book, "One World." I can think of no more useful way of returning to fundamentals on our quest for peace than by rediscovering the power and validity of what he was trying to tell us.[54]

That is a *most* revealing statement. Wendell Willkie was the "Republican" candidate defeated by President Roosevelt in 1940. Yet, as noted in an article in *Vista*, formerly the official monthly publication of the United Nations Association of the United States:

> Willkie had never been much of a Republican anyway. He had been a Democrat in his early adult years, serving as a delegate to the Democratic convention in 1924 . . . and he had voted for Roosevelt when the New Deal came along. . . . Even when he joined the Republican Party he did so as a maverick, taking anti-isolationist, pro-interventionist positions that even outdid F.D.R. He won the 1940 Presidential nomination by a fluke. . . . His foreign policy views were not so much in opposition to Roosevelt's as strongly in support.[55]

Vista noted that when Presidential adviser Harry Hopkins once made a slurring remark about Willkie, "President Roosevelt thundered, 'Don't ever say anything like that around here again. Don't ever think it. . . . He was a godsend to this country when we needed him most.' "[56] The article continues, "By 1944, Roosevelt, having used Willkie for morale-boosting missions to Britain in 1941 and around the world in 1942, was seriously considering him as his running mate in the forthcoming election even though Willkie was planning another try at the Republican Presidential nomination."[57]

That "around the world" trip in the late summer and early fall of 1942 subsequently served as the basis for Willkie's book,

One World (New York: Simon and Schuster, 1943). Essentially, the book is an outline of his wildly internationalist ideas, including a fervent plea for a post-war world of accommodation between the United States and the Soviet Union. His traveling companions had been Gardner Cowles, Jr., and Joseph Barnes, both members of the Council on Foreign Relations. Willkie wrote his book from notes and outlines provided by the two,[58] which is significant not only because of the CFR influence involved, but because

> in sworn [*Congressional*] testimony, Whittaker Chambers, Louis Budenz, Alexandr Barmine, Karl Wittfogel, and Hede Massing, swore of their own personal knowledge that they had known Barnes as a Communist agent.[59]

Such is the background and philosophy of the book whose "power and validity" Secretary-General Waldheim recommended as a guide to the fundamentals of "peace."

Following the admission of Red China to the United Nations, Kurt Waldheim fully concurred in the UN's *1984*-style drive to obliterate every last vestige of Free China. He supported the expulsion of Free China's press representatives from UN headquarters (an unprecedented move that had been taken by his predecessor, U Thant, following action by the General Assembly.)[60] He also went along with Red China's demand that there be no text or tables dealing with Taiwan's population, trade, industry, or any other data in future editions of the world organization's *Statistical Yearbook* — even though this was entirely inconsistent with past UN policy. (Figures for Red China, for instance, had been included in the yearbooks even prior to 1971.)[61] And it was Waldheim himself, acting under pressure from the Communists, who ordered the removal from the wall of the General Assembly chamber of a large plaque, featuring a quotation from Confucius, that had been donated by Free China in 1968.[62]

When Red Chinese Premier Chou En-lai died on January 8, 1976, Waldheim sent a message of condolence which asserted:

I have learnt with deep sorrow of the death of His Excellency Mr. Chou En-lai . . . . He was a most distinguished and esteemed leader who served his country and his people with great devotion for many decades. His dedication to the fostering of better understanding among nations and international peace is widely recognized. The world will be poorer for no longer having the benefit of his statesmanship in these critical times. Mr. Chou En-lai inspired admiration and respect among all who were privileged to meet him.[63]

All this praise for a man who not only played a major part in the slaughter of thirty to sixty million of his fellow citizens but who also instituted some of the most inhuman tortures ever devised in the process of forcing Communism on the peoples of China.

After the Communists were permitted to take all of Vietnam following conclusion of the lengthy no-win (for anti-Communists) war, Kurt Waldheim was urged by United States officials to use his good offices to convince the North Vietnamese to permit the safe evacuation of South Vietnamese refugees. Waldheim declined. Since the Communists said they would not release the three to four million displaced persons in the South, he claimed: "It is not in the interest of the United Nations to get involved in this political aspect."[64] Pressed on the matter, Waldheim claimed that any pressure on the Communists to release their civilian hostages might jeopardize existing UN humanitarian projects in the area. "Waldheim said the Communists contended the refugees would be aided in their territory and there was no reason for them to leave."[65] Waldheim, who thinks "Everything in life is relative,"[66] believed them.

Such is the record of the current leader of "mankind's best hope for peace."

Thus far, as we have seen, the United Nations has been headed by a Soviet spy, two self-proclaimed Socialists, a Burmese Marxist, and a former Nazi foot soldier. Each Secretary-General to date has been an aggressive enemy of limited government and free enterprise economics, and has used his talents and influence to expand the reach, influence, and control of government over the lives of people everywhere. And each has been sympathetic to the goals (and obedient to the demands) of the Communists — the greatest enemies of true peace, freedom, and prosperity the world has ever known.

If it is true that an organization can be judged by the quality of its leadership, the character of those who have held the post of UN Secretary-General becomes a rather compelling reason to *Get US out!* of the world body.

Chapter 3

War And Peace

Of all the clichés that have played a role in the historical development of the United Nations, none has been used more extensively than the claim that the UN is man's last and best hope for peace. Even today it is difficult to locate a pro-UN article, speech, or book that does not emphasize this central theme, despite the fact that not a single provision in the UN Charter contemplates an end to war.

The San Francisco Conference was not a peacetime conference; it was a wartime congregation, and each participant "was in a state of war when the Conference began. Many were engaged throughout the weeks of its deliberation in bitter and costly fighting."[1] Indeed, membership in the UN "was denied to Sweden, Switzerland and Ireland on the official grounds that they were not 'peace-loving' nations — as witness the fact that they had not fought in the World War."[2] The Charter was signed on June 26, 1945; yet within weeks the atomic bomb exploded on Hiroshima and Nagasaki.*

---

*In 1965, Luis Quintanilla (a former representative of Mexico in the UN General Assembly) "suggested that the atom bomb deserves the Nobel peace prize for having spurred mankind's efforts toward realization of a warless world." (*Christian Century*, August 11, 1965.)

Writing in *Foreign Affairs*, R. Keith Kane (CFR) explained:

> The Charter does not call on its signatories to renounce force;
> rather, it seeks to bring force under control by registering
> agreement on certain purposes and binding the contracting par-
> ties to refrain from the threat or use of force in any manner
> inconsistent with those purposes.[3]

In other words, the United Nations condones war as long as it
is fought to achieve a UN goal, in which case it becomes mag-
ically transformed into a "peace-keeping" operation. According
to Canadian historian Kenneth McNaught, also writing in *Foreign Affairs*:

> ...the program envisaged by the U.N. assumes that certain
> things are valued more highly than peace itself. . . . The entire
> machinery of collective security is based upon the assumption
> that force must be used (i.e. the peace must be broken) against
> any state committing aggression [*as defined by the UN*] upon
> those values which are held higher than peace [*as determined by
> the UN*].[4]

Professor McNaught continued: "It is the people of the
world who believe the peace mythology of the United Nations.
. . . it is a mythology which is perpetrated in true Machiavellian
style by their governments who do not for a moment believe it
themselves."[5]

This view has also been confirmed by former UN General
Assembly President Charles Malik: "When responsible representatives deliberated the United Nations Charter at San Francisco
in 1945 nobody ever thought for one moment that the new world
organization was going to abolish war for all time. . . . the
whole Organization . . . is predicated on the distinct possibility
of war."[6]

J. Reuben Clark, Jr. served for many years as U.S. Undersecretary of State and Ambassador to Mexico, and he was
widely recognized as one of our nation's foremost international

lawyers. Between June and August, 1945, Ambassador Clark composed an analysis of the UN Charter, concluding:

> . . . there is no provision in the Charter itself that contemplates ending war. It is true the Charter provides for force to bring peace, but such use of force is itself war. . . .
> The Charter is built to prepare for war, not to promote peace. . . .
> The Charter is a war document not a peace document. . . .[7]

Ambassador Clark further predicted:

> Not only does the Charter Organization not prevent future wars, but it makes it practically certain that we shall have future wars, and as to such wars it takes from us the power to declare them, to choose the side on which we shall fight, to determine what forces and military equipment we shall use in the war, and to control and command our sons who do the fighting.[8]

The UN's so-called "police action" in Korea five years later confirmed the accuracy of Ambassador Clark's perceptive analysis. Discussing Korea in a speech in Seattle on March 8, 1952, former American Bar Association President Frank E. Holman angrily exclaimed:

> . . . America is not allowed to win the war though we were put into it by United Nations action. Because of the conflicting interests and policies of other nations, America is not allowed to prosecute the war to a successful conclusion. . . . The chief objective of this United Nations war is to produce a stalemate and prolong the war instead of achieving victory. Thus, the United Nations in prolonging the war which might otherwise be concluded acts as a menace to peace.[9]

Remember that the Vietnam War was fought under the same UN-inspired, "no-win" ground rules, with results even more tragic for the cause of peace and freedom in the world.

In 1954, Clarence K. Streit, the Internationalist founder of the Atlantic Union movement, admitted: "Under guise of reducing the international anarchy, the United Nations really made it much more dangerous."[10] Similarly, Charles Malik claimed that "it is possible to show that the public and unlimited handling by the United Nations of certain cold war issues, far from having helped in easing them, has actually tended to aggravate them."[11]

Such aggravation has occurred, on occasion, because of the UN's tendency to draw uninvolved third parties into a fray and compel them to take sides. Columnist Paul Weaver has speculated:

> If the U.N. didn't exist, for instance, it is hard to imagine that hostilities in the Mideast would seriously engage more than the great powers, Israel, and its immediate neighbors — in all, maybe a dozen nations. But the U.N. does exist. . . . *[Its members]* spend a large fraction of their time at the U.N. . . . on the Mideast question. By now there is scarcely a handful of countries left in the world that haven't long since chosen up sides in that conflict and acquired something of a stake in its outcome.[12]

When the whole world is enticed to choose sides on issues which divide hostile nations, factions and competing power blocs are spawned which in time

> take on a life of their own, quite apart from the specific issues that gave rise to them, and they tend to politicize matters that would otherwise be unobjectionable. It is a truism that to minimize conflict, issues should be treated separately, questions defined narrowly, and the number of participants kept as small as possible. The U.N. pushes in the opposite direction; it is by nature an exacerbator and spreader of conflict.[13]

In a speech delivered in West Branch, Iowa on August 10, 1962, former U.S. President Herbert Hoover (CFR) recalled that he had urged ratification of the UN Charter, but lamented that it had become necessary to recognize that the UN had failed to offer even a remote hope for lasting peace. "Instead," he acknowledged, "it adds to the dangers of wars which now surround us."[14] And he was right, for it could hardly be otherwise when the world's most notorious arsonists — the Communists — were (and are) firmly entrenched in positions of great influence on the very commission charged with extinguishing the flames of war.*

The three main weapons used to promote Communist-style totalitarianism throughout the world during the past two centuries have been money, hatred, and war. Money is an obvious necessity for the fueling of any movement. Carefully-cultivated hatreds and antagonisms (whites *vs.* blacks, men *vs.* women, young *vs.* old, Christian *vs.* Jew, Catholic *vs.* Protestant, *etc.*) help tear apart existing societies and prepare them for reconstruction along new, Marxist-oriented lines. And then comes war.

Among other things, war enables governments to divert popular attention from troublesome difficulties and problems at home to the war effort abroad, in line with the advice Shakespeare's King Henry IV gave to Prince Henry: "Be it thy course to busy giddy minds with foreign quarrels; that action, hence borne out, may waste the memory of the former days."[15] War also conditions populations to accept government intrusions (such as wage and price controls, rationing, wild deficit spending and its accompanying inflation, *etc.*) which they would vigorously resist in calmer times. And, war psychology conditions people to exchange liberty for security. Goodrich and Hambro claim:

> ...the [UN] Charter would not have been possible if the peoples and governments which participated in the making of the Charter had not been motivated by a common desire to maintain peace and security in a world devastated by war.... It was the unity born of the experience of war which in the last analysis produced this common effort in the cause of peace.[16]

---

*"In view of the cold war, the presence of Soviets and Americans under one roof posed a novel problem for Western diplomacy. In a time when we were struggling to organize a world-wide defensive coalition against the Communist threat, we had to meet and negotiate with our allies in the presence of the enemy." (Lincoln P. Bloomfield [CFR], *Foreign Affairs*, July 1958, p. 598.)

And Charles Malik adds that the war "generated a sufficient political and spiritual impetus to make possible the United Nations such as it is. If the birth of the United Nations had been delayed six months or one year, it is likely that it would never have been born."[17] As one prominent Internationalist put it, "When there is no crisis, no one gives a damn."[18]

Consider some of the effects of World War I, as generalized and summarized by socialist author Stuart Chase:

> Free enterprise within nations was replaced by planned economies, government controlled.
> Free speech was replaced by censorship and propaganda.
> Free world markets were replaced by government control of exports and imports. . . .
> The gold standard was abandoned.
> The whole credit structure was wiped out in some countries, distorted in all, while relations between debtors and creditors were shattered by inflation and devaluation.[19]

And James Avery Joyce, long-time member of the British Fabian Society, adds: "One result of that war was to magnify in thoughtful minds the need for worldwide institutions and a supranational outlook. . . ."[20]

Clearly, some aspects of the internationalist philosophy contribute to the view that war is a frightful blessing in disguise. This attitude may be gleaned from the writings of prominent "world citizens" involved in World War II. One recalls, for instance, the startling statement made by Secretary of War Henry Stimson (CFR) regarding his initial reaction to the bombing of Pearl Harbor:

> When the news first came that Japan had attacked us my first feeling was of relief that the indecision was over and that a crisis had come in a way which would unite all our people. This continued to be my dominant feeling in spite of the news of catastrophes which quickly developed.[21]

Stimson admitted that at a White House Cabinet meeting on

November 25, 1941 — less than two weeks prior to Pearl Harbor — the question discussed "was how we should maneuver them [*the Japanese*] into the position of firing the first shot without allowing too much danger to ourselves."[22]

A few years later, in his book *One World*, Wendell Willkie asserted: "For I live in constant dread that this war may end before the people of the world have come to a common understanding of what they fight for and what they hope for after the war is over."[23]

What are we to think of men who are relieved when wars start, and live in dread that they will end before the desired conditioning has been accomplished? Men who apparently elate in the extent to which "World wars are great promoters of co-operation and the chief occasion for talking about peace"?[24]

And what about peace, UN-style? As we have seen, even Secretary-General Thant admitted that the ideals of peace and peaceful coexistence held by Communist leader Vladimir Lenin "are in line with the aims of the U.N. Charter."[25]

The Communists, of course, use the word "peace" to mean an absence of resistance (and potential resistance) to Communism. As noted by Socialist Harold Laski in *Foreign Affairs*:

> Nor, Lenin argues, can revolutionary Communism halt at its own frontiers. The best defensive is the offensive method; it must attack other states lest they become centers of attack against itself.[26]

And an anonymous scholar, also writing in *Foreign Affairs*, recalled:

> It is an axiom with Stalin that capitalists are filled with envy and hatred, and that whenever they can and dare they will seek to intervene in the Socialist country and restore capitalism. This danger he dramatized as "capitalist encirclement," declaring that Socialism cannot be considered finally achieved as long as this danger of intervention and restoration persists.[27]

The UN record strongly implies that the world body has

indeed worked to shield the Communist world from that "danger of intervention and restoration." Its bloody war of aggression against anti-Communist Katanga was labelled a "peacekeeping" operation; its drive to pull down anti-Communist Rhodesia was branded a "peace" maneuver (and peaceful Rhodesia was smeared as a "threat to peace"); and expelling anti-Communist Free China, and welcoming as members the mass murderers of Red China, was a "move toward peace" by UN standards.

On July 24, 1975, former UN Ambassador Henry Cabot Lodge (CFR) told a Congressional Subcommittee that "since 1945 there have been 14 international and 24 civil wars, all with substantial casualties."[28] Actually, the record was far worse. Years earlier, the UN publication *UNESCO Courier* had reported: "More than 100 wars or other international and national conflicts have occurred since the end of the Second World War."[29] In response to such a distressing statistic, advocates of the UN usually express relief that, at least, there has been no *world* war since 1945. For example, Clark Eichelberger, former National Director of the American Association for the United Nations, claimed: "Every day since the Second World War there has been spasmodic fighting somewhere on earth, but these conflicts have not resulted in a Third World War. The United Nations has made the difference."[30] And, in 1975, a newspaper advertisement sponsored by the McDonnell Douglas Corporation (a company which treats UN Day as a paid employee holiday) asserted: "In the 30 years since [*the UN's founding*], those armed conflicts that have erupted have stayed contained, often with the help of the UN."[31]

We detect some hardening of the moral arteries in such arguments. It is as if such horrors as Korea and Vietnam, the bloodshed in the Middle East and in Africa, *etc.*, are somehow "acceptable" wars simply because they did not degenerate into "unacceptable" *world* wars. In the words of Ambassador J. Reuben Clark, Jr., "We have been so intrigued by the Concept and phrase that godless men coined — 'total war' — that we not only tolerate, but take pride in boasting about, butcheries of peoples that a generation ago would have shocked to the very core all but the most depraved."[32] Even Belgian Socialist Paul-Henri Spaak, who was the General Assembly's first President, acknowledged in 1957:

> In the present United Nations setup . . . everything short of war is allowed. Treaties may be violated, promises can be broken, a nation is licensed to menace its neighbor or to perpetrate any sort of trick on it, just as long as there is no actual war. . . .
> This brand of justice . . . amounts to rewarding any nation which is audacious enough to accomplish the most reprehensible act but which very cleverly stops short, not of violence, but of open war.[33]

The assertion that the UN has somehow staved off World War III is baseless speculation. The organization is totally incapable of preventing such an outbreak should a major power decide to launch it. Even Secretary-General Kurt Waldheim has admitted: "Past experience has shown that the United Nations cannot either successfully deal with disputes if the Governments concerned do not wish to do so, or, against their opposition, impose the settlement of a dispute."[34] And Alexander Dallin, Professor of Government and History at Stanford University, told the Senate Foreign Relations Committee on May 14, 1975: "In its entire history the UN has only rarely been able to constrain any combatant nation. It has never constrained any of the major powers. It must be recognized that it can do least where it would be needed most."[35]

The absence of World War III to date has been due to the motivations and inclinations of those nations capable of starting it, not to the exaggerated influence of a braggart United Nations. Even at the time of the UN's founding, Secretary of State Stettinius testified on July 9, 1945: "If one of these [*permanent UN member*] nations ever embarked upon a course of aggression, a major war would result, no matter what the membership and voting provisions of the Security Council might be."[36]

Rather than *curb* war, the UN has actually *contributed* to
hostilities. It is claimed by some UN advocates that the General
Assembly provides a forum for verbal assaults which reduces
the chances for war because "letting off steam" has a cathartic
effect on the speakers. Yet, as explained by Abraham Yeselson
(Chairman of the Political Science Department of Rutgers
University) and Anthony Gaglione (Professor of Political Science at East Stroudsburg [Pennsylvania] State College), "When
Jews are described as Nazis at the UN, Israelis become more
than ever convinced that war is the only means of dealing with
their enemies. . . . South Africans who are constantly reminded at the UN that their words are unworthy of being heard
by more civilized ears become even more hardened in their
positions."[37] Yeselson and Gaglione (both of whom support the
basic concept of the UN) conclude: "Real negotiations require
that the parties define differences as narrowly as possible,
avoid recriminations, exclude extremists from discussions. At
the UN, issues are widened, insults are common, and the most
violent spokesmen frequently dominate the debate."[38]

And columnist Paul Weaver has noted:

> By providing a first-class propaganda platform, an opportu-
> nity to make and mobilize allies, and other resources that are
> useful in conflict situations, the U.N. allows nations to postpone
> the day when exhaustion or defeat forces them to resolve their
> differences. Moreover, by making such resources available to
> every comer, the U.N. provides scores of impotent and impov-
> erished new nations with the wherewithal to engage in conflicts
> they would otherwise be unable to afford.[39]

In short, the very manner in which the UN serves as a public
forum for the airing of grievances, which has so often been
propagandized by UN advocates as a contribution to peace, is
actually a *roadblock* to peace. Cecil Crabb, Jr., points out:

> In recent years, informed students of international affairs
> have challenged the efficacy of "open diplomacy," as epito-

mized by discussions in the UN General Assembly. Particularly when deliberations are televised to millions of viewers and the galleries are open to the public, proceedings are apt to degenerate into propaganda contests, in which each side tries to outscore the other in verbal sparring. . . . Above all, officials think they must avoid the slightest intimation that they are "appeasing" the enemy or failing to "protect" the national honor.[40]

Conservative author G. Edward Griffin illustrates the point with an enlightening analogy:

> Consider what would happen if every time a small spat arose between a husband and wife they called the entire neighborhood together and took turns airing their complaints in front of the whole group. Gone would be any chance of reconciliation. Instead of working out their problems, the ugly necessity of saving face, proving points, and winning popular sympathy would likely drive them further apart. Likewise, public debates in the UN intensify international tensions. By shouting their grievances at each other, countries allow their differences to assume a magnitude they would otherwise never have reached. Quiet diplomacy is always more conducive to progress than diplomacy on the stage.[41]

So we see that the UN, whose proponents claim it was formed to stop war, curb international hostilities, and promote freedom, has compiled a truly miserable record. Sold to us as a forum of reason and cooperation, it has in practice seethed with hostility and wild rhetoric. Allegedly intended to replace war with the rule of law, its history has been drenched with blood. Supposedly founded to promote the cause of human rights, it has become an aggressive enemy of freedom. Accepted as a mechanism to enhance our nation's foreign policy, it has become instead the world's leading anti-American outlet.

There is also a paradox in those provisions of the UN Charter that have to do with economic cooperation. They are "based on the premise that a necessary condition of the maintenance of international peace and security is the creation generally throughout the world of 'conditions of stability and well-being.'

It is only under such conditions that 'peaceful and friendly relations among nations based on respect for the principle of equal rights and self-determination of peoples' can exist."[42] The economic system best equipped to contribute such stability and well-being is Free Enterprise, with its emphasis on the production of new wealth and the right of individuals to own and control private property (thus enhancing their incentive to produce). But the United Nations is an advocate of Socialist economic policies, with an emphasis on redistribution of existing wealth. A few years ago, former Senator Jacob Javits (R.-New York; CFR), a staunch defender of the UN, served as one of twenty members on a United Nations panel studying multinational corporations. The panel's findings, issued in a report on June 7, 1974, were typical. As described by Senator Javits:

> . . . the two implicit assumptions of the Report are that governmental involvement is preferable to private initiative, and that governments know best and will act always in the long run in the interest of their citizens. Based on long experience, I seriously question both assumptions.[43]

Leaders of the Socialist International have stated with good reason: "The ultimate object of the parties of the Socialist International is nothing less than world government. As a first step towards it, they seek to strengthen the United Nations."[44] The point, they say, "is that the United Nations as a concept is essentially a democratic socialist idea."[45]

As viewed by the UN, the lot of the poor can be improved by "ripping off" the rich. "From each according to his abilities, to each according to his needs,"[46] as Karl Marx put it. And since the wealthy victims are the very nations now footing most of the bill for UN expenses, the UN has itself created yet another threat to world peace, similar to that described by Alexander Hamilton: "There is, perhaps, nothing more likely to disturb the tranquility of nations than their being bound to mutual contributions for any common object that does not yield an equal and coincidental benefit."[47]

If the various specialized agencies of the UN were allowed to take everything we have and redistribute it to poor nations, overall misery in the world would scarcely be affected: There are simply too many of them, and too few of us. But if we could assist the backward nations in throwing off the shackles of Socialism that are keeping them backward, and adopting instead the basic economic techniques that have been responsible for our unprecedented abundance, we would be making an unparalleled contribution to world stability and well-being. The United Nations, unfortunately, stands as a serious Marxist roadblock to such a change, which must be removed before there will be much chance to cope realistically with the problems of world hunger and poverty.

Contrary to the implications of UN propaganda, prosperity is no sure guarantor of peace. Hunger, ignorance, disease, *etc.* are serious problems which merit concern and solution — but they are not the roots of war. After all, it takes armaments and large armies to fight a big war. Nations hovering on the brink of poverty and disease are too sick and hungry to produce sufficient armaments and effectively field armies, and too poor to keep a war going (unless, of course, their military preparations are assisted from the outside by the affluent nations or the UN). On the other hand, Germany's health, educational, economic, and social status ranked among the highest in the world prior to World War I, and there was little economic distress or unemployment in Germany at the start of World War II. History shows that it has been advanced nations, rather than backward nations, that have disturbed world peace.

Nor are wars prevented by increased understanding between nations. Surely, few nations on earth understood each other better than England and Germany, yet they fought bitterly in both world wars. As decent people learn more about reprehensible nations, movements, or individuals, they become increasingly repelled. The more understanding Jews gained about the Nazis, the greater became the breech between them. The more advocates of freedom learn about Communism, the more repulsive the Red record appears. And, as one disgruntled Republican observed, "Richard Nixon was admired and respected until the American people found out more about him than he wished them to know."

In 1949, George D. Stoddard (a member of the Board of UNESCO, the UN's Educational, Scientific and Cultural Organization) seemed to recognize this principle when he expressed relief that a Gallup Poll had shown that only one percent of the people had ever heard of UNESCO, because "It means that hardly anybody has been turned against it!"[48] As Charles Malik once observed, "human nature being essentially and mysteriously subject to envy, spite, pride, and inordinate ambition — a certain degree of 'distance' from a country or culture is sometimes preferable to too intimate an acquaintance with it. . . ."[49]

During a 1965 tribute to the United Nations, former NATO Ambassador Harlan Cleveland (CFR) wrote: "It is almost impossible even to *think* about a durable world peace without the United Nations."[50] Which may be true. But it is even *more* inconceivable to think about a durable world peace *with* the United Nations. Testifying before the Senate Foreign Relations Committee, Rutgers Professor Abraham Yeselson (who personally opposes U.S. withdrawal from the UN) declared:

> It will be extraordinarily difficult now to rationalize continued involvement in an Organization which sponsors wars, passes one-sided or unenforceable resolutions, provides forums for international insult instead of diplomacy, and is guilty of the most outrageous examples of selective justice.[51]

He speculated: "Perhaps it will be impossible for the American people to overcome disillusion and they will demand withdrawal from the world body."[52]

We'll keep our fingers crossed.

Chapter 4

Aggression

Article 2 of the UN Charter lists the chief obligations assumed by UN members and the principles on which the organization is founded. The fourth principle asserts that "All members shall refrain in their international relations from the threat or use of force against the territorial integrity or political independence of any state, or in any other manner inconsistent with the Purposes of the United Nations." As Secretary of State Stettinius noted in 1945, "This means that force may be used in an organized manner under the authority of the United Nations to prevent and to remove threats to the peace and to suppress acts of aggression."[1]

Suppressing aggression, most would agree, is a noble assignment. Assuming, of course, that the term "aggression" is defined in some rational manner, such as "initiating the use of force against another party." That definition, however, would clearly brand the UN itself as an aggressor for its action against Katanga and Rhodesia. Such an obvious and rational definition of the term would be incompatible with the long-range goals of a world body bent on using aggression to suppress opposition to its pro-Marxist brand of "peace." As a result, the UN's search

for a more pragmatic definition of "aggression" proved extremely difficult.

Attempts were made at the San Francisco Conference to
achieve agreement on a definition, but they were eventually
abandoned as futile. President Truman explained in a subsequent report to Congress:

> The United States and some other delegations advocated that
> the Assembly should discontinue its attempts at definition as no
> satisfactory one could be found. A definition which enumerated
> all possible acts of aggression *would necessarily be incomplete*
> *and could thus be harmful*; conversely, an abstract and general
> formula would be too vague to prove useful. Therefore, those
> states considered it preferable to leave the United Nations
> organs, which are responsible for determining an aggressor, full
> discretion to consider all circumstances of each case.[2] [*Emphasis*
> *in original.*]

In other words, the UN could not even define what it was
supposed to oppose, so simply left it up to each UN "organ" to
operate under its own definition.

During the next thirty years, additional attempts were made
to reach some sort of consensus. In 1952, the General Assembly
established a 15-member committee to formulate a definition,
but adjourned in confusion. A second committee, established in
1954, waited another two years before convening, and then
produced nothing. The General Assembly spawned a third
committee in 1957, but its meager task was simply to decide
when the Assembly should "consider again the question of
defining aggression."[3] It met only four times during the next
decade, and reached no decision.

In 1967, a fourth group (called the "Committee on the
Question of Defining Aggression") was created. Seven years
later, it finally produced a definition which was approved by
the General Assembly on January 14, 1975. Running three full
pages (which we shall simply excerpt here), the definition
begins as follows (Article 1):

Aggression is the use of armed force by a State against the sovereignty, territorial integrity or political independence of another State, or in any other manner inconsistent with the Charter of the United Nations.[4]

Note that this would not preclude the use of armed force by a conglomerate of states (*i.e.*, the UN itself), nor the use of aggressive force when it is *consistent* with the UN Charter.

Article II, in typical UN fashion, then makes the self-serving definition *totally* meaningless by permitting the Security Council to "undefine" aggressive acts as aggression whenever the inclination arises. It asserts:

The first use of armed force by a State in contravention of the Charter shall constitute *prima facie* evidence of an act of aggression although the Security Council may, in conformity with the Charter, conclude that a determination that an act of aggression has been committed would not be justified in the light of other relevant circumstances, including the fact that the acts concerned or their consequences are not of sufficient gravity.[5]

So, aggression once again becomes whatever the UN says it is — or is not. If the Soviet Union were to re-invade Hungary (as in 1956) or Czechoslovakia (as in 1968), and the Red Chinese were again to rape Tibet (as in 1959), their aggression could easily be excused and ignored under the UN's phony definition. Should the UN itself invade another country as it did Katanga in 1961, or conduct diplomatic aggression against other nations as it has Rhodesia, it could do so without the need to censure itself for being an aggressor.

On the other hand, the definition leaves the UN free to condemn as "aggressors" any countries which might attempt to defend themselves against pro-Communist aggression (as when Marxist rebels attacked Portugal's overseas provinces — and the UN condemned Portugal).

The UN's definition of aggression is obviously as duplicitous as its definition of "human rights" (see Chapter Ten). It may be accurately paraphrased as follows: "Aggression is whatever is harmful to the existence and spread of Communism; and any act which aids the Communist advance is not and never can be aggression." It is yet another reason why the UN is no place for sovereign nations or men of honor.

Chapter 5
Korea

North Korea invaded South Korea on June 24, 1950 (June 25, Korea time). The UN Security Council promptly passed a resolution fixing blame on the North Koreans and urging UN members to render assistance to repel the Communist aggression. Two days later, the Security Council approved another resolution calling on UN members to supply military assistance to the Republic of Korea. Soviet vetoes could have killed both resolutions, but none were cast.

Using the non-membership of Red China as an excuse, the Soviets had stalked out of the Security Council the previous January, and were still "boycotting" the Council when the war began. Most pro-UN accounts claim that the boycott represented a serious Soviet blunder because, contrary to "obvious" Soviet wishes, it permitted the UN to rush to the aid of the anti-Communists. For example, President Truman reported to Congress: "Only fortuitous circumstances had enabled the United Nations to take swift action against the North Korean aggression: . . . the Soviet delegate had boycotted the Security Council and therefore was not able to veto its recommendations."[1]

Another UN advocate wrote that the Soviet absence "enabled the Council, unhindered by a Soviet veto, to pass its celebrated resolution calling upon member states to assist in repelling aggression in Korea. Even the Russians can make mistakes."[2]

In the same spirit, former U.S. Secretary of State Christian Herter (CFR) claimed: ". . . by one of those curious accidents which can play such a large part in the world's history, the Russians were absent from the Security Council, and that Council voted without a veto to oppose the aggression of the North Koreans."[3]

And former Senator Margaret Chase Smith (R.-Maine), after telling her Senate colleagues that "United Nations intervention in the Korean conflict was perhaps its greatest achievement," asserted:

> But in all honesty, we must recognize that it was the fortuitous circumstance of a Russian boycott of the U.N. Security Council at the time. Had not Russia so boycotted the Security Council at that time but instead had been present to vote, undoubtedly Russia would have exercised her veto power and thus prevented the United Nations from intervening and going to the defense of South Korea.[4]

This "Russian blunder" hypothesis appeared plausible to many at first glance, but closer scrutiny exposed it as a hoax. Following is some of the evidence supporting the revisionist hypothesis that the Soviets were *not* caught by surprise by the North Korean invasion, but instead were deeply involved in planning and launching it; that they did *not* oppose the UN intervention, but were actually anxious for the UN to become involved in the Korean fiasco.

Article 27 of the UN Charter clearly states that decisions of the Security Council on non-procedural matters "shall be made by an affirmative vote of seven members including the concurring votes of the permanent members. . . ." The Soviet Union, as one of the "permanent members," cast no concurring vote. Its refusal to participate in the Council's deliberations was, under the terms of the Charter, equivalent to a veto. This important point, however, was simply ignored, and the Korean Resolutions

were implemented despite their conflict with the Charter. The
Soviets raised no meaningful objection.

Writing in his memoirs, former Soviet dictator Nikita Khrushchev revealed:

> About the time I was transferred from the Ukraine to Moscow
> at the end of 1949, Kim Il-sung [*North Korea's Communist
> leader*] arrived with his delegation to hold consultations with
> Stalin. The North Koreans wanted to prod South Korea with the
> point of a bayonet. . . . Naturally Stalin couldn't oppose this
> idea. . . .
> We had already been giving arms to North Korea for some
> time. It was obvious that they would receive the requisite quantity
> of tanks, artillery, rifles, machine guns, engineering equipment,
> and anti-aircraft weapons. . . .
> The designated hour arrived and the war began. The attack
> was launched successfully. The North Koreans swept south
> swiftly.[5]

Khrushchev then made a most revealing admission:

> . . . when Kim Il-sung was preparing for his march, Stalin called
> back all our advisors who were with the North Korean divisions
> and regiments, as well as all the advisors who were serving as
> consultants and helping to build up the army. I asked Stalin
> about this, and he snapped back at me, "It's too dangerous to
> keep our advisors there. They might be taken prisoner. We don't
> want there to be evidence for accusing us of taking part in this
> business. It's Kim Il-sung's affair." So our advisors were recalled.[6]

Writing in *Foreign Affairs* for October, 1950, *New York Times*
UN Bureau Chief Thomas Hamilton (CFR) acknowledged that
North Korea "clearly could not have launched its aggression
without its patron's [*the Soviet Union's*] full approval."[7]

One year later former Senator Paul Douglas (D.-Illinois;
CFR) asserted in *Foreign Affairs*: "The North Korean Commu-
nists, without doubt under Russian stimulation, crossed the 38th
Parallel. . . ."[8]

And in April, 1952, yet another *Foreign Affairs* contributor
declared that the North Korean aggression "was supplied and

equipped by the Soviet Union and could not have occurred without its instigation or approval."[9] Those words were written by then-Senator Adlai Stevenson (D.-Illinois; CFR) who would later, as our UN Ambassador, help promote the myth that the North Korean invasion caught the Soviets off-guard.

Additional evidence surfaced on May 15, 1954, when the U.S. Defense Department released a report entitled, "The Truth About Soviet Involvement In The Korean War." The document began by asserting that the Soviet-assisted military buildup in North Vietnam had begun in 1945, and that "When the North Korean Army had reached a degree of strength which indicated it could conquer all of Korea, the Russians gave it the signal for the attack across the 38th parallel."[10]

The study further charged:

> . . . when the tide of battle turned against the North Koreans and the Chinese entered the conflict and stayed in it for more than two years, it was Russian support that made it possible for the Communist forces to ward off complete defeat. Without that help, the Chinese with their inadequate industrial structure could not possibly have maintained effective military forces in Korea on their own resources.[11]

This means, of course, that the chief enemy in Korea was the Soviet Union. Yet, the issue of Soviet involvement was never formally raised by the UN. As we have seen, influential Americans such as Senators Paul Douglas and Adlai Stevenson admitted (in *Foreign Affairs*) that the Soviets had helped instigate the conflict. Why didn't they speak out and demand that the UN condemn the USSR as an aggressor along with the North Koreans and Chinese? Part of the answer lies in the fact that North Korea and Red China were *not* UN members, while the USSR was, and to condemn the Soviets would have placed the UN in the untenable position of warring with one of its most powerful member-states. The primary role played by the Soviets was therefore simply ignored by all concerned.

According to the Defense Department study, a North Korean major who had been captured as a prisoner of war confessed "that as the flow of Russian equipment into Korea increased during the period immediately preceding the initial attack, the flow of Russian advisors increased with it. All orders, he said, came from these advisors, and he, who spoke Russian, was given the job of 'translating them into Korean.' "[12] The report continues:

> Many Russian "advisors" were attached to the North Korean Army advance headquarters established in June, 1950. They wore civilian clothing, the Major added, and it was forbidden to address them by rank. They were introduced as "newspaper reporters" but they had supreme authority. They took the lead in making operational and mobilizational plans, and in commanding and manipulating troops. They treated the Korean officers who were nominally their chiefs, the Major said, "like their servants, or children."
>
> The North Korean Major identified two of these Russian "advisors" as Lieutenant General Vasiliev and Colonel Dolgin. Vasiliev, he said, apparently was in charge of all movements across the 38th parallel.[13]

Another prisoner "said he actually heard General Vasiliev give the order to attack on June 25."[14]

That Soviet general, Vasiliev, was the same man who from 1947 to 1950 had served as the Soviet representative on the UN's Military Staff Committee. His Soviet bosses had evidently moved him to a new assignment.

So the Soviets knew the attack was coming, because they had supplied and arranged it, which means they *wanted* to have us embroiled in the Korean conflict. Their absence from the Security Council was obviously nothing more than a contrived ploy to permit the UN to become involved in Korea under conditions that would camouflage the obvious Soviet desire that it do so. After all, the Soviets had one of their own men (Undersecretary General for Political and Security Council Affairs Konstantin E. Zinchenko) in charge of the UN Department responsible for application of UN enforcement measures. And it was clearly in the Soviet interest to have the supremely powerful United States Army placed under an international command in a war it would not be allowed to win. The "limited" war precedent thus established, which significantly neutralized U.S. military potential, would serve their purposes in many ways (as Vietnam subsequently proved).

The following excerpts from General Douglas MacArthur's autobiography give an idea of how little the Communists had to fear from the UN's Korean expedition. MacArthur, one of the most able and patriotic military leaders in our nation's history, had been placed in command of UN forces, then compelled by Washington to fight over and around artificially-imposed roadblocks:

> I was . . . worried by a series of directives from Washington which were greatly decreasing the potential of my air force. First I was forbidden "hot" pursuit of enemy planes that attacked our own. Manchuria and Siberia were sanctuaries of inviolate protection for all enemy forces and for all enemy purposes, no matter what depredations or assaults might come from there. Then I was denied the right to bomb the hydroelectric plants along the Yalu. The order was broadened to include every plant in North Korea which was capable of furnishing electric power to Manchuria and Siberia. Most incomprehensible of all was the refusal to let me bomb the important supply center at Racin, which was not in Manchuria or Siberia, but many miles from the border, in northeast Korea. Racin was a depot to which the Soviet Union forwarded supplies from Vladivostok for the North Korean Army. I felt that step-by-step my weapons were being taken away from me.[15]

Note the remarkable parallel between General MacArthur's situation and the "no-win" policy forced on our fighting men in Vietnam.*

---

*The only legal basis for our involvement in Vietnam was the entangling alliance called the Southeast Asia Treaty Organization (SEATO), a regional UN subsidiary set up under Article 52 of the UN Charter. In the *New York Times* for March 2, 1966, C.L. Sulzberger (CFR) revealed: "[John Foster] Dulles [CFR] fathered SEATO with the deliberate purpose, as he explained to me, of providing the U.S. President with legal authority to intervene in Indochina. When Congress approved SEATO it signed the first of a series of blank checks yielding authority over Vietnam policy." After serving its purpose, SEATO was disbanded in February, 1976.

On June 27, 1950, President Truman commanded U.S. air
and sea forces to supply cover and support to South Korean
troops and ordered our Seventh Fleet into the Formosa Strait,
allegedly to preclude any military action against Formosa by
Red China, and *vice versa*.[16] Most significant by far was the
effect the Fleet's presence had in precluding any action by
Formosa against the Mainland. In effect, beginning with the
second day of the war, our Seventh Fleet was assigned to protect
the Red Chinese who, five months later, would attack our forces
in Korea. General MacArthur was ordered

> to isolate the Nationalist-held island of Formosa from the
> Chinese mainland. The United States Seventh Fleet was turned
> over to my operational control for this purpose, and I was
> specifically directed to prevent any Nationalist attacks on the
> mainland, as well as to defend the island against Communist
> attacks.[17]

The decision to move across the 38th Parallel into North
Korea presented MacArthur

> with problems of the gravest import. It immediately raised the
> shadow of Red Chinese intervention. Actually, the possibility of
> such an intervention had existed ever since the order from
> Washington, issued to the Seventh Fleet in June, to neutralize
> Formosa, which in effect protected the Red China mainland
> from attack by Chiang Kai-shek's force of half a million men.
> This released the two great Red Chinese armies assigned to the
> coastal defense of central China and made them available for
> transfer elsewhere.[18]

On April 8, 1952, William C. Bullitt (former Ambassador to
both the USSR and France; CFR) testified before the Senate
Internal Security Subcommittee, reminding Subcommittee
members that "Chiang Kai-shek offered to send 30,000 troops
immediately, just as soon as the attack of the North Koreans
took place. Our Government refused to accept them. He not
only offered 30,000, he also offered to send as many more as we

wanted. I would have taken a great quantity of them. I think if you had taken them, and put them into the fight, we would have won it in the very early days. . . ."[19] Asked by Senator Arthur V. Watkins (R.-Utah) if the Free Chinese had a navy, Bullitt replied:

> Oh, yes, As a matter of fact, it has been quite an efficient force, although it is forbidden to act in any way by fiat of our Government which has given orders to our fleet to prevent it from stopping the Communist supply ships going up to Korea. They sail right by Formosa, loaded with Soviet munitions put in the Polish Communist ships in Gdynia. They come all the way around and go right by Formosa and sail past there taking those munitions up, taking those weapons up to be used to kill American soldiers in Korea, and by order of our Government the Chinese Navy is flatly forbidden to stop them on their way up there."[20]

Senator Watkins then asked: "Would the Chinese Navy have the power, except for that order, to intercept them and capture them?" Ambassador Bullitt replied, "Certainly, without question, without question."[21]

On September 29, 1954, General James A. Van Fleet, Commander of the Eighth Army in Korea, testified before the Subcommittee. Asked if the neutralization of Formosa by the Seventh Fleet had freed the Red Chinese for action in Korea, he replied: "Yes, it would certainly help them; give them a feeling of security that they could go north free from a threat in the south." Asked if that made any sense militarily, the General answered: "No."[22]

Additional evidence that the Seventh Fleet had been positioned primarily to protect Red China surfaced following the 1952 Presidential election when, in his first State of the Union message to Congress on February 2, 1953,

> President Dwight D. Eisenhower [CFR] announced the decision to lift the blockade of Formosa by the United States Seventh Fleet as a base for Nationalists' attacks on the Communist Chinese mainland. The President said that he was "issuing

instructions that the Seventh Fleet no longer be employed to
shield Communist China" from attack by Chinese Nationalists
on Formosa. He wanted "to make crystal clear this order implies
no aggressive intent on our part. But we certainly have no
obligation to protect a nation fighting us in Korea."[23]

Most of the damage, of course, had already been done.
The overall military situation was so incredible that General
Mark Clark* later speculated:

> . . . perhaps Communists had wormed their way so deeply into
> our government on both the working and planning levels that they
> were able to exercise an inordinate degree of power in shaping the
> course of America in the dangerous postwar era.
>
> I could not help wondering and worrying whether we were
> faced with open enemies across the conference table and hidden
> enemies who sat with us in our most secret councils.[24]

General Clark's concern was justified. General MacArthur,
having directly experienced the problem himself, had written:

> That there was some leak in intelligence was evident to
> everyone. [*Brigadier General Walton*] Walker continually com-
> plained to me that his operations were known to the enemy in
> advance through sources in Washington. . . . information must
> have been relayed to them, assuring that the Yalu bridges would
> continue to enjoy sanctuary and that their bases would be left
> intact. They knew they could swarm down across the Yalu River
> without having to worry about bombers hitting their Manchurian
> supply lines.[25]

General MacArthur then cited an official leaflet published
by Red Chinese General Lin Piao:

> I would never have made the attack and risked my men and
> military reputation if I had not been assured that Washington

---

*General Clark succeeded General Matthew Ridgway (CFR) in 1953 as UN
Commander in Korea. Ridgway had replaced General MacArthur in 1951 after
President Truman fired MacArthur for wanting to win the war.

would restrain General MacArthur from taking adequate retalia-
tory measures against my lines of supply and communication.[26]

During his Senate testimony cited earlier, General James A.
Van Fleet was asked if the Red Chinese would have entered the
war if they had not been assured that our military response
would be limited. He responded: "No, he would not have entered
Korea if he did not feel safe from attack in north China and
Manchuria."[27]

One source of some of those leaks was exposed in 1967 when a
British newspaper succeeded in tracking down in Washington a
secret report which State Department intelligence officers had
compiled in 1956 in an attempt to assess the damage done by two
Soviet spies who had operated in Britain. According to news
accounts, the confidential document (Why was it still secret in
1967?) showed that one of the spies, Donald MacLean, "had
full knowledge of the critical American determination to 'local-
ize the conflict,' and therefore of its decision not to allow the
United Nations forces under Gen. MacArthur to carry the war
against the Chinese coast."[28] MacLean had defected to the
Soviet Union in 1951 and was, as General Clark suspected, a
hidden enemy sitting with us in our most secret councils.

The Korean armistice agreement was signed on July 27, 1953.
More than 33,000 Americans had died, another 103,000 had been
wounded, and General Clark (who signed the agreement) was
compelled to lament that he had "gained the unenviable distinction of being the first United States Army commander in
history to sign an armistice without victory."[29]

Such was the war that would subsequently be touted by many
influential UN supporters as the organization's "greatest
achievement." From the Communist viewpoint, it probably was.

Chapter 6

Rhodesia

United States involvement in the UN has twisted our foreign policy to the point where it actually works against our country's best interests. The UN-provoked boycott of Rhodesia, briefly mentioned in Chapter Three, is a prime example of this.

The story begins on November 11, 1965, when Rhodesia declared her independence from Great Britain in a manner similar to our own nation's declaration of two centuries before. The UN General Assembly condemned Rhodesia that same day,[1] and the Security Council followed suit the day after.[2] On November 20, the Security Council formally branded Rhodesia "a threat to international peace and security."[3]

Applying the Communist definition of "peace" (*i.e.*, an absence of resistance to Communism), Rhodesia could indeed have been classified as such a threat. But according to the concept of "peace" held by most people, the action of the Security Council was incredible. Indeed, when Britain first called for UN sanctions against Rhodesia, the resolution submitted did *not* contain a finding that Rhodesia was a threat to peace. That conclusion was simply inserted — with no supporting facts — and the resolution sent on its way, *after* it was pointed out that such a finding was necessary before the UN could take action.[4]

Rhodesia had never had a large, aggressive armed force; had never threatened her neighbors with aggression; and had never posed a military or economic threat to world peace or security. Yet it was claimed, with her internal racial policies cited as an excuse, that some other nations that disagreed with those policies might someday attack Rhodesia. This, by United Nations standards, made *Rhodesia* the threat to peace! It was like blaming the chickens for the gleam in the eye of the fox — or, in the words of one Congressman, "like saying that a law-abiding home is a dangerous threat to law and order in the community because some criminal may rob or burglarize it. . . ."[5]

The November 20, 1965, Security Council Resolution called for *voluntary* sanctions against Rhodesia, but met with little success. So, on December 16, 1966, the Council voted to impose *mandatory* sanctions,[6] an action that stands to this day as the only time in UN history that such sanctions have been applied. This is *quite* revealing. After all, the UN was founded in 1945. Since that time the Communists have instigated aggression after aggression, including the two major wars in Korea and Vietnam, and have forcibly enslaved more than one billion human beings along the way. Yet, when the UN finally moved to impose sanctions against a "threat to peace," it selected as its target the small, benign, pro-Western, anti-Communist country of Rhodesia. The Rhodesians had had both the courage and the wisdom to take their affairs into their own hands and achieve *real* independence before the United Nations, the socialist government of Britain, and our State Department could arrange for them the sort of completely phony and chaotic "independence" that has plagued most of the African continent in recent years — and which has so often served as the excuse and the means for placing ever more of the earth's population under Marxist control.

The UN crowd simply couldn't stand for it.

The Constitution of the United States gives Congress — not

the President or the United Nations — the power to regulate our commerce with foreign nations.[7] Nowhere in that document is the expedient of the Executive Order even mentioned. Yet, on January 5, 1967, President Lyndon Johnson signed Executive Order 11322, declaring it to be a criminal offense for any American to engage in the import of a wide range of Rhodesian products, and severely restricting U.S. exports to that country.[8] On July 29, 1968, the President signed another Executive Order (Number 11419) barring all United States imports from, and exports to, Rhodesia.[9]

These unilateral actions by President Johnson placed our nation in a very peculiar and uncomfortable position. At the time, our men were being killed and maimed in Vietnam by Communists supplied primarily by the Soviet Union.* Rhodesia, in contrast, had offered to send troops to help us fight in Vietnam. Yet our government leaders were permitting extensive shipments of goods and materiel to the Soviet Union and other Communist countries comprising the arsenal of the Vietcong, at the very time they were refusing to ship those items to friendly Rhodesia. For example, in 1966 the State Department set forth the following policy, which was in effect throughout the Vietnam War:

> All American citizens should know that any American businessman who chooses to engage in peaceful trade with the Soviet Union or Eastern European countries and to sell the goods he buys is acting within his rights and is following the policy of his government. So, too, is any American citizen who chooses to buy such goods. . . .
>
> But any organization, however patriotic in intention, that undertakes to boycott, blacklist, or otherwise penalize or attack any American business for engaging in peaceful trade with Eastern European countries or the Soviet Union, is acting against the interests of the United States.[10]

Yet, on October 17, 1973, during joint subcommittee hearings

---

*"They [the Soviets] furnish 80 to 85 percent of the sophisticated military equipment for the North Vietnamese forces. Without that assistance, North Vietnam would not have the capability to wage the major war they are against the United States." (President Richard Nixon, news conference, March 4, 1969: reprinted, *Weekly Compilation of Presidential Documents*, March 10, 1969, p. 367.)

in the House of Representatives, Congressman John Buchanan
(R.-Alabama), who appeared as a witness *against* continued
U.S. trade with Rhodesia, testified:

> . . . four individuals and two corporations were indicted by
> federal grand jury for violating the U.N. sanctions against Rho-
> desia last year. All pleaded guilty to planning to build a $50
> million chemical fertilizer plant in Rhodesia and to enter into a
> secret agreement with the Rhodesia regime to ship $5 million
> worth of ammonia to Rhodesia. All were fined.[11]

Fertilizer and ammonia? Consider:

> On January 19, 1966, the Commerce Department authorized
> shipment to the U.S.S.R. of technical data for the construction
> and operation of a plant to produce synthetic ammonia. . . .
> On March 2, 1966, the Department of Commerce issued a
> license to authorize sending technical information to the
> U.S.S.R. for three more fertilizer plants. . . .
> On August 3, 1966, a license was issued by the Commerce
> Department to authorize shipment to the U.S.S.R. of another
> ammonia plant.[12]

Indeed, "On January 28, 1966, the Department of Commerce
issued a routine announcement that it was licensing export of
technical data to enable a United States firm to build six
fertilizer plants in Soviet Russia. . . . That same week, in
Senate committee testimony, Secretary of Defense Robert S.
McNamara [*CFR*] revealed that volume shipments of war supplies — *including fertilizer* — were coming into the North
Vietnamese port of Haiphong from the U.S.S.R."[13]

In short, it was official policy to give aid and comfort to our
worst enemies while boycotting one of our best friends.

One result of this immoral double standard was to make us
increasingly dependent on the Soviet Union for chrome, a vital
strategic material. The world's three main sources of chrome ore
are South Africa, the Soviet Union, and — Rhodesia. The rest
of the world lags far behind, and practically no chrome ore is to
be found in the United States or elsewhere in North America.

Following the imposition of sanctions against Rhodesia, the Soviet Union greatly increased the price of its chrome ore, and we were soon paying an outrageous premium for the privilege of becoming dependent on an enemy for a material essential to the production of stainless steel and other high-performance steels and superalloys. (It is chromium that imparts to such metals their vital resistance to heat and corrosion.) As noted by one national news magazine:

> Ever since the U.S. slapped an embargo on Rhodesian chromium for diplomatic reasons, this country has been forced to rely on Soviet Russia for 45 percent of its entire supply of the strategic metal. Not only that, complain critics of the whole idea, but the Russians have upped the price from $30.50 to $72 a ton.[14]

It was primarily this situation that prompted Senator Harry F. Byrd, Jr. (I.-Virginia) to make a determined bid to reinstate Rhodesia as a source of supply for chrome ore. In 1971, Congress approved an amendment submitted by Senator Byrd that permitted the United States to import strategic materials from Rhodesia if those materials were also imported from Communist nations. It was a modest, sensible proposal that was clearly in tune with our country's best interests. As explained by Senator Byrd:

> The legislation did not make it impossible for the executive branch to prevent importation from Rhodesia.
> What the legislation did say . . . is that the importation of chrome from a Free World country cannot be prohibited if that same strategic material is being imported from a Communist-dominated country. . . .
> So if the President of the United States does not want to have chrome imported from Rhodesia, he can stop the importation of chrome from Russia. . . . So there is a way, if the President of the United States so desires, that the importation of this strategic material from Rhodesia can be prevented.[15]

Nevertheless, the Byrd Amendment immediately aroused the Internationalist Left to a frenzy of opposition because it permitted a partial circumvention of the UN sanctions against Rhodesia.

The Byrd Amendment became effective on January 1, 1972. It was promptly challenged, and upheld, in the courts. On May 16, 1973, the Communist newspaper *Daily World* published an editorial calling for its repeal, asserting: "The crucial step today is to compel Congress to repeal the pro-imperialist, pro-racist position it adopted, legalizing violation of the U.N.'s embargo in 1971." Later in the year, then-Senator Gale McGee (D.-Wyoming; CFR) admitted:

> The central issue is not chrome from Rhodesia. The central issue is not repealing something just to repeal it. The central issue is, what is going to happen to the United Nations? It is the United Nations that is on the line. . . .
> . . . every Member of this body [*the Senate*] ought to know what he is voting. He is voting to start getting out of the U.N.
> . . . if the United States is to go back under the Charter of the United Nations . . . this amendment must be repealed. That is the whole issue.[16]

Remember that the basis for the UN's Rhodesian embargo was the claim that Rhodesia was "minority-ruled" and a "threat to peace." Our leaders were calling for repeal of the Byrd Amendment, while at the same time advocating increased trade with the minority-ruled, peace-threatening Soviet Union. On March 7, 1974, during hearings before the Senate Finance Committee, the following revealing exchange took place between Senator Byrd and Secretary of State Henry Kissinger (CFR):

> Senator Byrd. Do you recognize our action in embargoing trade with Rhodesia as being just?
> Secretary Kissinger. Yes.
> Senator Byrd. Do you regard the Soviet Union as being governed by a tight dictatorship, by a very few persons over a great number of individuals?
> Secretary Kissinger. I consider the Soviet Union, yes, as a dictatorship of an oligarchic nature, that is, of a small number of people in the Politburo.

Senator Byrd. In your judgment, is Rhodesia a threat to world peace?

Secretary Kissinger. No.

Senator Byrd. In your judgment, is Russia a potential threat to world peace?

Secretary Kissinger. I think the Soviet Union has the military capacity to disturb the peace, yes.

Senator Byrd. In your judgment, does Russia have a more democratic government than Rhodesia?

Secretary Kissinger. No. . . .

Senator Byrd. . . . you have testified that you do not regard Rhodesia as being a threat to world peace.

Secretary Kissinger. That is correct.

Senator Byrd. And then you know, of course, that under the United Nations Charter action can only be taken against a country in regard to an embargo, if that country is judged to be a threat to world peace.

And so my question to you is do you think the United Nations acted improperly?

Secretary Kissinger. I had not thought that the United Nations had acted improperly, but in the light of what you have said, I would have to review the particular positions of the embargo.[17]

Secretary Kissinger never did come up with a rational basis on which to brand Rhodesia a "threat to peace." He simply continued to advocate repeal of the Byrd Amendment. The Congress, however, rejected attempts to repeal the Amendment on a number of occasions between 1972 and the end of 1976. But in early 1977 it buckled under the pressure and voted to scrap the Byrd Amendment and place our nation once again in compliance with the UN's immoral and illegal boycott. On March 18, 1977, President Jimmy Carter stated:

I'm very grateful this morning to have a chance to sign House Resolution [sic]* 1746, which gives me the authority to reestablish

---

*Actually, it was a *bill* (H.R. 1746), not a resolution. The prefix "H.R." does not designate "House Resolution," as is widely believed, but rather "House of Representatives" the body in which the bill originated. House Resolutions are abbreviated "H. Res."

the embargo against the purchase of chrome from Rhodesia. . . .
I think it puts us on the side of what's right and proper.[18]

You will recall that in 1961 it was an anti-Communist *black*
regime in Katanga which the UN and American Internationalists sought to destroy for seeking a "premature," non-Marxist
independence. From 1965 to 1980, it was the anti-Communist
white regime in Rhodesia. It should be quite obvious that the
common denominator is not race, but anti-Communism. Ka-
tangans resisted Communism, were branded a "threat to peace,"
and saw their province invaded by a UN army which bombed
hospitals and bazookaed ambulances[19] until "peace" was restored. Rhodesians resisted Communism, were branded a threat
to peace, and were subjected to UN sanctions and widespread
UN-condoned attacks by guerrilla terrorists. For Rhodesia, like
Katanga, the incredible pressures loosed against her by the UN
and other subdivisions of the International Marxist Conspiracy
proved to be too much. On April 18, 1980, she officially died
and became the terrorist-ruled, Communist-backed, nation of
Zimbabwe.

The time is approaching when those African nations that
are still free will be engaged in a life-or-death battle against
Communist subjugation. The role of Rhodesia's loyal anti-
Communists in this fight remains to be seen. But one thing is
certain: If this brave little country had not been betrayed by her
allies, foremost among whom we must count the United States,
she would undoubtedly be alive and well today — and her
survival would have marked a significant turning point in the
battle for freedom.

Chapter 7

They Love Me?
They Love Me Not?

It may seem absurd today, but a key argument used by UN advocates until just a few years ago was the claim that the United States should support the UN because the Communists were anxious to destroy it. This false premise was in turn used as the basis for claiming that anti-Communist Americans who opposed the UN were working for the same goal as the Communists. Here, for example, is how former Senator Frank Church (D.-Idaho; CFR) manipulated the argument during a Senate speech:

> If you tell them [*UN haters*] that their objective of getting the United States out of the U.N. is just what Khrushchev would like to see happen; that it was the shoe-pounding Khrushchev who tried to bully his troika plan through the General Assembly, with the purpose of undermining the office of the Secretary General, so that the U.N. might be rendered as impotent as its predecessor, the League [*of Nations*], they grow angry and abusive as they grope for the answers they cannot find.[1]

We will not become angry and abusive as we "grope for the

answers." As we find them, however, we may become just a little indignant at having been deceived for so long by propagandists like Senator Church.

In 1955, the State Department was claiming that "The United States has never been defeated in any important political question in the United Nations. On the other hand the Soviet Union can usually count on only 5 out of 60 votes in the General Assembly."[2] Similarly, former UN Ambassador Henry Cabot Lodge (CFR) once asserted that the Communists do not dominate the UN because "The United States has never been defeated on any important political question in the United Nations."[3]

Since those statements were made, Red China has been admitted to (and Free China expelled from) the UN, the terrorist Palestine Liberation Organization (PLO) has been welcomed and glorified by the world body, and the UN General Assembly has launched an hysterical anti-American crusade that now makes us feel lucky if we attract as many as 5 votes out of 154 (as of November, 1980) in its chambers. Indeed, the UN "almost automatically lines up alongside Moscow's 'three antis': anti-colonialism, anti-imperialism and anti-racism. The fact that the United States winds up on the losing side of almost every such U.N. argument is a welcome bonus to the leaders of the Kremlin."[4]

The UN's alleged "anti-Communist" cover has been blown for good; yet its apologists continue to offer such absurd rationalizations as that of former Senator Gale McGee (D.-Wyoming; CFR): "For the first time since the founding of the United Nations, the U.S. has to work for a vote. . . . This is an important development *and it is good for us*, since it requires a greater effort and participation in the U.N. to achieve our goals."[5] (Emphasis added.) Obviously, no matter *how* deranged and anti-American the UN becomes, there always will be semantic magicians conjuring up ways to justify the continuation of our support.

Communist support of the UN has been evident from the

start to those not blinded by misleading pro-UN propaganda. In 1942 Earl Browder, former General Secretary of the Communist Party, USA (and twice its candidate for the Presidency of the United States), wrote of the wartime anti-Axis alliance that served as a key landmark on the road to San Francisco: ". . . the American Communists worked energetically and tirelessly to lay the foundation for the United Nations which we were sure would come into existence."[6] The goal, of course, was to have the Soviet Union become a wartime ally of the United States so it could take political advantage of the alliance both during and after the war. As far back as July 19, 1935, U.S. Ambassador to the Soviet Union William C. Bullitt (CFR) had sent the following dispatch to Secretary of State Cordell Hull:

> It is . . . the heartiest hope of the Soviet Government that the United States will become involved in war with Japan. . . . To think of the Soviet Union as a possible ally of the United States in case of war with Japan is to allow the wish to be father to the thought. The Soviet Union would certainly attempt to avoid becoming an ally until Japan had been thoroughly defeated and would then merely use the opportunity to acquire Manchuria and Sovietize China.[7]

That was an incredibly accurate projection of exactly what happened. At the Yalta Conference, the Soviets had been assured control of the Manchurian railroads. (It was well known that whoever controlled the railroads would dominate Manchuria.) Two days after the A-bomb was dropped on Hiroshima (six days before Japan's surrender), Russia declared war on Japan. Subsequently, after grabbing Manchuria and looting its industrial equipment, the Soviets turned it over to Mao-Tse-tung as an operational base for the Red Chinese (along with tons of arms, ammunition and supplies taken from the defeated Japanese). It was a crucial beginning step, as planned more than a decade earlier, to facilitate the eventual Communist subjugation of Mainland China.

Dr. Bella Dodd, a former top official of the Communist Party, USA, who eventually defected, has revealed:

When the Yalta conference had ended, the Communists prepared to support the United Nations Charter which was to be adopted at the San Francisco conference to be held in May and June, 1945. For this I organized a corps of speakers and we took to the street corners and held open-air meetings in the millinery and clothing sections of New York where thousands of people congregate at the lunch hour. We spoke of the need for world unity and in support of the Yalta decisions.[8]

Political Affairs is the monthly theoretical journal of the Communist Party, USA. Two months before the San Francisco Conference, that journal told its readers: "Great popular support and enthusiasm for the United Nations policies should be built up, well organized and fully articulate. . . . The opposition must be rendered so impotent that it will be unable to gather any significant support in the Senate against the United Nations Charter and the treaties which will follow."[9]

"Popular support" for the Charter was indeed well organized. Francis O. Wilcox (CFR), a member of the U.S. delegation at San Francisco, later reminisced:

During my years on Capitol Hill I can recall only a few instances when mail in foreign policy questions made any heavy impact on the Foreign Relations Committee. One instance concerned the ratification of the U.N. Charter, when the flood of letters and telegrams made it unmistakably clear that the great majority of Americans in all walks of life strongly favored U.S. membership in the new world organization. If any serious doubts had been lurking in the minds of the committee, they should have been dispelled by that outpouring of popular sentiment.[10]

Indeed the opposition was rendered so impotent that only two Senators, William Langer (R.-North Dakota) and Henrik Shipstead (R.-Minnesota), voted against the Charter. (The tally was 89 to 2 on July 28, 1945.) In fact, the Associated Press had reported on June 24, 1945, — even before the Charter was completed — that fifty-two of seventy-five Senators interviewed had already gone on record favoring its ratification.[11] In other words, a majority of Senators committed themselves to voting for a crucial foreign policy document before they could possibly have read it, since it had not yet been finished.

At San Francisco, "The Soviet Government took an active part. . . . Noteworthy is the fact that Soviet Russia was willing to compromise, as the *New York Times* pointed out in an editorial, on at least ten important issues in order to assure the prompt and successful establishment of the U.N."[12]

On March 23, 1946, Josef Stalin was quoted in *Pravda* as having declared: "I attribute great importance to U.N.O. since it is a serious instrument for preservation of peace and international security."[13] And the Soviet publication *Bolshevik* for November, 1946, asserted: "The masses know that peace is possible only on the basis of cooperation among the existing states. . . . The Soviet Union is fighting to have the United Nations as effective as possible."[14]

In 1947, Soviet Deputy Foreign Minister Andrei Vishinsky proclaimed: "The policy of the U.S.S.R. with regard to the United Nations calls for strengthening that body, extending and reinforcing international cooperation, unfaltering and consistent observance of the Charter, and the implementation of its principles."[15]

In 1954, the Communist *Daily Worker* pointed out to its readers that ". . . it's not the UN that merits your scorn and active opposition, but the policies that have undermined the UN."[16] And in 1957, the Communist Party, USA adopted a Constitution, the Preamble of which asserted that "the true national interest of our country and the cause of peace and progress require . . . the strengthening of the United Nations as a universal instrument of peace."[17]

During his visit to the United Nations in 1960, Soviet Premier Nikita Khrushchev told the General Assembly: "Experience of the work of the United Nations has shown that this body is useful and necessary. . . ."[18] The next year, as Communist support of the UN began to surface even more forcefully in the wake of increasing antagonism within the United States toward the world body, the West Coast Communist Party newspaper *People's World* declared:

The UN commands a great reservoir of support in our country.
This support should now be made vocal.
People should write President Kennedy, telling him —
Do not withdraw from UN.
Restore UN to the Grand Design of Franklin Roosevelt — the
design for peaceful coexistence.[19]

In early 1962, *The Worker* (no longer a daily) ran an article
headlined, "Birchers Take Warpath Against UN Peace Hopes,"
telling its readers: "The John Birch Society has instructed its
members to prepare a hate campaign against the United Nations." *The Worker* article described this development as "insid-
ious business."[20]

In late 1964 and early 1965 the Xerox Corporation (whose
Board Chairman, Sol Linowitz, was a member of the CFR)
sponsored a television series consisting of the most blatant sort
of UN propaganda. In commenting on one of these programs,
the Communist *People's World* for January 23, 1965, noted:
"It's not a little horrifying that in our country at this time a
pitch is needed for the UN and for peace, but that is the case,
and we're all for figuratively hitting people over the head with
the message. The [*Xerox*] program did that."[21]

A few months later, Soviet spokesman Mikhail Sergeyevich
Lvov told a Moscow radio audience:

> There can be no doubt that with the United Nations consti-
> tuted as it is at present, the consistent line of the Soviet Union in
> pressing for the United Nations to face fully up to the problems
> of strengthening peace and insuring freedom is producing more
> and more positive results.[22]

And in 1973, an article in *Political Affairs* asserted:

> As for the positive role of the United Nations in international
> relations and in the affairs of its member-states, the list of its
> accomplishments is extensive. . . .
> To further the continuation and strengthening of this trend of
> United Nations activities, support of the people is necessary, and
> especially the support of the majority of the people of the United
> States.[23]

Clearly, the belief that the Communists *ever* opposed the UN cannot withstand the massive evidence to the contrary.

All of this does not mean, of course, that the Communists did not *pretend* to oppose the UN on occasion. To the contrary, the Communists realize better than anyone else how repulsive their system is to the vast majority of mankind, and they are perfectly willing to attack the UN and its policies from time to time if that will help to rally public opinion in non-Communist countries behind policies they really want. An example of this strategy, taken from another context, was reported in *U.S. News & World Report*:

> Soviet Premier Nikita Khrushchev to Stewart L. Udall, U.S. Secretary of the Interior, while the two men posed for news photographers in Moscow: "If it will help you out, you can go ahead and shake a finger in my face."[24]

Two former UN Ambassadors helped confirm this tactic as it relates to the organization. Henry Cabot Lodge (CFR) once asserted:

> I've seen it happen many times — the free nations, being free, start to drift apart, and everyone follows his own way. The politicians in the free nations start attacking each other. But when it gets to that point, the Soviet representative will say something that is so monstrous, so shocking, so irritating that the free people start pulling together again.[25]

And Adlai Stevenson (CFR) told the UN Security Council on February 15, 1961:

> . . . the Soviet Union has attacked the United Nations, has refused to pay its share of the Congo expenses, and has laid siege to the institution of the Secretary-General. Thus, *as often before, the Soviets have pressed their attack at a moment when the [UN] community seems most divided against itself.* But, once again, that very attack makes the members realize more deeply that they are members of a community *and causes them to draw together.*[26] *[Emphasis added.]*

Note that Stevenson's reference to Soviet attacks on the post of Secretary-General is similar to that of Senator Church which we quoted earlier. You will recall that Soviet demands for a *troika* were very firm until Secretary-General Dag Hammarskjöld was killed in a plane crash. But rather than use the opportunity his death presented to hamstring the UN, "The Soviet Union gave up for the time being its attempt to impose a three block 'troika' agreement, and the assembly elected Thant unanimously."[27]

Another unintended confirmation of this Communist duplicity was given on March 3, 1966, when pro-UN news commentator Howard K. Smith spoke at Brigham Young University in Provo, Utah. Mr. Smith made this point: "The Russians attacked us bitterly over the Congo, but the key fact is they voted for U.N. intervention in the Congo. The Russians attacked us bitterly over the Cyprus crisis, but the main thing is they did not veto U.N. action; they let it go in."[28]

And in 1964, when the Afro-Asian block at the UN was pressing for an increase in membership on various UN councils, the Communists pretended to oppose the move in public debate, but then quietly reversed themselves when it counted:

> The Soviet Union quietly backed down in its opposition to Afro-Asian demands for an expansion of the United Nations Security Council and economic and social council. . . . During the assembly's debate on these resolutions, the Soviet Union and the entire Communist bloc . . . opposed the proposal.[29]

Also in 1964, Associated Press writer Max Harrelson commented on this Communist tactic, noting:

> Those who have observed Soviet actions at the United Nations over the past 18 years are sure only that the Russians can — and do — change their minds.
> They may walk out of a U.N. body today and return without so much as a word to explain their reversal.
> Over the years they have made many threats they have never carried out, and they have suddenly abandoned policies which they previously held to be absolutely unchangeable.[30]

Many additional examples of pretended Communist opposition could be cited, but these few should make it clear that the UN propaganda network not only covered up the extent to which the Communists support the UN, it even worked in concert with them to create a false impression of Communist *opposition* to the organization. This deception helped effectively to neutralize anti-Communist opposition to the world body.

The UN is invaluable to Communist purposes as a base for Soviet intelligence operations. As early as 1952, informed estimates were suggesting "that as many as one-half of the 1,350 administrative executives in the UN are either Communists or people who are willing to do what they want."[31] Even "Liberal" columnist Jack Anderson admits: "Indeed, the U.N. is the main Soviet espionage center in this country."[32] A top-secret training manual for the Soviet KGB, obtained a few years ago by a Western security service, asserts: "In the U.S., in addition to ordinary cover, we use various international organizations and our representations in them. The most important of these is the United Nations and its branch institutions."[33]

Incredibly, the American taxpayer is being forced to help finance such Communist subversion. According to John Barron:

> The KGB derives still another advantage from placing its officers on the United Nations payroll. Since the United States pays 25 percent of the entire U.N. operating budget, it pays 25 percent of the bountiful salaries granted KGB officers insinuated into the U.N. jobs. American taxpayers are thus compelled to finance KGB operations against themselves and the non-communist world. Moreover, the Soviet Union requires its citizens paid by international organizations to rebate the greater part of their salaries to the government. Thus, it actually makes money each time it plants a KGB officer in the U.N.[34]

In addition to the protection it affords Communist spies within our country, the UN guarantees the continued enslavement of the millions of people imprisoned behind the Soviet Iron Curtain. As explained by historian Charles Callan Tansill:

In Article 42 of the United Nations Charter it is provided that

the Security Council "may take such action by air, sea or land
forces as may be necessary to maintain or restore international
peace and security. Such action may include demonstrations,
blockade and other operations by air, sea or land forces of
Members of the United Nations." As long as the Soviet government does not assume an active role in any breach of world peace,
this military force will help to protect its far-flung empire of
satellite states from outside aggression.

It is obvious that under these conditions, the role of America
has been reduced to one of mere containment. . . . The United
Nations was created to help Russia, not to hurt her.[35]

One of the most important posts within the UN (Secretary-
General Trygve Lie described it as "the most important assistant
secretaryship"[36]) is that of Undersecretary for Political and
Security Council Affairs:

> It is the function of this department to work permanently with
> the Security Council on any problem which may affect interna-
> tional peace. There is no territorial, military, or juridical dispute
> in the world that would not come to . . . [*this*] department for
> documentation. When any member of the Security Council or of
> the Military Staff Committee needs any special data, he turns to
> this department for help.[37]

From the beginning, this crucial position has been held by a
Communist. Here is the list (as of November, 1980):

1946–1949	Arkady Sobolev (USSR)
1949–1953	Konstantin Zinchenko (USSR)
1953–1954	Ilya Tchernychev (USSR)
1954–1957	Dragoslav Protitch (Yugoslavia)
1958–1960	Anatoly Dobrynin (USSR)
1960–1962	Georgy Arkadev (USSR)
1962–1963	E.D. Kiselev (USSR)
1963–1965	V.P. Suslov (USSR)
1965–1968	Alexei E. Nesterenko (USSR)
1968–1973	Leonid N. Kutakov (USSR)
1973–1978	Arkady N. Shevchenko (USSR)
1978–	Mikhail D. Sytenko (USSR)

Trygve Lie wrote that Soviet representative Andrei Vyshinsky was first to inform him of the decision by the Big Five to appoint a Soviet national as Undersecretary for Political and Security Council Affairs: "The preservation of international peace and security was the Organization's highest responsibility, and it was to entrusting the direction of the Secretariat department most concerned with this to a Soviet national that the Americans had agreed."[38] And what did our leaders seek for our own country? Lie continued: "To my surprise, they did not ask for a department concerned with comparable substantive affairs, like the economic or the social. Rather Mr. Stettinius proposed that an American citizen be appointed Assistant Secretary-General for Administration and Financial Services."[39]

Is it conceivable that the Communists could object to an arrangement like that?

Chapter 8

A Matter Of Opinion

In a letter dated July 3, 1952, accompanying his report on UN activities for the previous year, President Harry S Truman asserted: "In the United Nations no country can escape the judgment of mankind. This is the first and greatest weapon against aggression and international immorality. It is the greatest strength of the United Nations."[1]

Similarly, UN Ambassador Henry Cabot Lodge claimed in 1954: "And the Soviet Union, while it maintains an iron dictatorship wherever it has the legal [sic] power to do so, is very sensitive to public opinion in the world outside its borders."[2] In December, 1962, a State Department publication claimed: "The one great asset and powerful weapon of the United Nations, of course, is the moral force of world public opinion. . . . this force cannot be overestimated. It acts as the collective conscience of mankind. No nation can lightly accept a position of open defiance to this powerful moral force."[3]

In 1963, former UN General Assembly President Charles Malik wrote: "The force of public opinion generated at the United Nations and as a consequence throughout the world, has often exerted considerable pressure . . ."[4] The next year, the Board Chairman of the United Nations Association of the United States went so far as to claim: "In the final analysis, the whole force and power of the UN depend upon public opinion."[5]

Many more examples could be cited to illustrate how an alleged world public opinion has been used to convince Americans that the UN deserves support as a powerful moral force for peace. Yet on May 8, 1975, another influential UN advocate, former Senator J.W. Fulbright (D.-Arkansas), told the Senate Foreign Relations Committee (which he chaired for many years): "The assumption . . . that the moral weight of world opinion expressed through the General Assembly, would have a moderating effect on the deplorable events and practices has not been borne out by events."[6]

For once, Senator Fulbright had correctly analyzed a situation. The world opinion argument has been, from the start, a misleading hoax that has hurt our nation and the free world in many ways. While the United States has meekly revamped its foreign policy to meet the demands of an alleged United Nations "world opinion," the Communists have simply continued with their job of taking over the world, shrugging off world opinion all along the way.

Moral pressure elicits response only from those who are morally sensitive. The Communists are not morally sensitive: they view so-called world opinion as a myth, and therefore dismiss it entirely unless it happens to coincide with their goals. In contrast, the very Western nations that invented and popularized the world opinion concept were so successful in convincing their people of its existence, and the need to abide by it, that they soon found themselves confronted with the alternative of either going along with the collectivist UN majority or violating a principle of their own creation. This, in turn, has encouraged anti-American regimes around the world fearlessly to stick out their tongues at us, and vote against us, because they know we will not retaliate in any way that might offend world public opinion. On the other hand, these same nations cower before the

Soviet bloc, since they know that group ignores such nonsense.

Hamilton Fish Armstrong wrote in the April, 1961 issue of *Foreign Affairs*:

> Those that need to turn to both East and West for help with their social and economic problems are always under temptation to talk and vote against the United States; they know they can do it with impunity, and they know that opposite behavior would awaken damaging Soviet displeasure.[7]

Part of Secretary-General U Thant's own openly-expressed contempt for the United States, and go-easy attitude toward the Communists, was apparently attributable to this phenomenon:

> Although he [*Thant*] lost few opportunities to speak out about Vietnam, American diplomats found him somewhat less forth-right in his criticism of Communist behavior. . . . He seldom found cause for strong rebuke of Hanoi.
>
> Some analysts put this down to the underlying facts of U Thant's situation. The Soviet Union held the mortgage, as it were, on the workings of the U.N.; by withdrawing support or threatening non-cooperation, Moscow could cause paralysis. Thant knew that the U.S. was unlikely to resort to such tactics.[8]

In 1957, Henry Kissinger (CFR) had written a book titled *Nuclear Weapons and Foreign Policy*, which was the culmination of his two years of service as director of nuclear weapons and foreign policy studies for the CFR. Kissinger pointed out:

> Because Soviet doctrine teaches the inevitable hostility of the non-Communist world, no potential gain can be sacrificed to win an illusory good will. . . .
>
> As a result, the Soviet leaders never give up the chance to fill a vacuum, real or imagined, for the sake of winning the good will of the non-Communist world.[9]

He then reminded his readers: "The immense reservoir of sympathy built up [*by the Soviets*] during World War II was sacrificed without hesitation to obtain a bastion in Eastern

Europe."[10] For example, as noted by Professor Hans J. Morgenthau (CFR) in *Foreign Affairs*, "The Soviet Union put the success of the intervention [*in Hungary in 1956*] above all other considerations, and succeeded. Its prestige throughout the world suffered drastically in consequence. But Hungary is today a communist state within the orbit of the Soviet Union, and Soviet prestige recovered quickly from the damage it suffered in 1956."[11]

Harry Hopkins, influential advisor to President Roosevelt, once attempted to convince Soviet dictator Josef Stalin that he (Stalin) should be less abrasive in his comments about the United States, lest he offend public opinion in America. Writing in *Foreign Affairs*, McGeorge Bundy (CFR), who later became a Hopkins-type advisor himself in the administrations of John F. Kennedy and Lyndon Johnson, revealed:

> If Generalissimo Stalin understood this point, he never showed it. . . . He never asked why Americans were disturbed, or what Soviet Russia might do to calm them down. American public opinion, whose controlling influence in all American policy Hopkins was trying to communicate, seemed to Stalin either a weapon in bargaining or a problem for management by western statesmen. Neither the value of its support nor the cost of its opposition seems to have struck him as very important.[12]

Following the Yalta Conference in 1945, Andrei Vishinsky, who would later represent the Soviet Union at the UN, intervened personally to help install a puppet Communist regime in Rumania. In January, 1946, while visiting Bucharest, he was told that the methods he was requiring the Rumanian authorities to use would undoubtedly prove offensive to the United States and Britain. According to McGeorge Bundy, he replied curtly: "Let the sparrows twitter."[13] Bundy further describes Soviet behavior after Yalta as "a policy characterized by an apparent decision to disregard as unimportant the good will of the non-Communist west and to proceed as energetically as possible to expand and consolidate Communist power."[14] That's exactly what it was.

When the Soviets moved to suppress the Hungarian uprising in 1956, they ignored world opinion entirely. On April 9, 1958, during a speech at the Csepel Iron and Steel Works in Hungary, Nikita Khrushchev acknowledged:

> We knew that we might be reproached for having allegedly intervened with our armed forces in the internal affairs of the Hungarian People's Republic. . . . We knew that the imperialists would shout wildly that we interfered in the Hungarian people's internal affairs, but we also knew . . . that there was only one correct road open before our Soviet country: to extend our assistance to our Hungarian class brothers.[15]

Likewise, when the Soviets suppressed the rebellion in Czecho-Slovakia in 1968, they ignored world opinion. Again, their image was briefly tarnished, but Czecho-Slovakia remains Communist to this day.

UN apologists continued nevertheless to make absurd claims such as this excerpt from the pen of former British Labour Party leader Hugh Gaitskell:

> But even for dictatorships the importance of world opinion should not be underestimated. The Soviet government itself . . . cannot ignore its own reputation . . . and if, as in the case of Hungary, it is denounced by the Assembly, then its power and influence . . . suffers a setback."[16]

In contrast to Hungary and Czechoslovakia, when the British, French, and Israelis invaded Suez in 1956 after Egypt's pro-Communist dictator, Gamal Abdel Nasser, seized the Suez Canal, they were quickly pressured by world opinion to withdraw, leaving the Canal under Nasser's control. Clark M. Eichelberger (CFR), a staunch defender of the UN and a member of the five-man committee that prepared the first working draft of the UN Charter, wrote:

> The British, French, and Israelis, responding to an appeal of world opinion in the United Nations, agreed to withdraw their troops. . . .

In comparison, the simultaneous emergency session to secure the withdrawal of Soviet troops from Hungary was a disappointment. The Soviet Union was not responsive to public opinion as were the British, French and Israeli governments.[17]

Of course it wasn't. As President Eisenhower (CFR) told a joint session of Congress in January, 1957:

> The United Nations was able to bring about a ceasefire and withdrawal of hostile forces from Egypt because it was dealing with governments and peoples who had a decent respect for the opinions of mankind . . . But in the case of Hungary the situation was different. The Soviet Union vetoed action by the Security Council to require the withdrawal of Soviet armed forces from Hungary. And it has shown callous indifference to the recommendations, even the censure, of the General Assembly.[18]

Some observers believe that the spectre of world opinion played a role in affecting U.S. policy during the tragic Bay of Pigs venture in 1961:

> The United States had an interest in eliminating the political and military power of the Soviet Union. . . . The United States also had an interest in avoiding whatever would jeopardize its standing in the new and emerging nations. The United States failed to assign priorities to these two interests. In order to minimize the loss of prestige, the United States jeopardized the success of the intervention. . . . In consequence, the United States failed thrice. The intervention did not succeed; in the attempt we suffered the temporary impairment of our standing among the new and emerging nations; and we lost much prestige as a great nation able to use its power successfully on behalf of its interests.[19]

Remember, the world opinion myth was planted and cultivated by our home-grown Internationalists, and has been used to hamstring our own foreign policy (and that of the West in general), while leaving the Communists free to do as they please. It has been a "heads I win, tails you lose" proposition favoring the Communists. We must demand that our leaders start making foreign policy decisions on the basis of what is right and best for America — not what will affect a chimerical world opinion.

Advocates of the UN have consistently asserted that the "force of world public opinion" is the UN's greatest strength. It is a strength which has, in practice, been exerted entirely against the free world.

Chapter 9

Article 19

American Internationalists, as we have seen, are strongly inclined to place the interests of the UN ahead of those of our own nation whenever the two conflict. The controversy over enforcement of Article 19 of the UN Charter during the early 1960s is a revealing example.

Article 19 states:

> A member of the United Nations which is in arrears in the payment of its financial contributions to the Organization shall have no vote in the General Assembly if the amount of its arrears equals or exceeds the amount of the contributions due from it for the preceding two full years. The General Assembly may, nevertheless, permit such a member to vote if it is satisfied that the failure to pay is due to conditions beyond the control of the member.

On January 1, 1964, the Soviet Union, which had refused to pay its share of the cost of the UN's war in Katanga despite a ruling by the International Court of Justice that it was obligated to do so, fell more than two years behind in paying its UN dues.

The Soviets did not contend that their failure to pay was the result of conditions beyond their control, the only excuse recognized by the Charter. Indeed, as reported by *U.S. News & World Report*: "At present, Russia owes $5,793,331 more than the total amount of two years of obligatory assessments. Russia says it is quite able to pay this amount but does not choose to do so."[1] Under terms of the UN Charter, the Soviets should have been automatically and immediately stripped of their votes in the General Assembly.

During an appearance on NBC's "Meet the Press" broadcast, UN Ambassador Adlai Stevenson (CFR) was asked what the consequences would be if the Soviets refused to pay. He said it was his opinion they *would* pay. (Ambassador Stevenson habitually gave Russians the benefit of American doubts.) He was then asked if the United States would move to strip them of their votes if they did *not* pay, and he replied:

> Oh, yes. I don't think there is any question about that. If the organization is going to survive, we have to comply with the terms of the charter, and the charter is explicit on this subject. It is not a question of interpretation.[2]

Similarly, former Senator Frank Church (D.-Idaho; CFR) explained in a Senate speech:

> The charter is crystal clear.
> . . . there are no "ifs, ands, or buts." A nation which is 2 years behind "shall have no vote." . . . The U.S.S.R. thinks that when the showdown does come, many nations will be afraid of depriving Russia of her vote, and that some way will be found to "chicken out" on these very specific provisions of the charter.
> . . . The Congress of the United States has made its own position unmistakenly clear: the Soviet Union must either pay what she legitimately owes, or relinquish her vote in the General Assembly. We can take no other stand.[3]

Indeed, on October 2, 1962, Congress had approved a $100 million UN bond issue on the basis of a firm pledge that our government would not back down on this matter; otherwise the bond money would, in effect, be covering Soviet debts. Deputy Assistant Secretary of State for International Affairs Richard N. Gardner (CFR), for example, asserted:

> There are some people who oppose our coming to the aid of the United Nations in its present financial crisis on the grounds that we will be paying for the Soviet share. This charge is completely incorrect. On July 20th [*1962*] the International Court of Justice confirmed the obligation of United Nations members to pay assessments denied by the General Assembly for the expenditures incurred in the conduct of the United Nations Emergency Force in the Middle East and the United Nations Operation in the Congo. If the Communist bloc countries continue to refuse to pay their arrearages on these accounts, they stand to lose their votes in the General Assembly as of January 1, 1964, in accordance with Article 19 of the charter.[4]

Other officials also assured Congress time and again that the bond purchase could be approved in complete confidence that there would be no temporizing on the Article 19 issue.

On August 17, 1964, the U.S. House of Representatives voted unanimously (351 to 0) to urge the UN either to collect the debts of its deadbeat members or deprive them of their votes. On October 8th, a State Department memorandum made it perfectly clear once again that the United States would demand that the Soviets pay their debt or lose their votes, declaring: "The consequences of not applying it [*Article 19*], if it becomes applicable, would be to undermine the very integrity and capacity of the U.N."[5] That same day, Ambassador Stevenson sent a memo to Secretary-General U Thant, declaring there "is no alternative" to application of Article 19. Stevenson claimed that failure to apply it "could be a violation of the Charter which would have far-reaching consequences," that it would "be a repudiation of the International Court of Justice," that it would "undermine the constitutional integrity of the United Nation."[6] And on October 24, 1964, Undersecretary of State George Ball (CFR) told a UN Day dinner in Kansas City, Missouri:

. . . let no one confuse the desire to preserve the United Nations membership intact with vacillation on the basic issue of the powers of the General Assembly. When the chips are down, we are convinced that the members will uphold the integrity of the charter. . . . Any other course is a prescription for progressive deterioration and dissolution.[7]

Similar statements of the U.S. position were made during the next ten months, until everyone, everywhere, had been made aware of America's unswerving intention to stand firm.

And then, we backed down.

The late Leftist columnist Drew Pearson telegraphed the turnaround in his column for July 1, 1965:

Meanwhile you can write it down as certain that Article 19 is dead and will be quietly forgotten. The view is unanimous inside the Administration not to tell the Russians what they should do and how much they should pay. We'll let our position wither away and, we hope, be forgotten during the summer.[8]

On August 16, 1965, Arthur J. Goldberg (CFR), who had succeeded Stevenson as our UN Ambassador, announced that we were throwing in the towel, reversing our position, and would not even try to have the matter brought to a vote. Addressing the UN Special Committee on Peace-Keeping Operations, he phrased the surrender in these words:

The United States regretfully concludes, on ample evidence, that at this stage in the history of the United Nations the General Assembly is not prepared to carry out the relevant provisions of the charter in the context of the present situation. . . .

Therefore . . . the United States recognizes, as it simply must, that the General Assembly is not prepared to apply article 19 in the present situation and that the concensus of the membership is that the Assembly should proceed normally. We will not seek to frustrate that consensus, since it is not in the world interest to have the work of the General Assembly immobilized in these troubled days.[9]

Goldberg was simply admitting in typical bureaucratese style that all prior statements committing our nation to enforcement of Article 19 were a joke, that Congress had been deceived by the State Department, and that it was worth a disgraceful capitulation by the United States, on a matter where we were legally and morally right, to keep the UN going its illegal, immoral way.

Administration spokesmen attempted to soften the blow of our ignominious capitulation by claiming that, after all, if we couldn't compel Russia to pay, she couldn't compel us to pay, either.[10] Big deal! It reminded one observer of the story about the reprobate in church who, becoming increasingly uncomfortable during a discussion of the Ten Commandments, suddenly brightened as he recalled with relief that he had made no graven images. Yet another observer noted that "This major American concession brought to an end one of the most serious crises in the history of the United Nations."[11] Of course. Just like our "concession" to the Communists in Vietnam ended *that* serious crisis. *Any* serious crisis is terminated when one side surrenders.

On the day following Ambassador Goldberg's address, the *Washington Evening Star* reported that United States officials were bracing themselves for expected Congressional criticism in the wake of the sell-out, since "Congress had been assured for more than two years that the Russians would be forced to pay their dues," and "had gone along with the recent U.N. bond issue on the understanding that the United States would not yield on the dues issue."[12] Congress sputtered and fumed a bit, but took no effective counter-action, apparently caring little that the tax money it had voted for UN bonds had, indeed, been used indirectly to cover Soviet debts. Shortly thereafter, the *Washington Post* carried a dispatch which wrapped up the whole fiasco in a fitting manner:

> The Soviet Union had promised a substantial contribution as soon as the United States agreed to sweep the controversy over Article 19 under the rug, but no donation has been forthcoming

since the United Nations dropped its challenge under Article 19
last August.[13]

It is important to note that the black eye we suffered did not
result so much from anything the Communists did as from
what our own leaders did — first committing us to a firm
position, then backing down. Actually, a vote by the General
Assembly was not even required under Article 19, since it states
that a delinquent nation "shall" lose its vote — not "may" lose
its vote. Rather than raise this point, we went along with the
view that a vote was needed, then failed to demand one. (A
recorded vote would at least have given the world a specific list
of those nations willing to violate the Charter openly.) In short,
our policy was carried out in a manner which maximized damage
to our own reputation, while protecting the UN and enhancing
the position of the victorious Soviets. Some think it was planned
that way from the start. At the very least, it was yet another
revealing example of the destructive influence which our association with the UN has had on both our foreign policy and our
reputation in the world.

Max Jacobsen, writing in the *Saturday Review World*, described the Article 19 mess as "the beginning of an American-
Soviet *détente* in the United Nations context."[14] This is basically
true, since it involved our total capitulation to a Soviet demand
— and that is the very essence of *détente* with the Communists.

Chapter 10

Just Like US

A counterfeit, to be effective, must come as close as possible to the real thing. A dollar bill colored red, white and blue with a caricature of Archie Bunker in the center is unlikely to fool your local bank teller. Color it green and substitute George Washington, and your chances of getting away with the deception increase appreciably.

The United Nations has for over three decades been hawking carefully contrived counterfeits intended to mislead Americans into believing that the world body stands four-square with our Founding Fathers. To one UN apologist, "The UN Charter is founded on principles that parallel those of our own Constitution. The aims of the organization and its specialized agencies are akin to our own."[1] Another had claimed, "In its origin the United Nations had been largely an American conception. Its underlying philosophy showed the influence of American traditions. . . ."[2] If you want democracy, "the spirit and the methods of the U.N. are second nature to American democracy. . . ."[3] Or, if you prefer a republic, "It will be just as easy for nations to get along in a republic of the world as it is for you to get along in the republic of the United States."[4] One Senator even asserted: "Our own Congress is about as near to or similar to the U.N. as any significant political institution in the world."[5] And, in November, 1948, American Bar Association President Frank E. Holman wrote to various top-level government officials (including the Secretary of State) to urge that the American people be advised of what was being done in their name at the Paris convention that was formulating the UN's Declaration of Human Rights. He later wrote:

> The naive answer was to the effect that if the American people and American lawyers would think of the Declaration as analogous to our own Declaration of Independence, then they would not be disturbed.[6]

Quite often, UN advocates even try to draw a parallel between the federation of nations under the UN and the federation of American colonies under the Constitution. But there is no real parallel. John Jay, writing in *The Federalist Papers*, described some of the unique characteristics which favored federation of the American colonies:

> It has often given me pleasure to observe, that independent America was not composed of detached and distant territories, but that one connected, fertile, wide-spreading country was the portion of our western sons of liberty. . . .
> With equal pleasure I have as often taken notice, that Providence has been pleased to give this one connected country to one united people — a people descended from the same ancestors, speaking the same language, professing the same religion, attached to the same principles of government, very similar in their manners and customs. . . .[7]

Compare that situation with that of the United Nations, as described by UN supporter Morris B. Abram (CFR) in *Foreign Affairs*:

> Even among the nations which originally constituted the

United Nations . . . there were significant differences in values
and outlook. They included the communist nations of Eastern
Europe and the capitalist nations of Western Europe and America. They were both developed and underdeveloped nations.
These differences sharpened when the cold war shattered the
big-power anti-Nazi alliance, and they multiplied when a large
number of new states in Asia and Africa — nonwhite, non-
Christian, culturally different and economically underdeveloped
— were admitted to the U.N.[8]

In 1974, the Associated Press carried a brief dispatch that
illustrated rather well a fundamental difference between UN
and U.S. institutions:

UNITED NATIONS, N.Y., April 23 (AP) — About half the
United Nations' interpreters called in sick today in protest against
long working hours, forcing cancellation or postponement of
most meetings at U.N. headquarters.[9]

An exhaustive search has failed to uncover evidence that any
sessions of the United States Congress have been cancelled due
to a shortage of interpreters.

Senator Robert A. Taft (R.-Ohio) surveyed the UN structure
and exclaimed:

Here we would be attempting to unite peoples who do not
understand even how their new fellow citizens begin to think; we
would join democracies with dictatorship, Moslem states with
Christian states, the Brahmin with the Rotarian, men who talk
only Japanese with men who talk only English. We would attempt
to unite the most highly civilized with the aborigines, the work-
man who earns twenty dollars a day with the coolie who earns
twenty cents a day.[10]

The problem of holding together such diverse elements under
one government is obviously insuperable. How would *you* medi-
ate between the Hindu who views cattle as objects of holiness
and an American who views them as raw material for McDonalds?

It is important to remember that, despite the remarkable

compatibility of our early states, it was less than a century before they were fighting a lengthy, bloody civil war, thus proving that mere political federation is no guarantee of peace. Despite the many limitations that our Constitution placed on the power of the Federal Government, the usurpation of authority by ambitious and evil men has nevertheless led to a concentration of power in Washington, and encroachment on our personal liberties, that would have appalled our Founding Fathers. Yet for thirty years we have been asked to believe that an international union under the economic, political, cultural, geographic, and linguistic Tower of Babel on New York's East River can save us from the scourge of war and protect our personal liberties! It is an incredibly unrealistic, and dangerous, assumption.

Yet another misleading UN counterfeit is found in the Preamble to the UN Charter, which begins: "We the peoples of the United Nations. . . ." It sounds very much like "We, the people of the United States" that launches the United States Constitution. It was planned that way. "The insertion of these words in the Charter," notes one pro-UN source, "was proposed by the Delegation of the United States. . . . The proposal was inspired by the opening words of the Constitution of the United States."[11] The purpose was to make plausible such counterfeit claims as: "With its opening words, 'we the peoples,' the Preamble shows that it is speaking for the peoples of the world instead of merely for their governments."[12] And again: "The Charter opens with the phrase, 'We, the peoples of the United Nations. . . .' It is, in a sense, an agreement between peoples rather than between governments. The opening phrase marks, in some respects, the most fundamental distinction between the Charter and the League of Nations Covenant."[13]

An actual reading of the complete Preamble, and the Charter itself, makes it abundantly clear that "peoples" have no real say in the UN's decision-making process at all.

While the Preamble to the Charter opens with the words "We the peoples of the United Nations," the concluding words of the Preamble, "Accordingly our respective Governments, through representatives assembled in the city of San Francisco," etc., make it clear that the Charter is not a constituent act of the peoples of the United Nations, but rather an agreement freely entered into between governments.[14]

Even more to the point is the observation of yet another author who favors the concepts of internationalism and world government:

> "We the people [sic] . . ." — these symbolic words of demo-
> cratic government — do not belong in the San Francisco Charter.
> Their use in the preamble is in total contradiction to everything
> else in it, and only historians will be able to decide whether they
> were used from lack of knowledge or lack of honesty. The simple
> truth requires that "We, the people . . ." in the preamble of the
> charter be accurately read: "We, the High Contracting Powers.
> . . ."[15]

By using a phrase dear to the hearts of Americans who revere their own Constitution, the instigators of the UN were merely attempting to make their counterfeit come close to the real thing.

Perhaps the most dangerous and far-reaching attempt by the UN to mislead Americans has involved the drive to create the impression that rights under the UN are protected as they are in our Bill of Rights. A 1962 pro-UN propaganda piece asserted, for example: " 'Human Rights Day,' now observed annually on December 10, grew out of The Universal Declaration of Human Rights, the first such international statement in history. So many of its principles are embodied in our own Constitution that America must take deep pride in its existence."[16] Another, issued in 1963, claimed: "The guarantees of freedom in the Bill of Rights provide a familiar framework which serves well for a study of the Universal Declaration of Human Rights."[17] In 1964, Assistant Secretary of State for International Organizations Richard N. Gardner (CFR) wrote: "The Universal Declaration is a comprehensive affirmation of basic political and economic rights found in the Constitution and basic legislation of the United States."[18]

Even our Chief Executives have helped to perpetuate the deception. Former President Richard Nixon, while declaring Human Rights-Bill of Rights Day on December 9, 1971, claimed: "The Universal Declaration of Human Rights . . . is in the tradition of our Constitution and its Bill of Rights."[19] President Gerald Ford, in a similar proclamation issued December 3, 1974, alleged: "The link between it [*the Universal Declaration*] and our Bill of Rights is clear."[20] And President Jimmy Carter stated on December 9, 1977, that our "experience of successful struggle for human rights in our own country . . . propelled us into a leading role in the adoption of the Universal Declaration of Human Rights by the United Nations."[21]

Despite these prestigious observations, the philosophy of rights under the UN is diametrically *opposed* to that of our Constitution and Bill of Rights. There is simply no compatible link between the two.

The two basic concepts of the origin of human rights are (1) that they derive from government, or (2) that they come from a source outside of government. The first view was ably stated during debate on the Universal Declaration in the UN General Assembly on December 10, 1948, by Soviet spokesman Andrei Vishinsky: "The rights of human beings cannot be considered outside the prerogatives of governments, and the very understanding of human rights is a governmental concept."[22] This attitude toward human rights was explained more recently by William Korey, director of B'nai B'rith's United Nations office:

> In Communist ideology, the individual's rights are not counterposed to the state but, rather, are an integral part of it. A basically similar view prevails among most of the developing countries of the Third World. . . . A revealing document is the official summary of the UN-sponsored human rights seminar on Africa held in Tanzania in 1973. Protection of the rights of the individual was frankly acknowledged to be secondary as compared to the needs of the state.[23]

In contrast to the Communist view that rights come from government (which, as we shall see, is also the UN view) is the

traditional American concept that rights are endowed by a
Creator (*i.e.*, a Source outside of government), and that government's job is simply to *protect* — not to infringe, manipulate, or
otherwise violate — them. In the words of Dr. Clarence B. Carson: "If government can create rights, it can withhold and destroy rights. The practical consequences of this fact are that if
rights are derived from governments, there are no rights."[24]

"Human rights" are mentioned in the UN Charter, but
"There is no attempt made in the Charter to define the 'human
rights' and 'fundamental freedoms' to which reference is
made."[25] Delegates at the UN's founding conference simply
couldn't agree on a definition for the phrase "human rights."
As noted by another prominent Internationalist and UN supporter:

> Conflicts of meaning exist in the United Nations charter
> itself, as well as in speeches delivered under its auspices. Take
> the expression "human rights," for which a definition was
> actually sought in San Francisco. The Russians wanted "the right
> to work" included, which was frowned upon by some, and both
> the British and Russians opposed the American wish to include
> "the right to free enterprise"; both also grew perplexed when it
> was proposed to bring in practically the whole Bill of Rights. The
> search was quickly abandoned for the sake of expediency. . . .[26]

Despite having failed even to define human rights at the
Charter level, the UN later adopted its vague, non-binding
Declaration of Human Rights on December 10, 1948. According
to former UN General Assembly President Charles Malik:

> The Universal Declaration of Human Rights, adopted by the
> General Assembly in Paris in 1948 without a single dissenting
> vote, is one of the fundamental documents of this age. . . . The
> message does not come from this or that positive legal system,
> this or that special religion, this or that special outlook on life.
> The message comes from the combined and considered views of
> all systems, all religions, all cultures, and all outlooks.[27]

Think about that for a moment. Could anything be more
ridiculous and futile than attempting to pour the "views of all

systems [*Communist and Capitalist*], all religions [*Christian and Moslem*], all cultures [*Western and Hottentot*], and all outlooks [*moral and immoral*]" into a melting pot and come up with anything resembling a decent human rights policy? The only meaningful precedent we can think of is Dr. Frankenstein's renowned attempt to piece things together. He, too, created a monster.

The UN Declaration grants all sorts of human rights in its early Articles, then emasculates them with this language in Article 29:

> (2) In the exercise of his rights and freedoms, everyone shall be subject only to such limitations as are determined by law solely for the purpose of securing due recognition and respect for the rights and freedoms of others and of meeting the just requirements of morality, public order and the general welfare in a democratic society.
>
> (3) These rights and freedoms may in no case be exercised contrary to the purposes and principles of the United Nations.[28]

Suppose you are a Hitler, a Mao Tse-tung, or an Ayatollah Khomeini. Would the UN Declaration stand in the way of your oppressive rule? Of course not — because all you would need to do is claim that your opponents were threatening "public order," harming the "general welfare," or violating the "just requirements of morality."

The UN's collectivist philosophy of human rights was later drafted into various covenants, conventions and declarations. On November 20, 1959, for instance, the General Assembly adopted a "Declaration on the Rights of the Child" that asserts (Principle 7): "The child is entitled to receive education, which shall be free and compulsory, at least at the elementary stages"[29] and (Principle 10): "The child shall be protected from practices which may foster racial, religious and any other form of discrimination."[30] This means, if words have any definition at all, that parents could be in serious trouble should they advise their children that (for instance) Catholicism is superior to

Protestantism (or *vice versa*),, Mormonism is superior to Christian Science (or *vice versa*), Christianity is superior to Buddhism (or *vice versa*), — for such would be religious "discrimination."

On December 12, 1974, the UN General Assembly adopted a "Charter of Economic Rights and Duties of States" which grants each State the "right" (Article 2) to "nationalize, expropriate or transfer ownership of foreign property. . . ."[31] Article 7, a socialist directive urging government involvement in each key area of our lives, asserts: "Every State has the primary responsibility to promote the economic, social and cultural development of its people. . . ."[32] And Article 26 begins: "All States have the duty to coexist in tolerance and live together in peace, irrespective of differences in political, economic, social and cultural systems, and to facilitate trade between States having different economic and social systems,"[33] which would commit us not only to permanent "coexistence" with our Communist (and other) enemies, but to trading with them as well.

On December 21, 1965, the General Assembly approved an International Convention on the Elimination of All Forms of Racial Discrimination, which was signed by President Lyndon Johnson on September 28, 1966, and submitted to the Senate by President Carter on February 23, 1978. Sidney Liskofsky, Director of the American Jewish Committee's Division of International Organizations, told a House Subcommittee on February 11, 1976, that "racial discrimination as defined in article I of the [*Race Convention*] . . . is sufficiently broad to encompass any discriminatory condition, however small and however unintentional. Not one UN member is free of discrimination under its definition, not to speak of states where the grossest discriminations exist, but which the UN, under its selective morality, overlooks."[34]

Article 4 of the Race Convention demands that "States Parties condemn all propaganda and all organizations which are based on ideas or theories of superiority of one race or group of persons of one colour or ethnic origin, or which attempt to justify or promote racial hatred and discrimination in any form," and declares that the States:

(a) Shall declare an offence punishable by law all dissemination of ideas based on racial superiority or hatred. . . .

(b) Shall declare illegal and prohibit organizations, and also organized and all other propaganda activities, which promote and incite racial discrimination, and shall recognize participation in such organizations or activities as an offence punishable by law;

(c) Shall not permit public authorities or public institutions, national or local, to promote or incite racial discrimination.[35]

The threat to free speech and freedom of the press becomes obvious when the UN travesty is compared with Article I of the United States Bill of Rights, which unqualifiedly asserts:

Congress shall make no law respecting an establishment of religion, or prohibiting the free exercise thereof; or abridging the freedom of speech, or of the press; or the right of the people peaceably to assemble and to petition the Government for a redress of grievances.

William Korey, writing in *Foreign Affairs* shortly after the Race Convention was adopted, took note of arguments that parts of it "clash with the American Constitution and that Article 4 . . . threatens freedom of speech and association," and admitted that "the imprecision of the language does raise a serious question."[36] It certainly does!

On December 9, 1948, the General Assembly adopted an International Convention on the Prevention and Punishment of the Crime of Genocide (hereafter "Genocide Convention"), which was signed by the United States two days later and submitted to the Senate by President Truman on June 16, 1949.

Article II of the Convention states that "genocide means any of the following acts committed with intent to destroy, in whole or in part, a national, ethnical, racial or religious group. . . ."[37]

Dr. Alfred J. Schweppe, a designated representative of the American Bar Association,* testified before a Senate Foreign Relations Subcommittee on March 10, 1971:

---

*The ABA vigorously opposed the Genocide Convention from 1949 to 1976. On February 17, 1976, it suddenly reversed its stand. This despite the fact that there had been no changes made in the Convention since 1949 to lessen its dangers.

As originally drafted, the Convention included "political" as well as "national, ethnical, racial and religious groups." The Soviets announced that they wouldn't play unless "political groups" were expunged from the draft. They insisted on preserving the right to assassinate and exterminate the political opposition as essential to the safety of the state. . . . Result: the United States yielded, and "political groups" were eliminated from the draft.[38]

American delegates also tried to have the phrase "with the complicity of government" included in the definition, since they knew that genocide could never have occurred in Nazi Germany or Communist countries (nor anywhere else) unless deliberately directed, encouraged or condoned by government. The Soviet Union again objected, the United States yielded, and the important phrase was dropped. As a result, a Convention allegedly intended to outlaw genocide exempts the very Communist governments that have long engaged in genocide on a vast scale — as in Cambodia.[39]

The specific acts of genocide listed under Article II include: "(a) Killing members of the group" (such as a Black Panther by a policeman?); "(b) Causing serious bodily or mental harm to members of the group" (such as criticizing Communists or Nazis, thus causing them "mental harm"?); "(c) Deliberately inflicting on the group conditions of life calculated to bring about its physical destruction in whole or in part" (such as refusing to grant the amount of welfare benefits deemed desirable?); "(d) Imposing measures intended to prevent births within the group" (such as the many State laws which authorize court-ordered sterilization of lawbreakers who are feeble-minded or otherwise unfit to procreate normal children?); and "(e) Forcibly transferring children of the group to another group" (such as forced busing of school children for racist purposes?).

If the examples of potential "genocide" cited in parentheses sound too far-fetched to be taken seriously, consider this statement by former Senator Sam J. Ervin (D.-North Carolina):

... demands have already been made that the United Nations investigate the slaying of Black Panthers by police officers on the ground that their slaying constituted genocide under article II(a), and that the United Nations investigate the action of the legislature of one State in respect to welfare benefits on the ground that the legislative action constituted genocide under article II(c).[40]

In 1951, the Civil Rights Congress (a Communist Front) prepared a two hundred-page complaint formally accusing the President and other high U.S. officials, and the officials of eleven Southern states, of genocide against Negroes. The alleged basis was Article II(c) of the Genocide Convention. The complaint was presented to the General Assembly at Paris by William Patterson (a Communist who was Secretary of the Civil Rights Congress) in 1951.

The UN could take no action because the United States was not a party to the Genocide Convention, but the accusation is still pending before the UN, awaiting Senate ratification of the Convention.[41]

On October 17, 1970, the Communist newspaper *Daily World* carried a "Petition to the United Nations to End Genocide" which had been circulated by another Marxist front, the Emergency Conference Committee. The petition asserted, in part:

> The racist planned and unplanned terror suffered by more than 40 millions of black, brown, red and yellow citizens of the United States cannot be regarded solely as a domestic issue. . . .
> On the basis of simple justice, it is time for the United Nations to call for universal action to apply economic and political sanctions against the United States Government until such time as the United States will abide by the Genocide Convention and the Declaration of Human Rights.[42]

This wildly inflammatory document was signed by, in addition to Communist William Patterson, such luminaries as Mrs. Martin Luther King, Jr., the Reverend Ralph Abernathy, Representative Shirley Chisholm (D.-New York), comedian Dick Gregory, and Black Panthers Huey Newton and Bobby Seale.

Ratification of the Genocide Convention would not only
endanger many of our basic Constitutional rights, but would
also open the UN floodgates for a new surge of anti-American
propaganda.

Equally dangerous, if not more so, are the UN Covenant on
Civil and Political Rights (hereafter "CP Covenant") and the
Covenant on Economic, Social and Cultural Rights (hereafter
"ESC Covenant"). Both were adopted by the General Assembly
on December 16, 1966, signed by President Carter on October 5,
1977, and submitted to the Senate on February 23, 1978.

By definition, "The obligation of a state ratifying the [*ESC*]
Covenant would be to take steps for the promotion of conditions
for economic, social, and cultural progress and development."[43]
In other words, this Covenant would also commit the federal
government to involve itself further in the economic, cultural
and social affairs of our nation, at a time when increasing
numbers of Americans are recognizing that what is actually
needed is a cut back in government's role in these very areas.
Article I, for example, commits nations to take steps, "to the
maximum of its available resources," to achieve progressively
the "rights" set forth in the Covenant;[44] Article 7 commits
governments to provide a minimum wage and "decent living" to
workers; Article 9 asserts a right to "social security, including
social insurance"; Article 11 requires governments to assure
adequate "food, clothing and housing"; Article 12 mandates
socialized medicine through "creation of conditions which
would assure to all medical service and medical attention in the
event of sickness"; and Article 13 provides for government
control of education, and the use of schools as pro-UN indoc-
trination centers, by asserting that *all* educational institutions
must "further the activities of the United Nations" and con-
form to such standards "as may be laid down by the State."

These examples are by no means exhaustive. There is hardly
an area of human society left untouched by the ESC Covenant's far-reaching statist provisions. Paragraph 2 of Article 2
requires participating governments "to guarantee that the rights

enunciated in the present Covenant will be exercised without discrimination of any kind as to race, colour, sex, language, religion, political or other opinion, national or social origin, property, birth or other status." This is as all-inclusive as one could possibly make it. Presumably, if "other status" means a convicted murderer in prison, or a willfully indolent freeloader who refuses to work, his "right" to exercise (and benefit from) his myriad so-called "rights" could not be denied. The ESC Covenant is a socialist blueprint that encourages open-ended, unlimited government meddling of the sort on which dictatorships thrive.

Whereas the ESC Covenant "can only be implemented progressively, depending on the resources available to the State party," the even more sinister CP Covenant "deals with rights that are legally enforceable" and whose "obligations are meant, by and large, to be carried out immediately upon ratification by a State."[45] Article 20 of the CP Covenant "requires States parties to prohibit by law any propaganda for war and any advocacy of national, racial or religious hatred that constitutes incitement to discrimination, hostility or violence. . . ."[46] In the United States, the right to preach, print, and propagandize even wrong-headed views has been one of our most cherished and vigorously defended freedoms. The UN's CP Covenant, however, would require Congress to pass the very sort of laws suppressing free speech which Article 1 of the Bill of Rights presently prohibits.

Other Articles in this incredibly ominous Covenant grant alleged "rights," but then, in the spirit of the UN Declaration of Human Rights cited earlier, destroy them with vague, weasel-worded exceptions. For example:

Article 18
1. Everyone shall have the right to freedom of thought, conscience and religion. . . .
2. Freedom to manifest one's religion or beliefs may be subject only to such limitations as are prescribed by law and are necessary to protect public safety, order, health, or morals or the fundamental rights and freedom of others.

Article 19

2. Everyone shall have the right to freedom of expression; . . .

3. The exercise of the rights provided for in Paragraph 2 of this article carries with it special duties and responsibilities. It may therefore be subject to certain restrictions, but these shall only be such as are provided by law.

Article 21

The right of peaceful assembly shall be recognized.

No restriction may be placed on the exercise of this right other than those imposed in conformity with the law.

Article 22

Everyone shall have the right to freedom of association with others.

No restrictions may be placed on the exercise of this right other than those which are prescribed by law and which are necessary in a democratic society.[47]

It is little wonder that the Soviet Union has enthusiastically approved the UN's phony CP and ESC Covenants. As noted in our newspapers at the time:

> The Soviet Union said today [*September 28, 1973*] that the two international human rights covenants that it has just ratified gave it specific authority to limit the right of emigration, the free flow of ideas and other individual liberties.
>
> Two major articles in Communist party publications used the covenants today to justify existing restrictions rather than to offer any hope that Moscow was preparing to relax its rules.[48]

It is clear that the UN's "human rights" documents are cleverly-contrived counterfeits to mislead the unwary. Their totalitarian spirit is in total conflict with the free spirit of our Constitution and its Bill of Rights.

Chapter 11

The Charter

When its ratification was being considered by the United States Senate in 1945, the UN Charter was widely propagandized as a great political document which would serve as the basis for solving the world's major ills. For example, Judge L. Stauffer Oliver, Chairman of the Board of the United Nations Council of Philadelphia, told the Senate Foreign Relations Committee on July 12, 1945, that the Charter "comes as close to being a perfect document as can be prepared in a practical and imperfect world. We think that it is a marvelous document, notable for its directness, simplicity, and completeness."[1]

On that same date, Clark M. Eichelberger (CFR), Director of the American Association of the United Nations (AAUN), testified that his organization supported the Charter "because it believes that it offers a workable, practical means for the achievement of political security, justice, and economic and social cooperation." He described the Charter as "an excellent document."[2]

Livingston Hartley, director of the AAUN's Washington office, followed with the claim that "American entry into the United Nations Organization will give the United States leader-

ship and unparalleled influence among the nations of the
world."³ At the time, we already had such leadership and
influence. Today, thanks in large part to our involvement in the
UN, we have lost it. Mr. Hartley went on to claim that, should
the Senate reject the Charter, "it will set in motion forces of
power politics which would tend to create exactly the type of
world system most dangerous to our future, an eventual world
balance of power between two great regional blocs."⁴ He included with his testimony a chart which claimed that a "Yes"
vote by the Senate on the Charter would, among other things,
strengthen our security, enhance U.S. leadership, improve relations with our allies, lead to a decrease in taxes, and strengthen
democracy abroad.⁵

The Senate voted "Yes."

We now find ourselves (1) increasingly insecure in the face
of the Soviet-bloc military buildup, (2) in trouble with allies
everywhere (as we have actively worked to undermine some of
them — such as Free China and Rhodesia — in accord with pro-
Marxist UN policies), (3) taxed nearly to death (in part to
bolster the UN network), and (4) reminiscing about the many
countries which, relatively free in 1945, have fallen under
Communist rule. Indeed, figures compiled by the "Liberal"
organization Freedom House indicated, at the start of 1976, that
"only 19.8 per cent of the world's 4.06 billion people now live in
freedom, 35.3 per cent are partly free and 44.9 per cent are not
free."⁶ Yet, it was a vote *against* the Charter that UN propagan-
dist Livingston Hartley had claimed would endanger our security, reduce U.S. leadership in the world, antagonize our allies,
keep our taxes high, and cause a decline in democracy abroad!

Not everyone testified in favor of the new Charter. On July
13, 1945, for instance, economist and author John T. Flynn took
note of the massive propaganda campaign on behalf of Charter
ratification:

> It has been a grand job. As one who has been watching
> propaganda for a great many years, I take off my hat. You
> cannot turn on the radio at any hour of the day — morning, noon

or night — whether you listen to the Metropolitan Opera or to a horse opera, a hill-billy band, a commentator or a newscaster, that you do not hear a plug for this great instrument for peace.[7]

Mr. Flynn astutely noted that hardly anyone had actually read the document that was being trumpeted to the sky. "It is the kind of propaganda," he claimed, "that Hitler taught the world so effectively — 'Don't argue with the people. Just put your idea in a slogan or a phrase and repeat it a dozen times a day until they take it for granted.' "[8]

Years later, even some of the key figures who helped sell the Charter in its early years admitted they had greatly exaggerated its merits. In 1952, for instance, Adlai Stevenson (CFR) wrote: "Obviously the United Nations has not fulfilled all the high hopes that some people entertained when it was founded. The idea that it would automatically usher in an era of sweetness and light was exaggerated at the start."[9]

Another UN Ambassador, Henry Cabot Lodge (CFR), claimed:

> Even at the founding of the United Nations, some people in 1945 in San Francisco, and some of the people who followed them, undertook to get the idea spread around that here was an automatic peace producer, an automatic war preventive, like a patent medicine — you could take a swallow of it, and the disease would be cured. Well, of course, there isn't any such thing, and there never will be any such thing.[10]

In 1964, former Senator Frank Church (D.-Idaho; CFR), another vigorous UN backer, also confirmed the deception:

> . . . one wonders how so infirm an infant as the United Nations could ever have received so auspicious a christening. The supporters of the U.N., then and now, bear a responsibility for having oversold it to the American people. From the outset, we should have stressed that the U.N. by itself lacked the power to preserve world peace. . . .[11]

And former Secretary of State Dean Acheson (CRF) wrote in his memoirs:

... the management of the hearings before the Senate Committee on Foreign Relations regarding its [*the Charter's*] ratification
fell within my field of responsibility. I did my duty faithfully
and successfully but always believed that the Charter was
impracticable. Moreover, its presentation to the American people
as almost holy writ and with the evangelical enthusiasm of a
major advertising campaign seemed to me to raise popular hopes
which could only lead to bitter disappointment.[12]

In other words, the UN Charter as presented and explained to
the American people — and the U.S. Senate — was largely a
propaganda hoax. As a result, in the words of two latter-day
Senators who strongly favor the UN, "Once the Charter was
formally adopted and the institution became a reality, we
allowed ourselves to become caught up in a tremendous euphoria
as we came to expect things from the U.N. that it never had the
capacity for doing, such as playing a major peacekeeping role in
the world."[13]

The massive and misleading propaganda campaign on behalf
of the Charter compelled most Americans to consider only the
theoretical benefits if the Charter organization worked, instead
of the evils that would result if it failed. They were conditioned
to ask, "If it works, what will we get?" when they should also
have been wondering, "If it fails, what will we suffer?"

Since, as a practical matter, the Charter is not amendable,
those in the UN hierarchy have simply stretched and manipulated it to fit their purposes. As explained by authors Yeselson
and Gaglione:

> ... neither moral nor legal restraints flow from the invocation
> of Charter principles at the UN. National interest creates the
> necessary rationalizations. In the world forum, all states defend
> all policies by reference to the Charter. Appropriate clauses are
> selected to support policies on each issue, and states exchange
> positions easily. ... Charter principles are clearly convenient
> pegs on which to hang any foreign policy. This debasement of the
> principles causes them to lose whatever moral authority they
> might otherwise exert. Furthermore, victorious states are em-

boldened by the vindication of their policies, and losers are embittered by injustice.[14]

Even Adlai Stevenson admitted that "Every one of the main charter restrictions has been loosened," and speculated: "I suspect that, if in 1945 there had been proposed such a world organization, endowed with all the actual authority, and energy which the U.N. is showing today, the nations would never have agreed to it."[15] And former Secretary of State John Foster Dulles (CFR) claimed: "I have never seen any proposal made for collective security with 'teeth' in it, or for 'world government' or for 'world federation,' which could not be carried out either by the United Nations or under the United Nations Charter."[16] This is simply an admission, by one of the UN's founders, that the Charter in practice is whatever the most powerful bloc at a given moment wishes it to be. Even Hamilton Fish Armstrong (CFR) admitted in 1961 that "no one of the organization's key bodies — Security Council, General Assembly, Secretariat — is functioning today as was planned 15 years ago at San Francisco."[17]

The "Uniting For Peace" Resolution was a revealing example of the extent to which the Charter has been stretched to fit circumstances which a literal interpretation could never cover. According to Clark Eichelberger, the Resolution that was adopted by the General Assembly on November 3, 1950, "provides one of the most spectacular illustrations of a liberal interpretation of the Charter."[18]

The "Uniting For Peace" Resolution was yet another allegedly anti-Soviet move resulting from the Korean War which actually menaced the interests of the free world. The Charter as originally approved gave little effective power to the General Assembly to act against alleged aggression. Using frustration over Soviet abuse of the veto power in the Security Council as an excuse, Secretary of State Dean Acheson led a move to shift power from the Security Council to the General Assembly without formally amending the Charter. This was virtually an admission that the Charter's original provisions for collective security gave more comfort to aggressors than to the victims of aggression!

As summarized by the United Nations Office of Public Information, the proposed Resolution provided:

> Where there appears to be a threat to peace, breach of the peace or act of aggression, and where the Security Council fails to act because of a negative vote of one of its permanent members, the Assembly may meet in emergency special session within 24 hours at the request of the Council on the vote of any seven Council members, or at the request of a majority of United Nations members. In such a case the Assembly may make recommendations to members for collective measures, including, in the case of a breach of the peace or act of aggression, the use of armed force, to maintain or restore international peace and security.[19]

In effect, the "Uniting For Peace" Resolution asserts that if the Security Council is prevented by the veto from taking effective measures to deal with a situation, the General Assembly may act on behalf of the UN and authorize action by its members. Its main purpose was to circumvent the veto, and, as British Labour Party leader Hugh Gaitskell confirmed, "experience shows that this is just what it has done."[20] Of course, by eroding the Soviet veto it also eroded *our* veto. And that is indeed ominous considering the current Marxist makeup of the world body.

The Resolution was first used in 1956, with predictable results. According to Historian Cecil Crabb:

> When the Assembly had to deal with successive crises in Egypt and Hungary in 1956, the "Uniting For Peace" resolution was put into effect for the first time. It was of no avail in attempting to terminate Soviet oppression of the Hungarian revolutionary movement.[21]

Of course not. But, as we have noted earlier, it *was* successful in pressuring the English, French, and Israelis to withdraw from Egypt and leave the seized Suez Canal under Marxist control. As explained by Lincoln Bloomfield, "With Egypt being invaded, a veto by Britain and France blocked a cease-fire resolution in the Security Council. A majority of Council members . . . then voted to convene the General Assembly in emergency session, and it was the Assembly that created the new [*UN emergency*] force" that was sent to "stabilize" the situation — and merely precluded further effective action to free the Suez Canal.[22]

The "Uniting For Peace" Resolution was conceived by Americans who allegedly wished to halt Communist aggression. In practice, the Resolution merely shifted the UN's center of gravity from the Security Council to the increasingly Marxist and anti-American General Assembly.

The UN has accomplished so much extra-legally, and gathered so much power without Charter authority, that even some influential UN supporters readily acknowledge that any attempt to legalize formally what has been done would result in a fiasco. Professor Richard Gardner (CFR), for example, a former Deputy Assistant Secretary of State, has written:

> An attempt to rewrite its constitution would arrest the continued growth of the United Nations, for some of the members would be reluctant to give explicit endorsement to some of the implicit powers that have been granted to the organization over the years. The fact is that the Charter is a better instrument for the achievement of U.N. purposes than any that could be negotiated today.[23]

Further along, Mr. Gardner makes the startling assertion that "The day the members of the United Nations decide to be uncommitted to the principles of the Charter, the organization will cease to exist."[24] This means either Mr. Gardner is wrong or the UN is a mere figment of our imagination. As we have seen, UN members long ago abandoned any semblance of meaningful commitment to the Charter. The *real* threat to the UN's survival would be a serious attempt to compel its member nations to abide by the Charter's provisions.

Chapter 12
National Sovereignty

Article 2, Paragraph 7, of the UN Charter is the important provision that asserts:

> Nothing contained in the present Charter shall authorize the United Nations to intervene in matters which are essentially within the domestic jurisdiction of any state or shall require the Members to submit such matters to settlement under the present Charter; but this principle shall not prejudice the application of enforcement measures under Chapter VII.

As Goodrich and Hambro have noted, "This paragraph constitutes potentially the most substantial limitation that is to be found anywhere in the whole Charter upon the activity of the United Nations."[1] And James J. Wadsworth adds: "It is a foregone conclusion that had this provision been omitted from the Charter, literally dozens of prospective members in 1945 would have balked at ratification — certainly the United States would have been among them."[2]

Of course it would have. Any document authorizing an internationalist outfit to meddle in our domestic affairs would have been figuratively tarred-and-feathered and run out of town. It is therefore revealing (and frightening) to note the extensive campaign which has been waged to neutralize Article 2(7) and permit the UN to meddle in matters which are clearly the domestic concern of member states. A key strategy has been to promote the idea that nearly everything a nation does has at least an *indirect* impact on other nations, thus nullifying claims to domestic jurisdiction. As early as 1946, William Carr, a consultant for the United States delegation at the San Francisco Conference, wrote:

> Under modern conditions, few acts of a nation affect only its own people. . . . It seems clear that no nation which signs this [*UN*] Charter can justly maintain that any of its acts are its own business, or within its own domestic jurisdiction, if the Security Council says that these acts are a threat to the peace.[3]

Similarly, in April, 1949, UN staff member Moses Moskowitz publicly stated the ominous contention that

> once a matter has become, in one way or another, the subject of regulation by the United Nations, be it by resolution of the General Assembly or by convention between member States at the insistence of the United Nations, that subject ceases to be a matter being "essentially within the domestic jurisdiction of the member States." As a matter of fact, such a position represents the official view of the United Nations, as well as of the member States that have voted in favor of the Universal Declaration of Human Rights. Hence, neither the Declaration, nor the projected [*Human Rights*] Covenant, nor any agreement that may be reached in the future, on the machinery of implementation of human rights, can in any way be considered as violative of the letter or spirit of Article 2 of the Charter.[4]

That all-encompassing blueprint for converting the United States into a subservient UN milk cow is even more frightening in light of President Harry S Truman's claim in 1950 that "there is no longer any real difference between domestic and foreign affairs."[5]

The UN has often disregarded Article 2(7) to meet the demands of expediency. The explosive issue of racial *apartheid* in South Africa is one example. Regardless of one's feeling about the practice, there is little question about the domestic nature of a nation's racial policies. As Amelia C. Leiss noted, in a 1965 study that amounted to a blueprint for eventual UN military invasion of South Africa:

> Clearly, there are few things more "essentially within the domestic jurisdiction" of a state than its relationship to its own citizens, its constitutional form, and its laws, and administrative and judicial procedures. Yet these are the features of the present South African system that are under assault and that a majority of the UN insist be changed.[6]

Meanwhile Clarence Manion, former Dean of the Notre Dame Law School and one of our nation's most astute and respected Constitutional authorities, pointed out:

> Our slavish support of the United Nations' illegal interferences in the domestic affairs of independent nations has made us an accessory to crimes committed against our own allies in the cold war and turned over the management of our foreign policy to the direction of the United Nations General Assembly — a revolutionary body that now runs the United Nations in defiance of its charter.[7]

Dean Manion's contention was perhaps most dramatically documented by our participation in the UN's shameful and disgusting crusade to pull down the anti-Communist regime of Ian Smith in Rhodesia.

On September 9, 1972, the Washington newsweekly *Human Events* reported the incredible news that:

> By a 12-to-0 vote, with 10 abstentions, the United Nations Special Committee on Colonialism last week voted to put Puerto Rico under study as a colonial territory of the United States entitled to independence. . . .

The resolution to meddle in the internal affairs of the U.S. was approved despite overwhelming evidence [*that*] Puerto Rico citizens do not want independence.[8]

That "overwhelming evidence" consisted primarily of a 1967 referendum in which Puerto Ricans voted 698,396 to 4,205 *against* breaking away from the United States (a fantastic ratio of more than 166 to 1!).

Even closer to home is a startling dispatch carried by the Associated Press and datelined Memphis, Tennessee:

> The United Nations Commission on Human Rights will consider allegations of police brutality in Memphis that could "embarrass the country," a federal official said Wednesday [*September 6, 1978*] . . . .
> He [*Bobby Doctor, Southern regional director of the U.S. Civil Rights Commission*] said the U.N. Commission on Human Rights has placed on its Sept. 11 agenda a review of the charges. A U.N. spokesman in New York said the commission would meet Monday in Geneva, Switzerland.[9]

Even to "review" alleged "police brutality" in an American city is a flagrant violation of Article 2(7) of the Charter. As explained by Goodrich and Hambro:

> While discussion does not amount to intervention [*in domestic affairs*], the creation of a commission of inquiry, the making of a recommendation of a procedural or substantive nature, or the taking of a binding decision constitutes intervention under the terms of this paragraph [*Article 2(7)*]. To limit intervention to coercive measures would have the result of largely limiting the application of the paragraph to the field of the exception which obviously could not have been intended.[10]

A serious threat to our national sovereignty is the drive to repeal the important Connally Amendment that qualifies United States participation in the International Court of Justice (World Court). We automatically became a member of the World Court when we joined the UN, but were not bound by its jurisdiction until a Senate-ratified declaration to that effect was formally filed. That Senate resolution "recognizing as compulsory . . . the jurisdiction of the International Court of Justice in all legal disputes hereafter arising" provided that such World Court Jurisdiction would *not* apply to "disputes with regard to matters which are essentially within the domestic jurisdiction of the United States."[11]

This, however, was not enough, for who was to define "domestic jurisdiction" — the United States or the World Court itself? Senate Foreign Relations Committee Chairman Tom Connally (D.-Texas) wanted the resolution to pass, but feared it wouldn't unless this question was resolved in favor of the United States. So he succeeded in having these six words added to the resolution: *as determined by the United States*. The resolution, thus amended, passed by a vote of 62 to 2 on August 2, 1946.

As G. Edward Griffin has warned, those six little words — the Connally Reservation — "are all that stand between us and complete legal subjugation to the whims of fifteen or nine or five or even two men whose legal backgrounds and personal ideologies may be strongly antipathetic to the free world in general and to the United States in particular."[12] Nevertheless, every American President through Carter since 1945 has urged repeal of the crucial Connally Reservation!

The drive by Internationalists to chip away at U.S. sovereignty has also included a clever back-door approach that merits comment. Professor Richard N. Gardner (CFR), a former Deputy Assistant Secretary of State, is aligned with those who are realistically resigned to keeping the Charter largely as is, since it is nearly unamendable, preferring instead merely to "interpret" it liberally to fit circumstances. Writing in *Foreign Affairs* in 1974, he speculated that "we are more likely to make progress by pressing the existing instrument to the outer limits of its potentialities through creative use, seeking amendments only on carefully selected matters where they seem both necessary and capable of adoption by the constitutionally required majority."[13] Recognizing that world government cannot be achieved in the near future, Professor Gardner asserted that the "house of world order" will "have to be built from the bottom up rather than from the top down. . . . an end run around national sovereignty, eroding it piece by piece, will accomplish much more than the old-fashioned frontal assault. . . . The question is whether this more modest approach can do the job."

Believing that its chances are reasonably good, Professor Gardner continues: "The hopeful aspect of the present situation is that even as nations resist appeals for 'world government' and 'the surrender of sovereignty,' technological, economic and political interests are forcing them to establish more and more far-reaching arrangements to manage their mutual interdependence." He then lists a few of those arrangements that could prove especially useful to the cause of subtly surrendering national sovereignty to international institutions:

1. International monetary reforms, which will necessitate giving the International Monetary Fund (IMF) "unprecedented powers to create new international reserves and to influence national decisions on exchange rates and on domestic monetary and fiscal policies." He also notes that the IMF would probably be given power to back its decisions "by meaningful multilateral sanctions."

2. Strengthen the General Agreement on Tariffs and Trade (GATT) to cover hitherto unregulated "non-tariff barriers" in order to "subject countries to an unprecedented degree of international surveillance over up to now sacrosanct 'domestic' policies, such as farm price supports, subsidies, and government procurement practices that have transnational effects."

3. Increase resources of international development and technical assistance agencies. "This should enhance the authority of the World Bank, the regional development banks and the U.N. Development Program over the economic policies of rich and poor nations," explains Professor Gardner.

4. Environmentalism, leading to "new procedures to implement the principle of State responsibility for national actions

that have transnational environmental consequences. . . . At the same time, international agencies will be given broader powers to promulgate and revive standards limiting air and ocean pollution."

5. The so-called "population problem" could drain additional sovereignty as national programs aimed at zero population growth are established and implemented with the help of international agencies.

6. Food supplies, with the UN's World Food Conference likely to result in Internationalist efforts to maintain adequate food supplies as "reserves of food and arable land dwindle under the impact of crop failures and disappointing fish harvests." Of course, the socialist policies of government are primarily responsible for food shortages throughout the world — the same sort of socialist policies favored by the Internationalists who use the shortages as the excuse to expand their power.

7. Control of the world's oceans, once negotiated into the hands of "a new international regime," could necessitate "tough provisions to assure compliance as well as to provide for the compulsory settlement of disputes."

8. Communication technology is requiring new international regulatory institutions that "will probably be given new powers to allocate radio frequencies and satellite parking orbits among users."

9. Disarmament, moving beyond U.S.-Soviet agreements on strategic weapons to the more multinational matter of conventional weapons, could give international agencies "new responsibilities for the administration of these arms control and disarmament measures, including means of verification and enforcement."

10. Conflict containment, including "international peace-keeping arrangements to patrol borders, supervise elections and verify compliance with nonintervention norms."

According to Professor Gardner, "the case-by-case approach can produce some remarkable concessions of 'sovereignty' that

could not be achieved on an across-the-board basis." He predicted: ". . . while we will not see 'world government' in the old-
fashioned sense of a single all-embracing global authority, key
elements of planetary planning and planetary management will
come about on those very specific problems where the facts of
interdependence force nations, in their enlightened self-inter-
est, to abandon unilateral decision-making in favor of multilateral processes."

Numerous observers have claimed that many of our so-called
"crises" in recent years (in energy, environment, food, *etc.*) have
been largely and *purposely* manufactured and sustained by
governments. Professor Gardner's scenario presents one explanation of why certain influential individuals would favor such
"crisis" conditions as an excuse to expand their power even as
they undermine the national sovereignty of the United States
and other countries.

In an earlier article in *Foreign Affairs*, Professor Gardner
asserted: "The most basic division in the world today is not
between communists and non-communists, between blacks and
whites, between rich and poor or even between young and old. It
is between those who see only the interests of a limited group
and those who are capable of seeing the interests of the broader
community of mankind as a whole."[14] In other (less self-
serving) words, between defenders of national sovereignty and
advocates of World Government.

He is probably right.

Chapter 13

Patriotism

The drive to undermine our national independence has included a move to destroy the patriotic emotions and loyalties of
the American people. The campaign has included tactics ranging
from character assassination of the Founding Fathers to attrib-
uting nearly all of the world's evils to loyalty to one's country.
Atlantic Union advocate Clarence Streit once went so far as to
assert that "Cain was the first man known to love his country.
Before his time there was no fatherland."[1] This is absurd,
considering how Adam and Eve must have felt about Eden prior
to falling to temptations tendered by history's most influential
Internationalist. And it was the brilliant Marxist sympathizer,
Albert Einstein, who tried to discredit patriotism by referring to
nationalism as "an infantile disease" and "the measles of
mankind."[2] International collectivists know very well that the
nations of the world cannot be comfortably merged into a world
government until the patriotic loyalty of the citizens of those
separate nations has been replaced by loyalty to an international
entity such as the United Nations.

Probably none of the Founding Fathers of our nation has

been more extensively maligned with less real justification than George Washington. As military leader of the successful War for Independence and our first Chief Executive, he is rightly known as the Father of Our Country. Perhaps it is for this reason that so much time and effort have been expended by Internationalists to deface his memory.

Consider, for example, the vicious rumor instigated by the muckraking journalist Drew Pearson in July, 1965, to the effect that President Washington was guilty of a serious conflict of interest. Pearson alleged that while serving as Chief Executive the Father of Our Country had owned a Virginia quarry that sold sandstone to the government for use in construction of the U.S. Capitol building. The allegation was given further national publicity in August by television's David Brinkley (CFR), and turned up a few weeks after that in a news bulletin of the National Geographic Society. A number of newspapers also circulated the rumor before someone finally decided to verify Pearson's charges. Documents subsequently discovered in the National Archives proved that the quarry in question had been owned by a man named Henry Brent, and that Washington had held no financial interest in it whatsoever.[3]

One of the most bizarre charges against General Washington was made in 1971 when he, Thomas Jefferson (author of the Declaration of Independence), James Madison (father of the Constitution), and four other early Presidents were lumped together and accused of being marijuana smokers. The top medical officer of the Nixon Administration, Surgeon General Jesse Steinfield, told the National Commission on Marijuana and Drug Abuse:

> Indeed, Dr. Burke, president of the American Historical Reference Society and consultant to the Smithsonian [*Institution*] reports no less than seven U.S. Presidents smoked marijuana, including Washington, Jefferson, Madison, Monroe, Jackson, Taylor and Pierce.

Despite the serious implications of this claim, it went unchallenged by members of the Commission. Only later was it learned that there was no such person as "Dr. Burke," and that the Smithsonian Institution knew nothing of the so-called American Historical Reference Society. The hoax was eventually traced to the *Chicago Seed*, an underground newspaper of the New Left. The staff of the *Seed* didn't know any more about "Dr. Burke" or his "Society" than did anyone else. They had simply copied the seedy story from yet another underground paper, which had apparently made it up.[4]

Meanwhile the image of many of our nation's patriotic figures has been consistently undermined in America's school textbooks. One contemporary history book promoted at the high-school level was rejected by Texas school authorities who learned that, among other faults, it devoted five times as much space to Marilyn Monroe as to George Washington.[5] And when *This Week* magazine compared history books issued before 1920 with those issued after that year, it discovered a shocking tendency in modern texts to denigrate or eliminate some of the most impressive patriotic events in our national history. Former Secretary of Agriculture Ezra Taft Benson summarized the findings of *This Week*:

> *Nathan Hale* said, "I regret that I have but one life to give for my country," in eleven of the old textbooks, but in only one of the new textbooks. *Patrick Henry* said, "Give me liberty or give me death" in twelve out of the fourteen earlier texts, but in only two out of the forty-five recent texts. But *John Paul Jones* set the record. He said, "I have not yet begun to fight," in nine of the old books and in none of the new books.[6]

Probably the most effective mechanism used to attack the patriotic outlook of the American people during the past decade has been the Vietnam War. It would have seemed incredible to most Americans, prior to Vietnam, that a war against so natural and deadly an enemy as the Communists could have been turned into a means of *reducing* the American patriotic spirit. Yet, consider the obvious lack of desire on the part of our leaders to

win the war; the sedition they encouraged and permitted here at
home by open supporters of the enemies we were fighting in
Vietnam; their insistence on implementing policies which they
knew in advance would needlessly increase American casualties*;
the resulting loss of lives on the battlefield and disruption of
lives at home for clearly phony reasons; the massive flood of
aid by our government to those Communist nations comprising
the arsenal of the Vietcong; the increased war spending which
helped create the inflationary excuse for such dictatorial measures as wage and price controls; and a "conclusion" to the war
on terms so disgraceful and dishonorable as to include a
commitment by our leaders to pay what amounts to reparations.
All of these tragic events and policies combined to create the
widespread doubts, confusion, and despair which have replaced
real patriotism in the minds of many Americans, and which
have helped to erode many other American virtues that were
once taken for granted. The Vietnam War was used with
incredible effectiveness by Internationalists to condition the
American people to accept various parts of the One World
agenda as an "alternative" to future Vietnams.

Many major reviewers of books, movies, and plays have
similarly helped to undermine the spirit of patriotism in America by continually lauding works which promote Internationalism while attacking patriotism, even as they smear or ignore
those which promote love of country and respect for our
heritage.

*On February 1, 1968, for example, the late President Lyndon B. Johnson
asserted, during presentation of a Medal Of Honor to an Air Force Major: "Let
those who would stop the bombing answer this question: 'What would the North
Vietnamese be doing if we stopped the bombing and let them alone?' The
answer, I think, is clear. The enemy force in the South would be larger. It would
be better equipped. The war would be harder. The losses would be greater. The
difficulties would be longer. And of one thing you can be sure: It would cost
many more American lives." Two months later, on March 31, 1968, President
Johnson ordered a unilateral halt to the bombing of North Vietnam. Within one
year, not only had 13,000 additional American lives been lost in Vietnam, but
North Vietnam had completely repaired the damage inflicted by American
bombers prior to the bombing halt. (See *Weekly Compilation of Presidential
Documents*, February 5, 1968, p. 192, and April 8, 1968, p. 620; and *The Review
Of The News*, April 9, 1969, pp. 10–11.)

John Wayne, for example, was a talented and patriotic actor whose reputation was largely established in movies portraying him as an American fighting Japanese Fascism. At first no significant roadblocks were thrown in Wayne's path by the Left. But later, when Wayne remained consistent in his patriotic outlook and hatred of totalitarianism by opposing the Communists, the brickbats started coming thick and heavy.

In the early 1960s, for example, Wayne produced, directed, and starred in a $12 million extravaganza entitled *The Alamo*. It was a well-done, highly patriotic movie, with a cast of outstanding stars, and about as far removed from Hollywood's typical subversion and perversion as a movie could get. Apparently it was for this very reason that the Left began to howl against the film and to discourage Americans from patronizing it. So serious did the situation become that a number of patriotic organizations launched campaigns to encourage Americans to insist that their local theaters show *The Alamo*, and then to support it with their attendance. Fortunately, the film went on to become a box-office success, despite all the Left could do to scuttle it.

Another movie directed by John Wayne, in which he also starred, was *The Green Berets*, the only regular full-length feature film produced during the Vietnam War that reflected a pro-American, anti-Communist position. This exciting and well-acted movie was in the tradition of many of Wayne's World War II films, except that the enemy was Communism. "Liberal" reviewers from one end of the country to the other went to work to discredit *The Green Berets* in the same manner as they had *The Alamo*. Typical was this review from the *New York Times*:

> "The Green Berets" is a film so unspeakable, so stupid, so rotten and false in every detail that it passes through being fun, through being funny, through being camp, through everything and becomes an invitation to grieve. . . . Simplicities of the right, simplicities of the left, but this one is beyond the possible. It is vile and insane. On top of that, it is dull.[7]

Compare the tone of that vitriolic diatribe with the *Times* review a few weeks earlier of the degenerate "rock" musical *Hair*, a production that glorifies drugs and sexual perversion, desecrates the Flag, and ridicules religion:

> What is so likable about "Hair," that tribal-rock musical that Monday completed its trek from downtown, via a discotheque, and landed, positively panting with love and smelling of sweat and flowers, at the Biltmore Theater? I think it is simply that it is so likable. So new, so fresh and so unassuming, even in its pretentions.[8]

The very title, *Hair*, pronounced *ah-ee-r*, has nothing to do with what keeps us from being *bald*, but is the French verb meaning "to hate." Yet the *New York Times* described this movie as "panting with love" and "so likable." That's how the game is played. At times it is rough!

The most visible symbol of our national pride is the Flag of the United States. In recent years it has been a target of escalating Internationalist attacks. In early 1962, for instance, a U.S. Air Force recruiting poster was released which depicted a young man and a young woman in Air Force uniform walking down the street. It would be expected that such a poster, urging young Americans to join a branch of the U.S. military, would include the Flag of the United States. Yet, aside from the happy faces of the figures, the only other conspicuous item in the poster was a huge UN flag. Even the NATO flag was discernible! But Old Glory was conspicuous only by its absence.

Adverse public reaction eventually compelled Secretary of Defense Robert McNamara (CFR) to withdraw the offensive poster and order a return to the traditional use of the United States Flag on Armed Forces recruiting posters, but he never did offer a sensible explanation for eliminating the Flag in the first place.[9]

Another recent strategy to undermine national sentiment has been to demand modification of the wording of the Pledge of Allegiance to the Flag, on the grounds that the goals it sets forth have not actually been realized. The old *Look* magazine, for instance, carried, in 1970, a lengthy anti-Pledge article entitled, "Do We Need A New Pledge Of Allegiance?" The article referred to the Pledge's "unsupportable claims to national virtues we have not yet attained," specifically citing "its declaration that this is a nation indivisible, when proof to the contrary is all around us," and questioning why we must "pronounce that there is liberty and justice for all, when a person only has to look and to listen to realize we have yet to reach that goal." Similarly, in August of 1977 a federal judge struck down a New Jersey law requiring students to stand during the Pledge after a student refused to obey it on grounds that the phrase "with liberty and justice for all" is "a lie."[11]

Such specious reasoning reminds one of the argument that Christians shouldn't call themselves "Christians" because they all fall short of living that religion to perfection. The Pledge of Allegiance focuses on an ideal, not on an imperfect reality. The Republic for which our Flag stands is one thing; the democracy into which we are fast degenerating is quite another. And it is to the noble concept of a Republic united under God with liberty and justice for all that we pledge allegiance, and toward which we should strive. Demands that the Pledge be amended because we are not completely unified, or have yet to achieve perfect liberty or justice for all citizens, are mere excuses to erode respect for yet another of our patriotic symbols.

Even our national anthem, "The Star-Spangled Banner," has suffered increasing assault in recent years. Advocates of Black Power showed their contempt for it at both the 1968 and 1972 Olympic Games. The new chancellor of a major Western university cancelled the Anthem at his inauguration because he considered it "provocative."[12] In December, 1971, the president of another university outlawed playing of the Anthem at home basketball games for fear of arousing "racial tensions."[13] During that same month, the coach of yet another university basketball team participating in a holiday tournament at Madison Square Garden refused to allow his players on the court while the Anthem was played because, as he put it, "My team once honored the National Anthem this season and we lost. Now we just don't come out until it's played."[14] In January, 1973, a college track team was disqualified from a major meet when its players insisted on doing stretching exercises while the Anthem was played. But the very next month, directors of the Olympic Invitational Track and Field Meet at Madison Square Garden attempted to drop the Anthem from the Meet's agenda. They hastily reversed their decision after an angry and determined public outcry.[16]

There has also been a move to have "The Star-Spangled Banner" replaced by some other song. Critics promoting this line have ranged from the old *Life* magazine[17] to *Senior Scholastic*,[18] from the *Saturday Review*[19] to *Newsweek*,[20] from *Reader's Digest*[21] to *My Weekly Reader*,[22] and from *This Week*[23] to *Scholastic Teacher*.[24] Some of the arguments used against our present Anthem are designed to appear politically neutral, such as the one which claims it is too difficult to sing — a criticism which some view as reflecting lazy patriotism, similar to the insistence that Washington's Birthday and certain other holidays be celebrated on Mondays rather than on their actual anniversaries so we can extend the fun and games of a holiday weekend. After all, how many who consider the Anthem too hard to sing have ever taken time actually to *practice* singing it?

Indeed, most of the criticism of "The Star-Spangled Banner" grows out of radical "peace" propaganda which sees evil in anything martial, nationalistic, or conservatively rooted in our patriotic history. A typical example was an editorial in *Christian Century* which condemned the Anthem for being too war-like ("the rockets' red glare, the bombs bursting in air") and too piously belligerent ("Then conquer we must, when our cause it is just./ And this be our motto, 'In God is our trust.'"). The editorial also implied that the Anthem promotes "superpatriotic self-righteousness," and should be replaced by a song which would generate a sense of "common humanity" and "move out in a positive way toward other nations."[25] Thus we see once again the demand that a respected patriotic symbol be abandoned in favor of one more in line with the concept of UN-style world government.

Even the incredible tragedy at the 1972 Olympic Games, in which many members of the Israeli team were brutally murdered by Marxist terrorists, was turned by Leftists in our news media into a launching pad for additional anti-nationalist propaganda. Newscaster Walter Cronkite, for instance, concluded his CBS broadcast for September 8, 1972, with this observation:

> Maybe a little less flag-waving, a little less hysteria over national point-scoring, is what the Games need right now; a little more emphasis on true sportsmanship and a little less fanfare — the kind of puffing that builds up the Games until they become the natural forum and target for the type of people who carry machine guns, as they climb the fences around the Olympic compounds.[26]

This same line was expounded again over CBS on September 13 by commentator Eric Sevareid, who asserted: "What was designed to produce international spirit has produced blatant and bitter exhibitions of nationalism. . . . The next summer games set for Montreal in '76 . . . will have to downplay the national flags, anthems, and patriotic bands."[27]

Ignored in commentary of this sort is the fact that almost all of the trouble at the Olympics in recent years can be laid directly at the door of anti-nationalists. The Black Powerites who showed such contempt for our National Anthem could hardly be called patriots, while the examples of blatant referee bias that occur periodically during the Games are almost always the work of Internationalists representing Communist countries. Even the degenerates who slaughtered the Israeli athletes in 1972 were later found to be linked *internationally* with a revolutionary network of terrorists and assassins, and to have used Soviet-made AK-47 automatic rifles and ammunition in their bloody Olympic raid.[28]

To imply that true sportsmanship and nationalism are incompatible is to ignore the clear record of the Olympic Games prior to the 1960s. Spirited competition between individual nations in an atmosphere of unsurpassed sportsmanship was the rule, not the exception. Perhaps it is for this very reason that devotees of internationalism have been working so hard to undermine the traditional Olympic spirit, even arranging to heap blame for the results of their own agitation on the scapegoat of "nationalism."

Another important element in the drive toward world government has been the attempt to have Americans begin thinking in terms of international interdependence rather than national independence. President John F. Kennedy went so far as to travel to Philadelphia on July 4, 1962 — Independence Day — to propose a Declaration of *Inter*dependence. The late President declared: "But I will say here and now on this day of independence that the United States will be ready for a Declaration of Interdependence. . . . Today Americans must learn to think intercontinentally."[29] One week later, *New York Times* columnist James Reston (CFR) elated: "This year . . . President Kennedy went to Independence Hall, of all places, and on the Fourth of July, of all days, and virtually proposed to repeal the Declaration of Independence in favor of a declaration of international interdependence."[30]

On March 5, 1968, the Mayor and City Council of Minneapolis, Minnesota, signed, in conjunction with the Hennepin County Board of Commissioners, "A Declaration of World Citizenship" that recognized the "right of our citizens to declare that their citizenship responsibilities extend beyond our city and nation." It pledged the signers to "join with other concerned people of the world in a declaration that we share in this world responsibility and that our citizens are in this sense citizens of the world," and also resolved "that as a symbol of our obligations as world citizens we request the Municipal Building Commission to proudly display the United Nations flag on suitable occasions at the main entrance to the City Hall and the main entrance to the new county building."[31] The Declaration was endorsed by a dozen other prominent Minnesotans, including Governor Harold LeVander and Representative Donald M. Fraser (D.; CFR).[32]

On United Nations Day in 1975, the World Affairs Council of Philadelphia unveiled the notorious "Declaration of INTERdependence" authored by Internationalist historian Henry Steele Commager. The document called for "all nations to strengthen and to sustain the United Nations," and claimed that "To establish a new world order" it "is essential that mankind free itself from the limitations of national prejudice . . ."[33] Incredibly, the Commager Declaration was eventually endorsed by more than one hundred United States Senators and Representatives (see Appendix D).

The propaganda for interdependence has continued to escalate, even as many of our national leaders have advocated and implemented policies aimed at actually making us more dependent on other nations (including, in some instances, our enemies — as when the Rhodesian boycott made us increasingly dependent on the Soviet Union for chrome ore) for everything from military security, to the value of our money, to the everyday goods we buy.

It is important to keep in mind that neither hatred nor bitterness toward other countries is a characteristic of true patriotism. Rather, patriotism is the spirit that leads a citizen to love his own country best, while respecting all other countries that merit respect. As President Theodore Roosevelt once observed: "Patriotism stands in national matters as love of family does in private life. Nationalism corresponds to the love a man bears for his wife and children."[34] Surely, loving one's wife and children best does not imply hatred of all other women and children.

Former Pennsylvania Senator Joseph Clark, an Internationalist who became President of the United World Federalists in 1969 and was a vigorous sponsor of the Declaration of INTERdependence, once lamented, "Old-fashioned patriotism is surely an obstacle to world government."[35] It surely is! And it is the responsibility of us all to keep it that way.

Chapter 14

One World Government

Is it justified to brand the United Nations a One World Government? At the present time, it is not — but don't be fooled. From the start, it was merely intended as a first step in that direction. In his 1945 report to President Truman, Secretary of State Edward Stettinius (CFR) noted that "The Security Council is not the enforcement agency of a world state, since world opinion will not accept the surrender of sovereignty which the establishment of a world state would demand." The report continued:

> A similarly realistic acceptance of the facts of the actual world limits the General Assembly to discussion and deliberation without the power to legislate, since the power to legislate would necessarily encroach upon the sovereign independence of the member states.[1]

In "An Open Letter to the American People" that same year, a number of prominent Internationalists declared:

The San Francisco Charter, by maintaining the absolute
sovereignties of the rival nation-states, thus preventing the
creation of superior law in world relations, resembles the Articles
of Confederation of the thirteen original American republics.
We know that this confederation did not work. No league system
ever attempted in human history could prevent conflict between
its members. We must aim at a federal constitution of the world,
a working world-wide legal order. . . .[2]

American Internationalists favored some form of World
Government, and wished to have the UN eventually evolve into
one, but were sufficiently realistic to recognize widespread
public opposition to the concept. Allen W. Dulles (CRF) and
Beatrice Pitney Lamb, for example, concluded:

Although the ultimate need for an organization stronger than the
United Nations must be clear to any thoughtful observer, the
question of what type of organization is realistically possible at
the present time is the real issue. . . . There is no indication that
American public opinion, for example, would approve the establishment of a super state, or permit American membership in it.
In other words, time — a long time — will be needed before world
government is politically feasible. . . . this time element might
seemingly be shortened so far as American opinion is concerned
by an active propaganda campaign in this country.[3]

Another committed Internationalist, and a future President
of the United States, General Dwight D. Eisenhower (CFR), was
pleased with how military operations during World War II had
compelled nations to "pool a portion of their authority in a
single headquarters with power to enforce their decisions." He
wished to see this essentially dictatorial battle-front experience
applied to peace-time operations of the UN, but lamented that,
because its "application would have meant some form of
limited federated world government," it "was politically unacceptable to any of the great nations concerned."[4]

Ike's brother, Dr. Milton Eisenhower (CFR), was less pessi-
mistic. While acknowledging that the UN Security Council, for
example, was largely a paper tiger, he nevertheless recognized

that each member UN nation, by accepting *in principle* that the UN should be able to impose military sanctions to "keep the peace," had committed itself *in principle* to the sacrifice of individual sovereignty. He asserted that even this largely "theoretical commitment to limited sovereignty" marked "a considerable advance in our progress toward effective and orderly world government."[5]

John Foster Dulles (CFR), who would become President Eisenhower's first Secretary of State, also recognized the evolutionary role of the UN in the gradual drive toward world government. "The United Nations," he wrote, "represents not a *final* stage in the development of world order, but only a primitive stage. Therefore its primary task is to create the conditions which will make possible a more highly developed organization."[6]

One of the UN specialized agencies actively working to create those conditions is UNESCO. On one occasion in the UN's early years, when UNESCO was widely criticized for promoting One World propaganda, the *Saturday Review* candidly editorialized:

> If UNESCO is attacked on the grounds that it is helping to prepare the world's people for world government, then it is an
> · error to burst forth with apologetic statements and denials. Let us face it: the job of UNESCO is to help create and promote the elements of world citizenship. When faced with such a "charge," let us by all means affirm it from the housetops.[7]

If only *all* UN advocates would be that candid in their pronouncements!

It should be clear by now that the UN's founders and key supporters intended it eventually to evolve into a powerful agency of world government — even though for the time being, as Clark Eichelberger once put it, the UN is "in the shadowy area between an organization of States and a world government."[8] Yet some UN propagandists, anxious to keep Americans hoodwinked regarding the ultimate goal, have deceptively claimed: "It is plainly evident that the United Nations was never intended to be a super state. It was given no attributes of statehood; it has no power to conscript a soldier, levy a tax or enforce a decision."[9]

Of course, what the UN was initially, and what it was intended to become, are two different things. The fledgling UN was to become a superstate in the same sense that a child is to become an adult: one stage at a time.

What are some of the adjustments which must eventually be made to convert the UN into at least a limited world government? According to former Senator Joseph Clark (D.-Pennsylvania), onetime head of the United World Federalists:

> Among the major changes in the charter that would be required to create a limited world government with power to keep the peace [*or wage the war*] are (1) elimination of the veto in the Security Council; (2) substitution for the "one nation, one vote" in the General Assembly of a more realistic system that recognizes the vast disparity of both population and economic power of the nation-states; (3) a self-operating system of financing the UN, such as a license fee on concessions in the seabed, or a small tax payable directly to the UN treasury, on transactions in international trade; (4) a strong United Nations Peace-Keeping and Peace-Making Force, subject to the control of the secretary-general acting under instructions of the Security Council; (5) general and complete disarmament; and (6) compulsory jurisdiction over disputes between nations, whether justifiable or not, by the World Court (i.e., repeal of the Connally Amendment).[10]

A seventh reform cited by Senator Clark is "the admission of all nation-states to the U.N." in order to create "a universal federation of all the nation-states in a limited world government. . . ." And, at the same time, he would have the specialized UN agencies "acquire the power to deal with the problems of pollution, poverty, and population."[11]

Influential American Internationalists in government, education, the electronic and print media, and many other fields are actively promoting those goals at the present time. And they are not alone, for as Adlai Stevenson pointed out: "There is no possibility of doubting (and no reason for ignoring!) the fact that the Soviet objective is one world. . . ."[12]

Chapter 15

Democracy

Representative John H. Rousselot (R.-California) once observed that the best example of democracy he could think of was a lynch mob, since there was only one man against it. This point, that majority rule has no inherent relationship to morality, justice, or fair play, is nowhere more evident than in the manner in which "democracy" is practiced at the United Nations. As columnist Paul Weaver has noted, the UN is "an upside-down institution, in which the nations that are dominant in the world — by wealth, power, even population — are a tiny minority, and where the nations that are weak and unimportant are in a position of unassailable superiority."[1]

Indeed, the UN may well be the least-representative, most mal-apportioned political entity in the history of the world. "At the present time," testified former Secretary of State Dean Rusk (CFR) in 1975, "less than 10 percent of the world's population, with less than 2 percent of the financial contributions to the UN, can cast two-thirds of the votes in the General Assembly."[2]

A minority of nations contribute around sixty percent of the UN's budget. William Korey, Director of B'nai B'rith's International Council, has correctly branded the farce as "taxation without representation carried to the ultimate absurdity."[3]

Brandeis University Professor John Roche, former Chairman of the "Liberal" Americans for Democratic Action, also laments: ". . . the last time I did a count I discovered sadly that about 80 per cent of the member nations of the U. N. are run by regimes I despise — the democratic countries could caucus in my living room."[4]

And former Senator J. Glenn Beall, Jr. (R.-Maryland) once told his colleagues:

> It is interesting to note that the U. S. population — approximately 212 million [*in 1975*] — is greater than the combined populations of the 77 smallest countries represented in the United Nations. Each of these nations . . . has one vote in the General Assembly. The U. S. economy exceeds the total output of goods and services for the combined economies of 124 countries in the United Nations.[5]

Even Clarence K. Streit, the leading advocate of internationalism via Atlantic Union, recognized the danger inherent in attempting to bring democratic nations (even when they are roughly equal in population) under an umbrella like the UN or League of Nations, claiming that such an arrangement would actually encourage dictatorship among them. According to Streit:

> A league by giving an equal vote to the government of each nation in it allows the government least responsible and responsive to its people to maneuver best.
>
> The more democratic a people is the more it respects the minority [*sic*] and requires a government to explain policies to the people before committing them, and the more important the issue the more vigilant is its public opinion. But the more these conditions obtain the more handicapped the government is in defending the interests of its citizens in a league. The league system thus places a premium on whatever strengthens the government as regards its own people and a penalty on whatever strengthens the citizen's power to restrain his government.[6]

Mr. Streit also noted: "When 100,000,000 men league with 50,000,000 they lose power as regards the field of government they transfer to the league, for whereas each formerly had the power of 1 over policy in this field they now have only the power of one-half, since the league weights 50,000,000 and l00,000,000 alike. Because it thus shifts the unit in shifting the field of government, a league entails loss of power to the citizens of all but the least populous of the democracies in it."[7]

Clearly, the UN concept of one-nation, one-vote, has simply sanctified *minority* rule within the organization, but there is no realistic way to change the situation under the Charter. A two-thirds vote in the General Assembly, followed by ratification of two-thirds of all UN members (including two-thirds of all perm-anent Security Council members), is required to amend the Charter — a proposition that UN supporter Lincoln Bloomfield (CFR) labeled "a political impossibility."[8]

As a desperate alternative, some UN devotees have urged that the ballot box be totally abandoned in the General Assembly. Former NATO Ambassador Harlan Cleveland (CFR), for example, has argued:

> There is a remarkably simple solution to the "voting problem" in the General Assembly: Don't take any votes. The alternative mode — the action mode — is to decide by *concensus* among those whose action together is necessary to carry out any given interna-tional program.
>
> Once there is a consensus about action, a vote is unnecessary. When there is not yet a consensus about action, a vote dramatizes the difference and makes eventual reconciliation that much more difficult.[9]

This amounts to an admission, by a vigorous UN advocate, that majority rule in the United Nations is a dangerous, unwork-able fraud which makes not voting at all preferable to the one-nation, one-vote nonsense. The vast majority of UN members are weak states unable to contribute support in any meaningful or effective military or economic way. According to Clyde Eagleton

(CFR), these "nations" have little responsibility for what results, so "are tempted to vote through half-thought-out enterprises, the consequences of which must be faced by the few members strong enough to face them."[10] Vernon Aspaturian adds:

> In the United Nations, where majorities do not correspond to the actual distribution of population, wealth, power, or enlighten- ment, majority will is a synthetic contrivance expressing the lowest common denominator of interests and passions which temporarily and adventitiously shaped it, while majority rule, under these conditions, is an unmitigated vice.[11]

A few years ago the General Assembly voted, 102 to 1, for a Soviet-sponsored motion calling for an international convention to regulate satellite television broadcasts, a move that would include the "right" of states to veto broadcasts considered dis- tasteful. The lone negative vote was cast by the United States, primarily because of the obvious threat posed by such a move to our First Amendment guarantee of a free press.[12] On November 26, 1976 the Assembly voted 124 to 1 to condemn the United States for having vetoed Communist Vietnam's application for UN membership.[13] It is obvious that so-called "democracy" at the UN is predicated on the lynch-mob principle pin-pointed so perceptively by Representative Rousselot.

Chapter 16

Honestly!

Soviet dictator Joseph Stalin once asserted: "With a diplomat, words *must* diverge from acts. . . . Words are one thing and acts something different. . . . A sincere diplomat would equal dry water, wooden iron."[1]

In an address to the UN Security Council on February 15, 1961, during the UN's war against Katanga, U.S. Ambassador Adlai Stevenson attempted to reassure American critics of the UN that the United States was not supporting the conflict militarily. He asserted: "In contrast to others, the United States has never at any time provided a single tank, a single gun, a single soldier, a single piece of equipment that could be used for military purposes to anyone in the Congo."[2]

Ambassador Stevenson was simply behaving as Stalin had said diplomats must behave, for the U.S. government *had* been rendering military aid and comfort to the UN for its Congo caper. For example, *U.S. News & World Report* had earlier reported:

LEOPOLDVILLE — By July 22 [*1960*], the airport here had come to resemble an American military installation.

148 _The United Nations Conspiracy_

A whole fleet of U.S. Air Force planes was taking off and landing at all hours.

It was an impressive display of American air power — air power than can reach easily into the heart of Africa.

Incoming planes were bringing flour and United Nations troops to the Congo.

. . . Hundreds of tons of flour were unloaded, together with jeeps and other military equipment.[3]

Toward the end of the year, in its issue for December 19, 1960, _U.S. News & World Report_ ran an advertisement for the Lockheed Aircraft Corporation that boasted of the great job Lockheed planes had done to assist the UN in the Congo:

> The call came from the United Nations. Within hours huge airlifters were rushed to the Congo with hundreds of U.N. peace [sic] troops and tons of supplies. One airlifter proved outstanding: the Lockheed C-130 Hercules.[4]

A plane pictured in the ad, presumably being loaded in the United States or unloaded in the Congo with troops and trucks, was lettered "U.S. Air Force."

Another example of diplomatic duplicity at the UN occurred on November 16, 1972, when pro-UN Senator Gale McGee (D.-Wyoming; CFR), acting in his capacity as U.S. Representative in the Fifth Committee on Scale of Assessments for the Apportionment of the United Nations, introduced a proposal to cut back the U.S. share of the UN budget from approximately one-third to no more than twenty-five percent. This move to pacify growing public outrage over the unduly large U.S. portion of the budget was ballyhooed in the press as a new "get tough" attitude on the part of the administration. In fact, the opposite was true. As Senator McGee explained to the Fifth Committee:

> . . . there exists in some quarters the belief that the proposal I am introducing today . . . represents a shift in U.S. policy, reflecting a diminution of interest in and support for the Organization. I wish to assure you at the outset that this is not the case. . . . It is aimed not at weakening but rather at strengthen-

ing the United Nations as an institution and its varied operations
and important programs.[5]

The formal budget reduction was simply a ploy intended to
sooth anti-UN feeling within the United States to the point
where *greater* support could be secured from American taxpayers for the overall UN operation. As Senator McGee put it:
"The achievement of this objective [*budget reduction*] . . . will
remove a serious concern which, particularly in recent years, has
clearly had an adverse effect on the attitude of the American
public toward the United Nations. I should add, Mr. Chairman,
that were this concern not expunged, it is my considered opinion
that it would cause damage to the interests of this important
organization." But he made clear that "We do not wish to reduce
the traditional high level of the United States financial commitment to the activities of the United Nations."[6] The subtle
strategy was simply to reduce our formal budget assessment to
pacify U.S. taxpayers, while quietly increasing our "voluntary"
contributions to other UN agencies so that, when all was said
and done, as many — probably more — U.S. dollars would flow
into UN coffers as ever.

Former UN Ambassador (now Democratic New York Senator)
Daniel Moynihan was once asked by *Washington Post* correspondent Marilyn Berger if he had been telling the truth during
his sojourn at the United Nations. He replied: "Selectively, like
most people in diplomacy." Mrs. Berger then asked: "Is a
diplomat sent to the U.N. also to tell lies?" To which Moynihan
responded: "To lie abroad for his country, as they say."[7]

A few weeks later, Ambassador Moynihan was asked by CBS
news correspondent George Herman if he planned to resign his
UN post in order to run for the Senate from New York.
Moynihan replied:

. . . I would consider it dishonorable to leave this post and run
for any office, and I would hope that it would be understood that
if I do, the people, the voters to whom I would present myself in
such circumstances would consider me as having said in advance I
am a man of no personal honor to have done so.[8]

Moynihan subsequently resigned his UN post and, on June 10, 1976, announced his candidacy for the U.S. Senate.

Bribery and vote buying are among the sordid facts of life at the United Nations. *U.S. News & World Report*, for example, once quoted a former top U.S. representative at the UN as saying: "I know 30 delegates who will change their country's vote for a blonde, a case of Scotch or $5,000. Those representing the 'third world' countries don't get much money from home, so it's the 'freebies' that make being Ambassador to the U.N. worthwhile."[9]

Former Ambassador Moynihan was once asked, during a television interview with CBS correspondent Eric Sevareid: "Are votes on these things bought in the U.N.?" He replied: "I have never seen money change hands, but I know that money does change hands." He continued: ". . . last fall a vote changed hands at the U.N. for $600, and that was thought very bad for the reputation of the institution." And why was it bad for the UN's reputation? Not because it was *wrong*, but rather, in Moynihan's words, because "votes are supposed to be worth more than that."

Asked if he wanted to identify those involved in the bribery, Moynihan emphatically replied: "No, I do not."[10] Strangely, neither Sevareid nor any other "Liberal" media sources subsequently criticized Ambassador Moynihan for the cover-up, or hounded him further for names. It is a revealing example of the extent to which the UN's image is protected by its friends in the American press.

Semantics is yet another area where disingenuous games are played by the UN crowd to mislead the public. As explained by former Senator Joseph Clark (D.-Pennsylvania):

> Semantics plays an important part in advocacy of or opposition to world government. Everybody is, in theory, in favor of "peace." Most people are in favor of "world law" — as long as it is not enforceable. But if the concept is expressed in terms of "world government" or "yielding national sovereignty," most of these groups who think of themselves as having "a piece of peace" tend to shy away. The term "world order" tends to attract

more supporters, until its necessary connection with world government is explained.[11]

This apparently is why recent American Presidents, and a multitude of other leading Internationalists, ordinarily use the phrase "world order" when discussing foreign policy goals, rather than the more precise (but abrasive) phrase, "world government." It is important that we recognize the extent to which the terms are synonymous.

Chapter 17

Feathering The Nest

Bureaucrats employed by the United Nations are the highest paid in the world, surpassing those of any individual governments, including the United States. Indeed, *U.S. News & World Report* has told us:

> . . . the size of the U.N. Secretariat in New York keeps growing — having doubled in the last 10 years to more than 18,000, of which 6,622 are classed as "professional and higher-level staff." The number and size of U.N. agencies also are growing rapidly.
>
> More than 100 U.N. officials get higher pay than the $66,000 annual salary of a member of the U.S. Cabinet. About 1,000 earn more than $40,000 a year. . . .
>
> A State Department report . . . found: U.N. basic remuneration, plus employer contributions to health insurance and retirement benefits, exceed the United States by 45 per cent to 73 per cent. U.N. pensions exceed U.S. pensions by 23 per cent to 73 per cent. U.N. annual leave exceeds U.S. annual leave by 15 per cent to 131 per cent. U.N. sick pay, on a one-year basis, exceeds U.S. sick leave by 1,400 per cent to 1,900 per cent.[1]

What do the UN bureaucrats *do* to justify their pay? For one thing, they generate tons of reports, resolutions, memoranda, books, magazines, speech texts, news releases, and other documents. It is certain (and we are speaking from excruciating personal experience) that no entity in the history of the world has ever come close to churning out the endless flood of printed material which emanates from the UN and its affiliated agencies. Even Secretary-General U Thant acknowledged:

> The United Nations has been suffering from what I would call a "document explosion." There has been a vast increase in the number of meetings of United Nations bodies and conferences and, although efforts have been made, an effective means of controlling the conference programme has yet to be found. These meetings generate large quantities of documents, and there has been little reduction in the documentation of the permanent organs. The result is the continuous output, rising to a peak during the General Assembly, of an enormous mass of paper. . . . many delegations complain — privately and publicly — that they cannot digest the contents of the quantity of paper they receive.[2]

Consider, for example, the 1974 UN Law of the Sea Conference held in Caracas, Venezuela. Barry Newman of the *Wall Street Journal* reported:

> The volume of verbiage is staggering. There are actually three meetings — one dealing with coastal waters, one with the deep sea and one with pollution and ocean research — and each is struggling with several issues that would each merit conferences of their own. The UN has 90 mimeograph operators grinding away at 27 machines around the clock, spewing forth 250,000 pages of documents a day. Each is prepared in three, and sometimes five, languages by teams of translators and typists. . . . The list of documents produced so far is itself 160 pages long.[3]

What was the end result of that paper-besieged Conference? According to reporter Newman: "So after 70 days of talk about a law to govern the use of the oceans and their resources the conference is making only one firm decision: to hold more conferences."[4]

Clearly, environmentalists are hypocrites if they do not join the drive to abolish the UN in order to save the world's trees! Many have wondered what is done with those mountains of documents that hardly anyone reads. Well,

> The other day a mouse found out. During a meeting of the General Assembly's Economic Committee, the mouse presented itself at the microphone of the Maldives, then meandered over to the delegates from Malta. The delegates clearly could not tolerate such an affront to their dignity and decorum. So after much tumbling and scurrying, they flattened it with a hefty report. And that's what they do with those documents.[5]

On a more serious note, how are your taxes holding up? Outrageously high, we presume. But did you know that United States citizens employed by the UN pay, in essence, no income taxes? The phrase "in essence" is required for technical accuracy, since those UN employees do go through the motions of paying taxes. But the UN then reimburses the amount paid! As the *Washington Post* reported on June 9, 1966, "U.S. citizens working for the United Nations must pay Federal income taxes, but are reimbursed for the full amount by the U.N." An undated U.S. State Department memorandum entitled "Taxation of U.S. Nationals Employed by the United Nations" confirms:

> In the case of United States citizens employed within the United States by the United Nations the amount of tax paid by the individual to the United States is re-imbursed by the Organization in order to equate the citizens' compensation with the salary of other employees of the Organization who are not United States citizens.

A later missive from the State Department describes the policy in these terms:

> U.S. citizens who are employed by the UN in the United States do pay income taxes (Federal, State, local). In order to provide equitable treatment to all employees, the United Nations reimburses the income tax paid by American employees so that all have equal take-home pay for equal work.[6]

In the spirit of George Orwell's *Animal Farm*, all Americans are equal, but some are more equal than others. When *you* pay *your* taxes, the government gets the money and you get a feather-light wallet or purse. When your fellow Americans at the UN pay *their* taxes, the government gets the money and they get a complete refund. Need we remind you that a large part of the money that pays their salaries in the first place, and which reimburses their taxes, also comes from your pocket?

So much for equality.

Chapter 18
The Humanitarians

It is sometimes alleged, by observers who readily admit that the UN's political activities are (and have been) disastrous, that the United States should nevertheless maintain its affiliation with the world body because of the alleged good accomplished by certain UN specialized agencies. Of course, it is possible to find some good in almost anything if one's search is sufficiently thorough. Even snake venom, we are told, is at least five percent protein. Yet, while it is often a virtue to look for the good in things and discount the evil, at times it can be irrational and place a person (or nation) in mortal danger.

It would be possible, were we so inclined, to continue our support of specific specialized agencies after severing all ties with the UN's primary political apparatus (the Security Council and General Assembly). That kind of decision could be reached once we are certain how much actual good the UN's so-called "humanitarian" endeavors are accomplishing. Considering the enormous expenditures made over the years by such specialized agencies as the United Nations International Children's Emergency Fund (UNICEF), World Health Organization (WHO), and others, it is probable that some of the largesse has hit the proper targets on occasion. However, unlike private charitable operations here at home, which are constantly subjected to close inspection by the press and others for possible fraud or misuse of funds, the activities and expenditures of international agencies have been widely glorified, but sparsely scrutinized for waste and corruption. Most of our influential news sources merely parrot press releases from the various UN agencies, thus giving the general public little alternative but to swallow whole the reported claims and statistics.

A case in point is an article about UNICEF by a staff writer for the *Washington Star-News*, which appeared in that newspaper on October 30, 1974. Entitled, "UNICEF Has Enemies But Many Little Friends," it asserts at one point:

> C. Lloyd Bailey, executive director of the U.S. Committee for UNICEF, acknowledged in a telephone interview from New York yesterday that administrative and fund-raising costs are higher than other children's charities, like the Christian Children's Fund and Save the Children Foundation.

Yet, the reporter simply passed along Mr. Bailey's own self-serving explanation for the discrepancy (which had to do with the exorbitant cost of shipping, printing, and warehousing UNICEF Christmas cards). Elsewhere throughout the article, every statistic and explanation offered by Mr. Bailey (and other UNICEF spokesmen with whom the reporter talked) regarding UNICEF's activities and alleged accomplishments were presented in the same unquestioning, unchallenged manner. No attempt was made to investigate thoroughly the veracity of the pro-UNICEF claims.

Unfortunately, many investigators who would like very much to dig deeply into such matters simply cannot afford the expense of doing so. It is one thing to delve into the doings of a church charity in, say, Maryland, but quite something else to verify whether UNICEF really did save the life of that emaciated Mauritanian child pictured in your local newspaper. A panel established by the United Nations Association of the U.S.A. itself was compelled to conclude:

> Although our contributions to UN specialized agencies are rising, no entity in the U.S. government is adequately equipped to judge the effectiveness of particular programs. . . . international organization programs at the present time are not evaluated in a positive, systematic way. . . .[1]

All too often, UN agencies receive full credit for various projects when, at best, only partial credit is deserved. In most (if not all) cases, private agencies contribute significantly to the various humanitarian efforts. For instance:

> Over two decades, the UN has had many occasions to be grateful to its NGO [*non-governmental organization*] supporters. In 1946, when UNICEF was working to save the children of war-devastated areas, it called upon the Red Cross, church groups, relief agencies and many other citizens' organizations to help. World Refugee Year combined the efforts of the UN and citizens committees in many nations on behalf of the world's homeless people. Private industry around the world supports a continuing fertilizer program within the FAO's [*Food and Agriculture Organization's*] Freedom-From Hunger Campaign.[2]

And in 1976, news accounts described a buffet supper at UN headquarters announcing the development of a new high-protein food ("Ricetein") which could become a major weapon in the war against world hunger. In many newspapers, the accounts carried such headlines as "High-Protein Food Announced at U.N."[3] and "Sumptuous U.N. Buffet: 'Ricetein'."[4] Readers, skimming their papers quickly, may have gained the impression that the UN had scored another important humanitarian breakthrough. Yet, careful reading of the news stories made it clear that two *American* companies — Nabisco, Inc. of New York and Riviana Foods, Inc. of Houston — had developed the new, inexpensive blend of soybean protein and rice.

It is entirely possible that many of the UN specialized

agencies would find their activities enhanced if freed from the corrupting political influences of the Security Council and the General Assembly. A sizable percentage of the incidents justifiably cited by critics of the UN to demonstrate the harm done by this or that agency can be traced to the effects of the UN's perverse political pressures. The image of UNICEF, for instance, suffered a severe blow when, in 1961, funds earmarked for needy children were — with UNICEF's knowledge and consent — temporarily diverted to help finance the slaughter of innocent children during the UN's vicious war against anti-Communist Katanga. Former U.S. Representative H.R. Gross (R.-Iowa), a staunch Conservative critic of the UN, discussed the sordid matter on the House floor on June 19, 1961. He reminded his colleagues that, during hearings on the bill being debated, government witnesses had admitted that Secretary General Thant had borrowed from the Children's Fund to help finance the Congo operation. According to Congressman Gross:

> After the committee adjourned, the witnesses provided a statement showing that U.N. officials got $12 million from the United Nations Special Fund and grabbed $10 million from the United Nations Children's Fund, UNICEF.[5]

Another former Congressman and "Liberal" devotee of the UN and UNICEF, Richard D. McCarthy (D.-New York), explained to his House colleagues a few years later:

> In 1961, the U.S. Government allocated $10 million in support of UNICEF. Prior to actual payment, the Secretary General required emergency funds to carry on U.N. action in the Congo. Acting under U.N. Resolution 1341, authorizing him to borrow funds from special accounts, and after consulting with UNICEF and the U.S. Government, the Secretary General was advanced the $10 million, which was repaid in full to UNICEF before the end of the year.[6]

Even UNICEF's Executive Director, Maurice Pate, has admitted:

The loan to the U.N., made with the full knowledge and approval of UNICEF, came from U.S. government funds not yet turned over to UNICEF. That loan was repaid to UNICEF December 27 [*1961*].[7]

UNICEF dollars were actually earmarked to help reconstruct Communist-controlled areas of Vietnam as the no-win war (for our side) neared its tragic conclusion.

> UNITED NATIONS, N.Y., April 16 [*1974*] — The United Nations Children's Fund announced plans today for aid to North Vietnam and to areas held by the Vietcong in the South.
> The 3-year program was described in a report by Henry Labouisse, the fund's director, who called for $18-million to be spent in the North to help rebuild destroyed schools and $4.5-million to be spent in the South.[8]

Actually, UNICEF had provided sustenance to the Communists in Vietnam on many earlier occasions. In 1970, for example, the UNICEF Executive Board approved a $200,000 purchase of cloth, allegedly for North Vietnamese children's clothing. The cloth was purchased from the Soviet Union, with rubles held by UNICEF, and was delivered to North Vietnam by the Soviet Union (not UNICEF) in 1972.[9] Needless to say, no one (but the Communists) knows if that cloth went to children or to Red troops.

The blatantly pro-Communist bias of UNICEF's assistance to Vietnam was summarized by Colonel Robert D. Heinl, Jr., in *Human Events*:

> In programs purportedly established "to help children in Indochina," the United Nations' Children's Emergency Fund gave just short of two-thirds of its collections to North Vietnamese or to the "Provisional Revolutionary Government of South Vietnam," sometimes confused with the Vietcong.
> The exact numbers, conceded by a UNICEF spokesman, run as follows: UNICEF collected and disbursed a total of $13,649,433 for its Indochina children's programs. While smidges of this

from abroad, the overwhelming amount came out of the
.ets of U.S. taxpayers.
Of this eight-figure sum, $8,975,587 went to Communist
recipients. . . .
While Communists were thus getting 61 per cent of UNICEF's
largess, our ally, South Vietnam, got only $5,360,707, or 39 per
cent.[10]

Again, there was no proof at all that the supplies sent to the
Communists actually reached needy children. When Colonel
Heinl asked a UNICEF spokesman about the matter, he was
told: "UNICEF has no way to make sure the supplies to the
Communists got to children. They were dropped off at the
airports and docks and we assume they were used as we
intended."[11] That is truly incredible, considering that some of
those supplies, according to Colonel Heinl, included "trucks,
bulldozers, heavy engineer construction equipment, and construction tools and materials."[12]

Even so innocuous an international agency as the Universal
Postal Union has suffered from the UN's pro-Communist
political pressures. Established in 1874, the UPU was the oldest,
and possibly most efficient, of all international institutions. Its
assistance in helping to move the mails from one part of the
world to another was uninterrupted even by wars and natural
disasters. But in 1947 the UPU became a specialized agency of
the UN and had to surrender much of its autonomy to policies
set by the world body. Consider:

> Ever since the United Nations admitted Mainland China and
> expelled the Formosa Administration, there was a strong suspi-
> cion that the Universal Postal Union might follow this political
> action. Now it is certain, for the necessary procedures have been
> undertaken by the Executive and Liaison Committee for its
> annual gathering here. Taipei is out; Peking is in.[13]

Clearly, to the extent that some of them may be worth
keeping at all, the specialized agencies now associated with the
United Nations would be improved by the demise of the UN's

Marxist-biased political apparatus. For this reason, the increasingly popular slogan *Get US out!* most urgently means withdrawal of U.S. financial support from, and membership in, the UN Security Council and General Assembly.

Chapter 19
UNICEF — A Case History

The UN's most effective public relations front is the United Nations International Children's Fund (UNICEF). It is always risky to condemn an agency that professes to aid needy children, and whenever the General Assembly and Security Council behave outrageously, references to the alleged good done by UNICEF are erected as shields to blunt demands that the United States pull out of the UN.

The methods used to build up the UNICEF image are subtle and far-ranging. Best known, perhaps, is the annual "Trick-or-Treat for UNICEF" crusade during which thousands of little ghosts and goblins spend Halloween night collecting coins for UNICEF in addition to goodies for themselves. The amount collected is, of course, far less important to the One World effort than the brainwash that accompanies the project. As admitted by the U.S. Committee for UNICEF, "The truth in connection with this is that Trick-or-Treat for UNICEF is primarily an education program."[1] And Leftist baby doctor Benjamin Spock has confirmed:

> When a Trick or Treat for UNICEF program is well organized
> by a school system or a church group, the children study the
> conditions and needs of the countries that are to be assisted. Or
> they study the activities of UNICEF and other departments of
> the UN. This is not just educational in the conventional, academ-
> ic sense. It changes attitudes and feelings in a way that is likely to
> have permanence.[2]

Some of the methods used to sell UNICEF to American
children are ingenious. As one of the scores of examples that
could be cited, consider the October, 1972, issue of the quarterly
cartoon magazine, *Dennis The Menace Pocket Full Of Fun.* In
the fourth story ("The Substitute Santa"), the devious Dennis
wants a burro for Christmas and sets out to raise money to help
Santa pay for one. He sets up a panhandling operation to collect
money from passers-by under the guise that it will be used to
"Help a poor kid." Just as Dennis's alarmed parents arrive on
the scene, a passing policeman stops to make a donation and
commend Dennis for raising money for a poor child. He then
asks, "Where are you sending the money . . . to UNICEF?"
And Dennis's father replies with a sheepish falsehood, "Er . . .
yes! That's it!"

After the policeman departs, a bewildered Dennis is taken
into the house where his father proceeds with a detailed disser-
tation on the blessings of UNICEF. Eventually, Dennis agrees
to forget the burro and send the money to UNICEF. To
complete the advertisement, one of the cartoon panels portrays
Dennis holding an envelope imprinted in bold letters with
UNICEF's complete mailing address. The story then continues
to its uneventful conclusion.[3]

UNICEF also sells Christmas cards. For many years the cards
have been advertised and sold in U.S. post offices despite
vigorous opposition by irate taxpayers to such federal promotion
of UNICEF. Among other things, this "free" advertising and
sales promotion gives UNICEF a significant advantage over
free enterprise greeting card companies which are tax- and rent-
paying entities. In addition, the enormously one-sided publicity

given UNICEF makes it almost impossible for the card companies to register justified protests. We have in our files, for instance, a letter dated November 9, 1970, from the president of a major greeting card association to the association's members. At one point, it is noted that the association itself

> has always maintained a "hands off" policy regarding the UNICEF greeting card activity because the "charity" appeal of UNICEF seems to make it immune to adverse attacks.
>
> IN ADDITION, in every instance where an organization or group has tried to stop the UNICEF program, those making the attack have incurred serious unfavorable public opinion on the premise that they are putting down "charity."

So, a segment of American business that is being harmed by unfair competition from a UN agency and its own government is intimidated into silence by fear of reprisal from a public misled by one-sided, pro-UNICEF propaganda. It is a disgraceful situation.

In 1969, however, something remarkable happened. Public protest against UNICEF reached such a pitch that the Post Office Department actually canceled — for a while — authority for the sale of UNICEF cards in Post Offices. The story of how the decision was made, and how it was eventually reversed, provides an interesting case history of the stranglehold that the United Nations has over even our domestic affairs.[4]

During the latter part of 1969 the mounting opposition to the sale of UNICEF cards led the Post Office Department's Director of Creative Services to write a frantic letter (dated October 29, 1969) to the U.S. Committee for UNICEF that began: "Your help is urgently needed! We are being deluged by Congressional inquiries and letters from postal customers, all questioning the wisdom of granting UNICEF space in Post Office lobbies for the purpose of selling Christmas cards." A request was made for information related to such matters as Communist involvement in the UNICEF program, how funds are handled, and the nature of U.S. involvement in the UNICEF program.

The Committee's November 4, 1969, reply was only partially responsive to the request. On November 18, the Director of Creative Services wrote once again, this time to request specifics regarding proposed UNICEF aid to Vietnam. When the UNICEFers were unable to deny that such assistance was in the works, the Director sent a memorandum dated December 17 to the Postmaster General's Special Assistant for Public Information, declaring:

> The use of Post Office lobbies by UNICEF to sell greeting cards has created a public relations problem of the first magnitude.
>
> To date we have received about 500 letters of protest from postal customers and the flow shows no signs of abating. In addition, a few score letters to Congressmen have produced a like number of inquiries from the Hill. And an undetermined number of protests have been registered with individual Postmasters in the field.
>
> The reason for this outpouring . . . centers largely on recent newspaper reports to the effect that UNICEF has some plans to turn $200,000 worth of supplies over to the government of North Vietnam.
>
> I inquired on this point with the headquarters organization of the U.S. Committee for UNICEF and learned that it is true. . . .
>
> After a lot of due consideration I have come to the conclusion that it would be a grave mistake to continue the practice of allowing UNICEF access to post office lobbies in 1970. From a public relations standpoint it would be nearly suicidal. From a moral standpoint it would be at best questionable.
>
> Further, I think that I should start including in my replies to these protesting customers a statement saying that the POD will not be continuing this practice in 1970.
>
> It is my strong belief that such a statement would generate a high degree of public good will for us in general, and this administration in particular.
>
> Do you agree?

The memorandum was returned with this penned-in notation: "Yes — 1. Wholeheartedly. 2. Let's get them out now."

After the decision was announced, the U.S. Committee for

UNICEF and *one private citizen* protested the action. In his March 4, 1970, response to that single private critic, the Director of Creative Services asserted:

> Since last October we have received well in excess of one thousand letters of protest from our customers all over the country. In addition, we have received several score Congressional inquiries regarding this practice.
>
> These letters were not the products of an "irrational lunatic fringe," as you suggest in your letter. Rather, they were from what was obviously a solid cross section of the American public. And the bulk of this mail raised some tough, albeit fair, questions concerning the subject of communist involvement in UNICEF activities.
>
> . . . a number of our customers sent us a copy of an article, "The Truth About UNICEF," by William E. Dunham (copy enclosed). I personally obtained and read copies of the source material cited by Mr. Dunham in his article, and must report that I did not find any of this information to be in error or misrepresented. If such is the case, I would be most willing to have the facts pointed out to me.
>
> . . . a former UNICEF procurement officer was discovered (in 1966) to be involved in an attempt to illegally purchase classified space flight apparatus. Only a hasty exit from this country prevented his arrest. As some of our customers pointed out, there is no getting around the fact that a man who spends his time trying to procure accelerometers for space vehicles is not doing much to help the world's needy children.
>
> Perhaps the biggest bone of contention centered upon the publication of a news story calling attention to the fact that UNICEF had been dealing with the communist North Vietnam government concerning a possible aid program.
>
> I cite these few examples just to demonstrate that we did make an honest attempt to fairly examine the issue in which we found ourselves embroiled. As a consequence of this examination we have determined that the overall interests of all parties concerned will be best served if we simply do not again renew lobby privilege arrangements with the U.S. Committee for UNICEF.

By May 19, 1970, the Director was able to send the following summary memo to his superior:

Here are some quick statistics regarding the decision to terminate UNICEF card sales in postal lobbies.
1. We received 1500 individual letters of complaint from
customers. . . .
2. We have received Congressional inquiries from about two-
thirds of the House and Senate. . . .
3. We have only received eight letters of thanks for providing
lobby space for these card sales; in each case from a member of a
local UNICEF group.
4. We have received only one letter of complaint over our
decision to terminate the program. . . .
5. We have received 100-200 letters of thank you for terminat-
ing the program.
6. Opinion playback from field people generally indicates
that they would be happier if they didn't have to contend with
the program each year.

And that, you would have thought, would be that. But it was
not. For shortly thereafter Postmaster General Winton Blount
intervened personally to reverse the policy and *again* permit
UNICEF to use tax-financed post offices for its card sales.
This was despite overwhelming opposition to the program from
the public and substantial opposition to it from within the
Department itself!

The unfortunate reversal of policy led to the resignation of
the courageous Director of Creative Services. His August 17,
1970, letter to the Department's Special Assistant for Public
Information sadly declared:

This letter is to officially advise you of my resignation. . . .
My leaving is motivated purely on the grounds of personal
moral principle. The public relations or political reasons for
granting card sale lobby space to the U.S. Committee for
UNICEF aside, I am convinced that this action [*the reversal of
policy*] is morally wrong and injurious to the best interests of the
nation and its citizens.
I make this statement on the basis of an extensive examination
of the UNICEF operation, which I conducted as a result of our
receiving some 1,500 letters of complaint from customers all
across the country.

The more I investigated these complaints, the more obvious it became that, since its inception, the constant outpouring of humanitarian pronouncements with which UNICEF is wont to surround itself, have served as little more than a facade to hide sinister men and sinister motives.

In short, I was forced to conclude that it is morally wrong for an establishment of the U.S. Government to provide the means whereby UNICEF can further its financial and propaganda objectives.

In light of this conviction, I feel it only proper that I resign.

Once again, the American people were ignored and a dedicated public servant was compelled to quit under Leftist pressures from Internationalists at the top.

Chapter 20

Model UN — A Case History

Each year, in communities throughout the country, Model United Nations assemblies are convened for selected high school and college students. Participants, usually the cream of the academic crop, serve as "delegates" from the various nations, role-playing the probable attitudes and mannerisms of real-world delegates. The Model UN network is one of the most effective pro-UN propaganda ploys yet conceived.

As an example of how one Model UN assembly was conducted, we have selected the session held for Utah high school students on the campus of the University of Utah in 1963. We have done so, despite the gap in years, because that event is one for which we have, owing to unusual circumstances, been able to collect complete and comprehensive documentation (including original correspondence, tape recordings, media clips, etc.). And, at the time, the Utah gathering was both the largest and oldest high school Model UN assembly in the nation.

The story began in early 1963 when a group of concerned

citizens, represented primarily by a Conservative organization called the Citizens Information Committee (CIC), decided the time had come to present students attending Model UN assemblies with at least a smattering of information critical of the UN, as a counter to the complete domination of such events by adult pro-UN propagandists. In years past (1963 was Utah's ninth Model UN) attempts in that direction had failed. Now, it was decided to choose a modest, realistic goal and work for its achievement as a foundation on which to build in the future. The plan eventually adopted consisted simply of trying to have three single-sheet flyers passed out to the delegate-students sometime during the assembly. The flyers were to consist of:

1. A documented biography of James Avery Joyce, the assembly's keynote speaker who was also a long-time member of Britain's Socialist Fabian Society;

2. An editorial from the respected *Santa Ana (California) Register* newspaper which quoted various observers (such as humanitarian Dr. Albert Schweitzer) on the UN's war in the Congo; and

3. A comparison of the concept of human rights held by the UN with that of the Soviet Union by quoting from the proposed UN Covenant on Human Rights and the 1936 Soviet Constitution.

It was expected, since the assembly was to be held on the campus of the University of Utah and co-sponsored by a division of the university, that the spirit of academic freedom would prevail sufficiently to assure that each of the fourteen hundred Model UN delegates received a set of the informative flyers.

The two-day gathering was scheduled to convene on April 19th. On April 15th, an officer of the CIC called an assistant to the university's president to request permission to distribute the flyers. Surprisingly, the Committee was told that it would not itself be permitted to distribute the literature, nor could *anyone* distribute the flyer exposing James Avery Joyce — despite the fact that no errors in the flyer could be cited. It might, the Committee members were told, be possible for the university to arrange to have the remaining two flyers distributed to the students.

On that same date, a certified letter was sent to the university's acting president, summarizing the earlier phone conversation with his assistant, and asserting:

> If you will let us know to whom we should deliver the literature, we shall be happy to do so, in order that it may be passed out to the students. (While we cannot agree that the article on Dr. Joyce is of such a nature as to be withheld from the students, and wish it to be distributed, we shall provide only the other two items unless you give permission to distribute the Joyce item.)

Incredibly, the same assistant with whom the CIC officer had spoken earlier responded now on behalf of the acting president, asserting in his letter of April 17th:

> We feel that it is important to guard the integrity of programs which are arranged and presented on the campus, and that circulation of your literature on the campus at this time would be an infringement of the integrity of the Model United Nations activity. Therefore, I have been instructed to advise you that your statements will not be distributed as you have requested.

This ridiculous response completely ignored the fact that the CIC had agreed to let the university itself pass out the material, and that such distribution could easily have been accomplished following adjournment of the assembly as the students departed the premises. The university spokesman went on to offer the CIC a forum to present its views on the campus at some future date. But such an offer was meaningless, since the Model UN delegates would not be in attendance at such a forum.

Totally dissatisfied with the university's cavalier reply, a delegation from the CIC arranged to meet at the state capitol with Utah Secretary of State Lamont Toronto. Mr. Toronto, a courageous and principled public servant, was also serving as acting governor of Utah at the time, in the absence of Governor George D. Clyde. He was also a member of the university's Board of Regents.

Mr. Toronto told the CIC delegation that they had every right to distribute literature during the Model UN, as long as it was carried out in an orderly fashion and did not disrupt the proceedings. He cautioned, however, that such distribution should be terminated promptly if the university authorities became overtly nasty about it.

Armed with this support from the acting governor, the CIC went ahead with its plans.

On the evening of April 17th, Dr. James Avery Joyce appeared on a talk show broadcast over Salt Lake radio station KSL. The first caller set the tone for the evening by compelling Joyce reluctantly to admit to his twenty-five-year membership in the British Fabian Society. Other callers continued to expose various aspects of his Far Left background until the "distinguished" Englishman exploded with rage at one caller (who had merely asked how much, if any, tax money was involved in bringing him to Salt Lake) and branded those opposed to the UN "crackpots" who should be "locked up." He then stuffed his distinguished foot *completely* into his mouth by claiming:

> You [*Americans*] aren't doing anything. You're only helping yourselves. . . . You owe the rest of the world so much. You've lived on the backs of so many people. . . . You don't seem to appreciate the fact that you owe the world a living.

Subsequently, a KSL employee reported that the station received more unfavorable calls regarding Joyce's embarrassing appearance than it had for any other guest they could recall.

By the way, that single-page CIC flyer about Joyce, which so frightened the university hierarchy, simply supplied background on the Fabian Society from a book highly sympathetic to the Society (Anne Fremantle's *This Little Band of Prophets*); noted Dr. Joyce's membership in the group; and included an excerpt from the 1961 edition of the *World Book Encyclopedia* which simply noted that the Fabian Society

> was named for Quintus Fabius Maximus, a Roman general who avoided defeat by refusing to fight any decisive battles against Hannibal. The Fabians teach that socialism can be achieved gradually, through a series of reforms. They differ from the Communists, who believe that the people can gain ownership of the means of production only through revolution.

The point, of course, is that the *goals* of the Fabians and the Reds are the same; they differ only on the methods used to attain those goals. Yet, officials of the Model UN resorted to outright censorship to keep the students from learning this important aspect of their keynote speaker's background.

On the first day of the assembly, CIC members and friends arrived at the start of festivities, determined to distribute flyers during a mid-morning or lunch break (in order to avoid any disruption while the assembly was in session). But another serious problem became immediately evident. The assembly officials, in violation of federal law, had placed the United Nations flag superior to the Stars and Stripes. A message requesting that an adjustment be made was delivered by usher to the assembly's president (a "Liberal" Political Science Professor at the University). Incredibly, the message was ignored, whereupon two CIC members drove to the state capitol, explained the situation to Acting Governor Toronto, and waited while he had his secretary photocopy the federal flag code and type a letter *demanding* that the United States Flag be properly and legally displayed. The letter read:

> It has come to my attention that the United States Flag is improperly displayed on the University Campus. It was reported that the United States Flag is one of many United Nations flags displayed before the audience for the assemblies, which is contrary to Title 36, Section 175, Federal Code Annotated, attached copy. In all areas within our country, except the United Nations Premises in New York, the United States Flag should have the place of honor.

Kindly adjust your flag displays to comply with the Federal
Statutes.

The letter was immediately taken to the campus, handed to
an usher, and delivered to the assembly president. The assembly
was temporarily halted while the United States Flag was properly placed. While the change was in progress, the assembly
president asserted, "it seems to subvert what we are trying to do
here. . . ."[1] Just what *were* they trying to do there that would
have been subverted by proper display of the American Flag?

With that matter taken care of, the CIC cadre began passing
out flyers during a break in the morning's proceedings. Incredibly, the professor who was assembly president called on university and city police to stop the distribution!

So literature critical of the UN was suppressed. Once again,
the UN crowd had brought students through a Model UN session
unscathed by a balanced view of the world body. Yet, in a sense,
it was a victory for those who had worked so hard to give
students the other side. The police-state tactics used by the
Model UN authoritarians, the Flag incident, and the antics of
Dr. Joyce combined to raise serious and widespread questions
about the Model UN.

The controversy spread across state lines when a summary of
the key events in a daily Idaho newspaper was reprinted in the
Santa Ana Register for May 8, 1963. Referring to what it called
"United Nations propaganda with a vengeance," the commentary included an account of Dr. Joyce's radio outburst, the Flag
fiasco, and the assembly professor-president's "seems to subvert what we are trying to do" *faux pas*. It concluded: "If we're
at all concerned — as, certainly, we very well may be — we'll be
giving some pretty serious consideration to the question of what,
indeed, they were 'trying to do' there."

As a postscript, the CIC wrote to the acting president of the
university on May 3, 1963, asserting: ". . . we will be happy to
arrange for speakers to present our point of view as soon as we

receive written assurance from the University that arrangements will be made for the same high school students who attended and participated in this Model U.N. to attend our presentation." The letter concluded:

> We wish to go on record as believing that any group, be it for us or against us, should be allowed to distribute its literature either before or after any presentation we hold on the campus, or during intermissions. We will not call out either Salt Lake or campus police to stop such distribution, and would hope the University would follow suit.

On May 21st, the dean of the university's Extension Division responded: "It is a little late in the year for us to do anything now," suggesting that the CIC get in touch "next school year."

Meanwhile the April-May, 1963, issue of *The Utah Alumnus*, published by the University of Utah Alumni Association, carried a brief article summarizing festivities at the Model UN. Totally ignoring the embarrassing incidents we have described, it simply referred in general terms to the "antics" of "some right-wing extremists." Noting that "The Model UN operates just like its big brother on the East River," the article concludes: "The world will pay little attention to the decisions made at the ninth annual Model UN. But Utah's high school participants left the campus much wiser in the ways of the world."

Others left the campus much wiser in the ways of the UN.

Is it any wonder that so many Americans are coming to view the United Nations as a serious form of heir pollution?

Chapter 21

Out Of Site!

The decision to base the United Nations in New York City was greatly influenced by the Soviet Union, which obviously recognized the enormous value of having such a potential Trojan Horse located within the borders of its chief adversary. According to former UN Secretary-General Trygve Lie:

> As the Headquarters battle got under way in London. . . . The Russians disappointed most Western Europeans by coming out at once for a site in America.
> . . . Andrei Gromyko of the U.S.S.R. had come out flatly for the United States. As to where in the United States, let the American Government decide, he had blandly told his colleagues. Later the Soviet Union modified its stand to support the east coast.[1]

The final decision as to the exact site for the permanent UN headquarters was taken on December 14, 1946. "The dramatic offer of Mr. John D. Rockefeller, Jr.," wrote Leland Goodrich and Edvard Hambro, "of the sum of $8,500,000 for the purpose of acquiring a tract of land in the City of New York along the

East River, between 42nd and 48th Streets led to the adoption of
the proferred New York site."[2] And Thomas J. Hamilton (CFR)
added: ". . . the United States made an interest-free loan of
$65,000,000 to pay for the building."[3]

In all essentials, the seat of the United Nations is a state
within a state. According to Louis Dolivet:

> The United States has no jurisdiction. No representative of
> administrative, judicial, military, or police authority of the
> United States may enter that zone without permission of the
> Secretary-General. In short: as long as the seat of the United
> Nations remains within the United States, the area occupied by
> the United Nations is considered as extra territorial with full
> diplomatic privileges and immunities.[4]

There is evidence that it is all blatantly illegal.

On March 15, 1967 an executive session of the Senate
Internal Security Subcommittee heard testimony regarding the
status of the United Nations Headquarters Agreement. The
testimony was released from its secrecy injunction on November
29 and published on December 11 of that year.[5]

This hearing is very important indeed, for it presents a strong
case that the United Nations Headquarters Agreement does not
even exist. If that is the case, the presence of the United
Nations in New York City is illegal.

Testimony was given by the Subcommittee's Chief Counsel,
J.G. Sourwine, who confirmed that the controversial site agreement grants to the UN the right to act, in effect, as a sovereign
nation within the boundaries of the United States. The problem
is, however, that the UN Headquarters Agreement approved by
the General Assembly of the United Nations is not the same
agreement as the one approved by the Congress of the United
States. Following are the chronological details:

On December 14, 1946, the General Assembly authorized the
Secretary-General to negotiate the Headquarters Agreement. A
draft agreement was signed by the Secretary-General and our
Secretary of State on June 26, 1947, and sent by President
Truman to the Congress for approval on July 2.

On July 3, a Joint Resolution incorporating the draft agreement was introduced in the Senate. It was favorably reported by the Foreign Relations Committee *with an amendment* on July 14 and passed by the Senate three days later.

On July 26, the House of Representatives passed the Joint Resolution after accepting the Senate amendment (which was designed to protect our immigration laws) and adding its own amendment to protect the right of this country to safeguard its own security. The Senate passed the amended measure on the same day, and on August 4, 1947, the Resolution was signed by President Truman and became Public Law 357 of the 80th U.S. Congress.

On October 17, a subcommittee of the UN's Sixth Committee issued a report that officially transmitted the matter to the General Assembly. However, the agreement that was transmitted by the report was *not* the amended agreement that the U.S. Congress had approved: It was the original draft of June 26, 1947. On October 31 of that year the General Assembly approved the June 26 agreement and authorized the Secretary-General to bring it into effect. In other words, the General Assembly approved a Headquarters Agreement that did *not* include the congressional reservations of Public Law 357. As Chief Counsel Sourwine expressed it at the conclusion of his testimony:

> In the absence of . . . phony rationalization, it is impossible to point to one single document constituting a United Nations Headquarters Agreement which has been legally assented to by vote of the United Nations General Assembly and the Congress of the United States, and by any other effective and fully authorized actions of representatives of both parties. The only possible conclusion is that there is no United Nations Headquarters Agreement.[6]

On December 12, 1967, the State Department attempted to rebut Mr. Sourwine's explosive (and meticulously documented) testimony by claiming that an exchange of notes (dated Novem-

ber 21, 1947) between our Ambassador to the UN (Warren
Austin) and the Secretary-General (Trygve Lie) was sufficient
to validate the UN Headquarters Agreement. But, on December
13th, Senator Strom Thurmond (R.-South Carolina) pointed out
that the exchange of notes in 1947 actually "offers some of the
most convincing proof that the U.N. never accepted the terms
of Public Law 357."[7] The Senator entered the complete texts of
both notes into the *Congressional Record*, and the notes do
indeed confirm that the United Nations did accept a *different*
Headquarters Agreement than that which was passed and authorized by the Congress of the United States.

As Senator Thurmond suggested during a Senate speech two
days earlier:

> It is intolerable for the United Nations to be occupying its
> present site within U.S. territory without the proper legal arrange-
> ments. If the State Department cannot make the U.N. submit to
> our conditions, then the U.N. itself should seek a site in another
> part of the world.[8]

The saga of the Site Agreement stands as yet another tribute
to the essential lawlessness of the United Nations clique.

Chapter 22

Get US Out?

There is no provision in the UN Charter that permits member nations to withdraw from the organization. Neither, on the other hand, is there a provision requiring them to stay. When the Charter was in the draft stage, the only amendment offered on the subject would have precluded withdrawal. It was defeated.[1] Nevertheless, the Committee handling the matter included in its report the following clarifying statement, with which the U.S. delegation concurred, and which was eventually adopted at the San Francisco Conference:

> The Committee adopts the view that the Charter should not make express provision either to permit or to prohibit withdrawal from the Organization. . . . If, however, a Member because of exceptional circumstances feels constrained to withdraw, and leave the burden of maintaining international peace and security on the other Members, it is not the purpose of the Organization to compel that Member to continue its cooperation in the Organization.
> It is obvious, particularly, that withdrawals or some other forms of dissolution of the Organization would become inevita-

ble if, deceiving the hopes of humanity, the Organization was revealed to be unable to maintain peace or could do so only at the expense of law and justice.[2]

During the Senate hearings on the Charter, Foreign Relations Committee Chairman Tom Connally (D-Texas) questioned Dr. Leo Pasvolsky (CFR), Special Assistant to the Secretary of State for International Organization and Security Affairs, about the matter:

> **The Chairman.** Let me ask you a question right there: Is it not true that there is no application required if a nation desires to withdraw? Moreover, there is no specific procedure to be followed. The theory of the whole withdrawal proposal, as I understood it, was that the nation affected would have to be the judge of the circumstances which it claimed had altered its position, and the penalty would be simply a mobilization of world opinion as to whether its cause was a just one or an unjust one.
> **Mr. Pasvolsky.** That is quite right.
> **Mr. Chairman.** And that there was no compulsive power to keep a nation within the League if it desired to withdraw?
> **Mr. Pasvolsky.** That is right.
> **Mr. Chairman.** It was simply a question of leaving the world to judge whether they had adequate causes for withdrawal. They were the ones, however, to determine whether or not their circumstances had so changed as to make withdrawal justifiable.
> **Mr. Pasvolsky.** That is right.[3]

Pasvolsky later re-emphasized this crucial point under interrogation by Senator Walter F. George (D-Georgia):

> **Senator George.** Then, Doctor, is it your answer that the Member state has an absolute right to withdraw?
> **Mr. Pasvolsky.** Yes, Senator.
> **Senator George.** Absolute?
> **Mr. Pasvolsky.** Yes.
> **Senator George.** Unqualified?
> **Mr. Pasvolsky.** Yes.[4]

Further along in the hearings, the following exchange occurred between Senator Wallace H. White, Jr. (R-Maine) and
the State Department's Legal Advisor, Green H. Hackworth:

> **Senator White.** Mr. Chairman, I did ask a question some time
> back as to whether there were any precedents for a treaty which
> had no definite time of life stated in it or which made no
> provision for either denunciation or withdrawal of parties to the
> treaty. I thought if there were such precedents it might be well to
> have somewhere in the record a reference to them.
> **Mr. Hackworth.** There are, Senator White, certain precedents
> of that kind. Some of the old treaties with France, the 1778
> treaty, for example, contained no provision for termination.
> Congress by an act of July 7, 1798, declared the treaty to be no
> longer obligatory on the ground that France had repeatedly
> violated it.
> It is a general rule that where one of the parties to a treaty
> violates it, the other party has a right to regard it as terminated.[5]

That the State Department considers the Soviets to have
violated the UN Charter is a matter of public record, as
indicated by this notation by the Department's Assistant Legal
Advisor for Treaty Affairs:

> Charter of the United Nations, signed at San Francisco, June
> 26, 1945. (TS 993). (Comment: It is considered that the Soviet
> Union has violated various terms of this charter.)[6]

Some UN advocates have argued that there is no legal way
for the United States to withdraw from the United Nations. To
the contrary, as we have seen, both legislative history and legal
precedent are solidly on the side of the expanding body of
Americans who favor such withdrawal.

Chapter 23

Get US out!

Turtle Bay is the New York City neighborhood in which UN headquarters is located. Several skirmishes during the American Revolution were fought in the area, and American patriot Nathan Hale ("I only regret that I have but one life to lose for my country.") was hanged by the British near the corner of 46th Street and First Avenue. Today, that is the site of the offices of *The Inter Dependent*, official publication of the United Nations Association of the USA.[1]

That historical sidelight seems somewhat symbolic of the relationship between the United States and the UN since 1945. An honestly intended federation of nations, united for the legitimate purpose of increasing the freedom of individuals, goods, and cultures to cross national boundaries, and to decrease governmental restrictions on individuals, is something most Americans could support wholeheartedly, for it would be in line with Richard Cobden's penetrating observation that "peace will come to this earth when her peoples have as much as possible to do with each other; their governments the least possible."[2]

Withdrawal from the UN would *not* mean a retreat into so-called "isolation," anymore than absence of the UN prior to 1945 meant we were "isolated." As Robert White and H.L. Imel have noted:

> . . . we had developed many international ties by 1945 and earlier. As individuals, Americans had long maintained social and cultural contacts with people all over the world. More than 400 nongovernment organizations such as Rotary International, the Y.M.C.A., the Olympic Games organizations, and many others serve to create good will and to act as a force in international relations. International business and trade grew. By 1945 Americans had invested more than 13 billion dollars in foreign nations.[3]

At that time we were *far* more admired and respected than we are after nearly four decades of doing things the UN way. As columnist Henry J. Taylor once observed, UN diplomacy "is like a man walking in the woods who stopped when he saw a snake. It turned out to be a stick. But the stick he picked up to kill it with turned out to be a snake."[4]

It is sometimes argued that so-called "global" mechanisms are needed to handle global problems. That is the premise, for example, of Professor Richard Gardner's ten-point scenario described in Chapter Twelve. Another prominent Internationalist, C. Maxwell Stanley, President of the rabidly pro-UN Stanley Foundation, has claimed:

> No business would seek to solve country-wide problems in its branch offices. Nor does the United States solve its national problems at the state level. The need for global mechanisms is supported both by logic and by the fact that nation states have not found lasting resolutions to global problems.[5]

What nonsense! Of course nation states have not found lasting resolutions to global problems. They haven't even found lasting resolutions to *national* problems! Within the United States, our federal government has actually created and/or sustained most national problems by usurping increasing power and authority allegedly to "solve" them. *Governments don't solve problems; they create them.* People can solve problems — if they are let alone by government. There is absolutely *no* basis for believing that huge government entities at the international level can solve "global" problems any better than big national governments have "solved" such problems as rocketing inflation, depressing unemployment, oppressive regulation, and burdensome taxation.

Other UN supporters argue that it is in our national interest to have the organization's headquarters situated in New York City. Representative Edward J. Derwinski (R-Illinois), for instance, has claimed:

> The exposure of United Nations delegates and staff to the atmosphere of freedom and democracy that prevails in the United States offers a rare opportunity for the United States to exert a positive influence on the attitudes of those delegates. Hopefully, this will result in the development of free institutions around the world.[6]

Again — sheer nonsense! We have (thank goodness) a free press in this country. Unfortunately, most emphasis by the media is on the nation's warts and moles, not on its many positive aspects. United Nations delegates in New York have not been exposed to the good points of America in recent years. They have instead been inundated with Watergate, attacks against our FBI and CIA, public exposure of the immoral behavior of a few Members of Congress and many occupants of the Carter White House, and other depressing revelations too numerous to mention. All of this was amidst speculation that New York City may itself face outright bankruptcy.

The view of our country from Turtle Bay is horribly jaundiced, and hardly calculated to affect UN delegates in the manner desired by Congressman Derwinski.

Still other UN apologists argue, as does James J. Wadsworth (CFR), that abandoning the UN would leave the field of struggle to the enemy. Wadsworth claims: "If the United States should withdraw from the United Nations, the Soviet Union would then be the most powerful country in the organization and, therefore, in command of the field."[7]

This incredible logic implies that if the United States stays in the UN, *it* will remain the most powerful country and therefore "in command of the field." Since when have we "commanded the field" in the UN? If we leave, the Soviets would at best have "command" of a disjointed nonentity that they (instead of us) would have to finance. It would be *their* white elephant, and would likely leave the Soviets with the alternative of getting out themselves or collapsing financially. It is yet another reason why United States withdrawal from the UN would be one of the most significant anti-Communist actions we could take.

Then, there are those who insist that we stay in the UN for the sake of the alleged good done by the specialized agencies. Withdrawal from the primary UN political apparatus (the General Assembly and Security Council) would still leave us the option of supporting various specialized agencies should we desire to do so. There would be nothing, for example, to stop us from financing the training of witch doctors through the World Health Organization:

> Witch doctors and other traditional mystics play a crucial role in looking after the sick in much of the developing world, and should get more encouragement from the medical profession. So says the World Health Organization (WHO), the UN agency which fights disease around the world. Since these healers form the basic corps of primary health workers for about 90 percent of the rural population of the third world, WHO believes that they should be given supplementary health training.[8]

Or, we can continue to assist UNESCO in producing such historically enlightening publications as the one that aimed at acquainting the public "with one of the major social triumphs of our day, namely, the way in which the problem of nationalities has been solved in the Soviet Union." According to the UNESCO booklet:

It was the Communist Party which showed the peoples of Russia the way to free themselves from social and national oppression. . . .

Only the October Revolution made it possible to liquidate the system of oppression of minorities and give equal political rights to all the nationalities and all the races of the USSR. . . .

The Soviet Union is a brotherhood of free and equal peoples comprising 15 sovereign Soviet republics in voluntary association on a footing of complete equality. . . . Each of them embodies the collective will of its people and can decide its own future in entire freedom. . . .

In 1940, the Soviet régime was restored in the Baltic Republics (Lithuania, Latvia and Estonia), which voluntarily joined the Union.[9]

We could also contribute independently to UNICEF, adequately preparing it to assist the next Marxist enemy with whom we may become militarily engaged.

The point is simply that the *first* order of business — dissolving our financial and political ties to the Security Council and General Assembly — is largely unrelated to action that might (or might not) be taken against this or that specialized agency. No longer can the alleged good accomplished by such agencies be used as the excuse to justify our continuing participation in the UN's political mischief.

Author Marya Mannes, a former staff writer for the Leftist magazine, *The Reporter*, once wrote sarcastically:

In the literature of the American far right, the UN is nothing less than the tool of communism and nothing more than an assemblage of knaves, gabbing their way through interminable debates in elegant surroundings at the expense of the heaviest taxpayer, Mr. American.[10]

Precisely! The only significant flaw in that statement is the implication that such a view is held by only a few on the so-called "Far Right," when in fact Americans from all walks of life are now reaching the same conclusions. Secretary of State Dean Acheson (CFR), hardly a "Far Rightist," devoted an entire career to promoting the interests and policies of the UN, only to acknowledge in 1970: "I never thought the United Nations was worth a damn. To a lot of people it was a Holy Grail, and those who set store by it had the misfortune to believe their own bunk."[11]

Ralph Bunche (CFR), who promoted "brotherhood" at the UN for years, later confided: "There are a hell of a lot of people in the world — black *and* white that I wouldn't want even as distant cousins, much less as brothers."[12]

Even "Liberal" Senator Robert Packwood (R-Oregon) has expressed the belief that "The United Nations has shown that it does not take itself seriously as a body designed to try to keep world peace, let alone world morality, and I think the time has come when we can well ask the question: Does this nation any longer belong in that body?"[13]

Meanwhile Senator William L. Langer (R-North Dakota) had told his Senate colleagues as early as July 28, 1945, that he could not vote for the UN Charter because "I believe it is fraught with danger to the American people, and to American institutions."[14] He was right, but only one of his colleagues paid attention and joined him in voting "Nay." With many years of UN history as a guide, another U.S. Senator, Barry Goldwater (R-Arizona), has advised:

> . . . the time has come to recognize the United Nations for the anti-American, anti-freedom organization that it has become. The time has come for us to cut off all financial help, withdraw as a member, and ask the United Nations to find a headquarters location outside the United States that is more in keeping with the philosophy of the majority of voting members, someplace like Moscow or Peking.[15]

During an address at the University of Wisconsin on July 14, 1975, then Secretary of State Henry Kissinger (CFR) asserted: "Dag Hammarskjöld once predicted that the day would come when people would see the United Nations for what it really is. . . ."[16] It has been the purpose of this overview to hasten that day.

Lord Acton once observed: "Power tends to corrupt and absolute power corrupts absolutely."[17] Nowhere does power tend to become so concentrated, all-pervasive, and absolute as in government. The bigger the government — as measured by the taxes it collects, the land it owns, the people it employs, the citizens dependent on it, and the regulations it imposes — the more the corruption. The biggest of all governments would be, of course, an economically collectivist *world* government, with sufficient military power to coerce the earth's population to do its will.

The United Nations, as its founders intended, is on its way to becoming such a world government. We are confronted with the basic choice of either getting out or going under. As one of O. Henry's timeless characters put it, in a somewhat different context, "it is a rat trap, and you, madam and sir and all of us, are in it."[18]

Let's get out!

Chapter 24

United Nations Update*

ON JANUARY 30, 1981, the United Nations Postal Administration issued a set of three stamps commemorating the "Inalienable Rights of the Palestinian People." The political force behind the stamp project was the Committee on the Exercise of the Inalienable Rights of the Palestinian People (C.E.I.R.P.P.), a U.N. outfit spawned by a Resolution adopted by the General Assembly on November 10, 1975. According to *Facts On File*, that Resolution was "drafted by" the terrorist Palestine Liberation Organization (P.L.O.). Congressman Hamilton Fish Jr. (R.-New York) recently noted that the C.E.I.R.P.P. "is merely a front in

---

*This chapter originally appeared as "TIIE U.N.: Terrorists From Arafat to Zimbabwe" in *American Opinion* magazine for May, 1981.

The United Nations Conspiracy

the United Nations for the Palestine Liberation Organization."
And the new U.N. stamp series is at once a propaganda effort
on behalf of the P.L.O. and yet another example of how the
U.N. consistently glorifies and promotes the cause of international terrorists.

In the whole field of internal security the main threat to life
and property is terrorism. A few years ago the Central Intelligence Agency revealed that more than one hundred forty terrorist organizations, from some fifty countries on four conti-
nents, were now linked together to comprise a formidable
international terrorist network. And a State Department summary of the problem released in December of last year reported:
"From January 1968 to October 1980, there have been more than
7,300 international terrorist incidents. Of these, 2,700 [*thirty-
seven percent*] were directed at US citizens or installations.
During the same period, 173 Americans were killed and 970
wounded."

Most terrorist attacks have in recent years fallen into five
major categories. While completely up-to-date statistics are not
available, those at hand are sufficient to indicate the nature
and scope of the terrorism problem.

ASSASSINATIONS: According to the C.I.A., there were 283 incidents of terrorist assassination between 1968 and 1979, resulting
in the deaths of 355 victims. Approximately eighty percent of
all such assassination attempts result in the death of the intended victim(s).

SKYJACKINGS: Between January 1970 and November 1977
there were seventy-two terrorist skyjacking incidents which
resulted in thirty-seven hostage deaths and fifteen woundings.
Eventually, 1,707 hostages were released, 361 were rescued, and
eighteen managed to escape.

KIDNAPPINGS: During that same eight-year time frame there
were 347 kidnapping incidents which resulted in death for 133
victims. (Forty percent of the kidnapping victims were Americans.) The kidnappings led to the release, as demanded by the
terrorists, of 267 so-called "political prisoners" and the payment
of $146 million in ransom.

SEIZURE OF FACILITIES: Between 1968 and 1979 there were 290 incidents of terrorist attacks on, and the seizure of, such facilities as government offices, banks, and private residences. As a result, 358 persons were killed, 332 wounded, and 664 held hostage. Material damage to these facilities amounted to $31,300,000.

BOMBINGS: This most frequent form of terrorist attack accounts for nearly forty percent of all terrorist operations. Between 1974 and 1980 there were 1,947 significant terrorist bombings which took the lives of 1,010 individuals. Nearly half of those attacks were against U.S. citizens or property.

The days of simple bombings and skyjackings may soon be replaced (or at least supplemented) by such even more repulsive tactics as bacteriological warfare and the use of small *nuclear* devices. Police in Paris, for example, recently permitted publication of papers seized in an apartment occupied by a member of a terrorist organization who was posing as a student. Among the documents was a formula for introducing lethal germs into a city's water supply. And other reliable evidence indicated that a team of scientists based in Paris was working to produce a miniature nuclear weapon. Foreign affairs analyst Hilaire du Berrier recently drew the attention of his readers to a new report by French researcher Roland Laurent which, according to Mr. du Berrier, "contains disclosures so alarming that West European governments may move to restore the death penalty. The problem will surface as people learn the full extent to which terrorists have developed, diversified, and acquired the most sophisticated arms and methods." Conceivably, terrorist tactics of the future will make those of the recent past seem the equivalent of pillow fights.

The situation is *very* serious and fully merits the priority attention which the Reagan Administration has promised to give it. During his initial press conference, on January twenty-eighth, Secretary of State Alexander Haig declared: "International Terrorism will take the place of human rights in our concern because it is the ultimate abuse of human rights." International terrorism, he announced, was "the greatest problem . . . in the human rights area today."

If implemented, this policy change will be a welcome successor to the Carter Administration's incredible "human rights" ploy — which in practice served as a weapon to *destroy* human rights in one pro-Western nation after another. A State Department summary of the Carter Administration's policy on terrorism, released during December of last year, asserted at one point: "Because of the inhumane character of international terrorism . . . we have been actively working to combat terrorism in all its forms." Which must have appeared a wry joke to those victimized by Carter Administration policies which weakened and undermined the once-friendly Governments of Iran, Rhodesia, and Nicaragua, while permitting millions of U.S. tax dollars to be channelled to terrorists through our contributions to the U.N. and other international agencies.

Maybe this is a good place to pause and define that term "terrorism." The most precise and useful definition we have yet discovered was offered a few years ago by Representative Lawrence Patton McDonald (D.-Georgia), one of our nation's best-informed authorities on matters pertaining to internal security.

Terrorism, wrote McDonald, is "a violent attack on noncombatants of the community for the purpose of intimidation, to achieve a political or military objective."

That is an excellent description, for it makes clear that the essence of terrorist activity is the harm inflicted on defenseless civilian populations. It does *not* include unconventional (or guerrilla) warfare directed exclusively at military targets.

The United Nations has been striving off and on for years to settle on a definition of "terrorism," but without success, since any rational description always proves offensive to the terrorist-abetting nations which control the world body. The "Liberal" *Boston Globe* reported as far back as November 15, 1972: "The failure by the United Nations to accurately spell out what it means by the term 'terrorism' appears to have stalled any efforts by concerned countries to deal with the problem in the international community. The UN General Assembly's legal committee has taken up the issue but so far has been unable to come up with any concrete definition."

No meaningful progress has been made since that time. According to a Representative from Syria, in fact, "the international community is under legal and moral obligation to promote the struggle for liberation and to resist any attempt to depict this struggle as synonymous with terrorism and illegitimate violence."

In the context of the United Nations, one man's terrorism is simply another man's patriotism. It has proved difficult indeed to entice an organization controlled by foxes to condemn the ravaging of chickens.

On occasion, the United Nations has itself been an active participant in what can only be described as terrorist activity. The most notorious examples occurred during the U.N.'s war against the anti-Communist province of Katanga in the Congo early in the Sixties. So numerous were the atrocities inflicted on non-combatants by U.N. troops that the forty-six civilian doctors in the Katangan capital of Elizabethville prepared a heavily detailed report fully documenting the U.N.'s bombing of clearly-marked hospitals, its bazooka attacks on ambulances, its bayonetting of children and the elderly, *etc.* Regarding one such incident, the doctors wrote: "These U.N.O. snipers seemed to have no other motive of thus killing unexpectedly and without warning, than to terrorize the civilian population by shooting at peaceful citizens, going about their daily occupations, as though they were shooting at clay pipes at a fair!!!"*

One of the doctors, a former Harvard Fellow who was a professor of surgery at the University of Elizabethville, spoke for his colleagues in a telegram to the president of the Harvard Faculty of Medicine:

---

*The entire report, entitled *46 Angry Men*, was translated from the French and was published by American Opinion, Belmont, Massachusetts 02178 in 1962. (Out of print).

We urgently request your intervention in order to put a stop to
the killing of civilian coloured and European men and women
and children by U.N. forces — stop — Women have been shot at
and wounded in their homes, workers in the streets — stop — So
have Red Cross servants — stop — During last two days jet planes
have been shooting at civilian cars downtown and in the country
— stop — Mortars are systematically shelling residential areas —
stop — For the second time Prince Leopold general African
hospital has been shelled — stop — Please inform academic and
medical world and public opinion and insist on U.N. giving up
such repulsive methods — stop — In name of the 46 civilian
practitioners at Elisabethville.

In his important book on the U.N., *The Fearful Master*, G.
Edward Griffin described one especially revealing — and
revolting — incident. Griffin reports: "At the height of the UN
attack on Elizabethville, Mr. Georges Olivet, the Swiss international Red Cross representative there, cabled an appeal to his
Geneva office to persuade the United Nations to stop firing on
Red Cross vehicles. A few days later he disappeared while on a
mercy mission to UN headquarters. It was not until eleven days
afterward that his wrecked ambulance was found. It had been
hit with bazooka rockets and machine-gunned by United Nations troops. In an attempt to conceal the crime, the UN soldiers
had hurriedly buried Mr. Olivet and his two companions in a
shallow grave next to the road."

At first, the U.N. attempted to blame the European-led
Katangese Army for the atrocity. Later, in the light of irrefuta-
ble evidence, it admitted that the vehicle had been struck by
U.N. fire. When the Red Cross asked for an official investigation, the U.N. denied the request.

More than ninety percent of the buildings bombed by the
U.N. in this conflict were strictly civilian structures with no
possible military value. The Roman Catholic bishop of Elizabethville accused the United Nations of "sacrilegious profan-
ities" and revealed that its troops had deliberately destroyed and
looted churches and had brutally murdered innocent civilians.
And so it went, in one instance after another, as the U.N. waged
its "peacekeeping operation."

In its later drive to topple the anti-Communist Government of Rhodesia, the U.N.'s approach was largely economic and diplomatic rather than military, although there were instances where U.N. funds and supplies were channelled to the Patriotic Front terrorists butchering helpless civilians. Tragically, the United States sided with the U.N., providing one of the clearest examples yet of the malevolent influence our association with the United Nations has had on American foreign policy.

Rhodesia had declared her independence from Great Britain (in a manner similar to our own nation's declaration of two centuries before) on November 11, 1965. The General Assembly condemned Rhodesia that same day, and the Security Council followed suit the day after. On November 20, 1965, the Security Council formally branded little Rhodesia "a threat to international peace and security." It was a ludicrous contention, as evidenced by the fact that the original version of the condemnation Resolution had *not* contained a finding that Rhodesia was a threat to peace in any way whatsoever. Only when it was pointed out that such a finding was necessary before the U.N. could take action was the desired conclusion inserted — with no supporting facts — and the Resolution sent on its way.

That Security Council Resolution of November 20, 1965, called for *voluntary* sanctions against Rhodesia, but it met with little success. So, on December 16, 1966, the Council voted to impose *mandatory* sanctions. To this day, it stands as the only time in U.N. history that such sanctions have been applied.

On January 5, 1967, President Lyndon Johnson signed Executive Order 11322, declaring it to be a criminal offense for any American to engage in the import of a wide range of Rhodesian products, and severely restricting U.S. exports to that country. And on July 29, 1968, President Johnson went even further and signed Executive Order 11419, barring all United States imports from, and exports to, Rhodesia. Remember that this was at a time when, despite the Vietnam War, our government leaders were permitting extensive shipments of goods and material to the Soviet Union and other Communist countries that were arming the North Vietnamese forces killing American troops in the field.

One result of the Rhodesian embargo was to make us increasingly dependent on the Soviet Union for chrome, a vital strategic material. The world's main sources of chrome ore are Rhodesia and the Soviet Union. Following imposition of sanctions against Rhodesia, the Soviet Union greatly increased the price of its chrome ore, and we were soon paying an outrageous premium for the privilege of becoming dependent on an enemy for a material essential to the production of stainless steel and other high-performance steels and superalloys. It was this outrageous situation which prompted Senator Harry F. Byrd Jr. (I.-Virginia) to introduce his famous amendment, approved by Congress in 1971, to permit the U.S. to import strategic materials from Rhodesia if those materials were also being imported from Communist nations.

The Byrd Amendment immediately sent the International Left into a frenzy because it allowed circumvention of the United Nations sanctions against Rhodesia which were designed to turn the country over to the terrorists.

The Byrd Amendment went into effect on January 1, 1972, was promptly challenged in the courts, and was upheld as thoroughly Constitutional. A number of unsuccessful attempts were made in Congress to repeal the amendment between 1972 and 1976. On one such occasion, former Senator Gale McGee (D.-Wyoming), one of the Senate's most outspoken advocates of the United Nations, admitted: "The central issue is not chrome from Rhodesia. The central issue is not repealing something just to repeal it. The central issue is, what is going to happen to the United Nations? It is the United Nations that is on the line."

In early 1977 a post-Watergate Congress buckled under the pressure, voted to scrap the Byrd Amendment, and once again put our nation in compliance with the U.N.'s destructive and intensely immoral boycott of Rhodesia.

Finally, on April 18, 1980, Rhodesia officially became Zimbabwe after an election in February which established Communist terrorist Robert Mugabe as Prime Minister. At last, the United Nations and our State Department were satisfied. Red terrorists were in power.

Again and again we find the U.N. on the side of the terrorists. Since the United Nations Childrens Fund (U.N.I.C.E.F.) is the world body's most revered and respected agency, it may come as a shock to many to learn that U.N.I.C.E.F. funds and supplies have time and again gone not to needy children but to terrorists engaged in committing atrocities against such children. During the U.N.'s own terrorist war against Katanga, for instance, ten million dollars earmarked for U.N.I.C.E.F. were instead "temporarily" diverted to finance the war effort. As outlined by former Representative Richard D. McCarthy (D.-New York), a "Liberal" advocate of both the U.N. and U.N.I.C.E.F.:

> In 1961, the U.S. Government allocated $10 million in support of UNICEF. Prior to actual payment, the Secretary General required emergency funds to carry on U.N. actions in the Congo. Acting under U.N. Resolution 1341, authorizing him to borrow funds from special accounts, and after consulting with UNICEF and the U.S. Government, the Secretary General was advanced the $10 million.

During the Vietnam War as well, U.N.I.C.E.F.'s efforts consistently favored the Communist side. Colonel Robert D. Heinl Jr. reported in *Human Events* for June 7, 1975:

> In programs purportedly established "to help children in Indo-china," the United Nations' Children's Emergency Fund gave just short of two-thirds of its collections to North Vietnamese or to the "Provisional Revolutionary Government of South Vietnam," sometimes confused with the Vietcong.
>
> The exact numbers, conceded by a UNICEF spokesman, run as follows: UNICEF collected and disbursed a total of $13,649,433 for its Indochina children's programs. While smidges of this came from abroad, the overwhelming amount came out of the pockets of U.S. taxpayers.

Of this eight-figure sum, $8,975,587 went to Communist
recipients . . . .
While Communists were thus getting 61 per cent of
UNICEF's largess, our ally, South Vietnam, got only
$5,360,707 . . . .

Did the supplies sent to the Communists reach needy children? When Colonel Heinl asked a U.N.I.C.E.F. spokesman
about the matter, he was told: "UNICEF has no way to make
sure the supplies to the Communists got to children. They were
dropped off at the airports and docks and we assume they were
used as we intended." It was a ludicrous assumption, considering
that some of those supplies, according to Colonel Heinl, included "trucks, bulldozers, heavy engineer construction equipment, and construction tools and equipment."

In 1970 the U.N.I.C.E.F. Executive Board approved a
$200,000 purchase of cloth, allegedly for clothing to go to North
Vietnamese children. The cloth was purchased from the Soviet
Union, with rubles held by U.N.I.C.E.F., and was allegedly
delivered to North Vietnam by the Soviet Union (not by
U.N.I.C.E.F.) in 1972. Again, no one but the Communists know
if that cloth went to children or to support the terrorism against
the South. In most instances U.N.I.C.E.F. insists on controlling
the disbursement of its aid. But, as the Religious News Service
reported in April of 1975, "UNICEF officials in New York
acknowledge that this has not been the case in their dealings
with the Vietcong, North Vietnam, or the Khmer Rouge rebel
forces in Cambodia. In these areas UNICEF merely arranges for
the types of materials requested by those authorities to be
shipped to Hanoi. From there on the goods go into the field
without any further UNICEF control over it."

Supplies from U.N.I.C.E.F. also turned up in encampments
of the Patriotic Front terrorists in Rhodesia. In June of 1979,
for example, the Combined Operations Headquarters in Salisbury disclosed that terrorists entering the country had been
issued medical *combat* packs provided by U.N.I.C.E.F. According to the *Bulawayo Chronicle* for June 23, 1979, "A military

spokesman said a medical pack taken from the body of a dead
terrorist, killed in a recent contact with security forces, contained a variety of pharmaceutical products made in Western
Europe, as well as the usual communist-made items. He said the
labels on the items each bore makers' names and country of
origin. Each label also clearly bore the name UNICEF." The
dispatch continued:

> In May last year the UNICEF annual report showed that the
> organisation was providing "aid" to the four Southern Africa
> terrorist movements recognised by the Organization for African
> Unity.
> The report — presented by the organisation's Executive Direc-
> tor, Mr. Henry Labouisse — showed that UNICEF as well as
> providing cash support for the terrorists, was giving what the
> report described as "humanitarian aid and social service training"
> to members of the terrorist organisations.
> A senior officer at Combined Operations said that the cap-
> tured medical kit "was hardly of the type that a social worker,
> dealing with children's ailments, would carry.
> "The contents," he said, "indicate clearly that it was a combat
> pack."

Yet another example of support by U.N.I.C.E.F. for the
terrorists in Rhodesia surfaced on October 2, 1979, when a
dispatch in London's *Daily Telegraph* described the results of a
raid by Rhodesian forces on a terrorist encampment in Mozam-
bique. Discovered at one point along a half-mile line of trenches
and bunkers was an underground medical dispensary. A reporter
on the scene at the time later wrote that "Piles of medical
equipment from UNICEF . . . [were] littered throughout the
area."

In July of 1980, the *U.N. Monthly Chronicle* reported that
U.N.I.C.E.F. had recently given approximately $244 million to
such countries as Red China, Communist Ethiopia, Marxist
India, Communist Vietnam, and Communist Zimbabwe. That
additional aid to Zimbabwe is especially revealing. As columnist
John F. McManus commented at the time:

Its new leader, Robert Mugabe, waged a cold-blooded war on Rhodesia for a decade. Tens of thousands perished, many of them women and children who were victims of sheer terror. Before U.N. and U.S. pressures forced its demise, Rhodesia's government presented conclusive evidence that Mugabe's murderers were receiving supplies from UNICEF, specifically medical combat packs: Rhodesia never received anything from UNICEF, but now that the nation is Zimbabwe and it is run by the murdering Mugabe, millions of dollars in UNICEF funds will be delivered.

That is something to keep in mind next Halloween when the "trick or treaters" come calling at your door for U.N.I.C.E.F.

Still another terrorist gang receiving assistance from the United Nations is the South West African Peoples Organization (S.W.A.P.O.), whose goal is the wresting of control over Namibia (South West Africa) from South Africa. According to a detailed background paper on S.W.A.P.O. prepared in 1979 by London's Foreign Affairs Research Institute:

> The United Nations Commissioner for Namibia, his three offices in New York, Luanda and Botswana, the UN Council for Namibia, the UN fund for Namibia and the UN approved Institute for Namibia are all organizations which co-operate closely with SWAPO as the 'sole and authentic representative of the Namibian People.'* All are bodies in receipt of generous funds from the UN budget. The UN Commission for Refugees and the Economic and Social Council's United Nations Development Programme are other organisations providing "humanitarian aid" on a lavish scale for refugees and others from Namibia. The United Nations Development Programme (UNDP) provided $31,500 to SWAPO for "education and training in the field of public information" during the year 1976-1977. It has also provided $151,000 in general education assistance to SWAPO within Angola.

---

*Elsewhere, the F.A.R.I. report asserts: "Despite its [*S.W.A.P.O.'s*] lack of military success, incessant lobbying at the United Nations resulted in the astonishing decision [*by the General Assembly*] to grant it recognition as the *sole* legal representative of the Namibian people despite the known minority nature of its support."

Almost as an aside, the report states: "During the course of raids by the South African Army on SWAPO bases in Angola during the summer of 1979, food cartons . . . originating from the UN's world food programme were found in the camps."

On October 2, 1978, S.W.A.P.O. president Sam Nujoma told a meeting of non-aligned nations in New York that S.W.A.P.O. shared a common bond of militant comradery and solidarity with Rhodesia's terrorist Patriotic Front, the terrorist P.L.O., and "other gallant forces of liberation." Remember, U.S. taxpayers pay one-fourth of the bill for the U.N. largesse which finds its way into the hands of such terrorists.

The U.N.'s love affair with the world's premier terrorist gang, the P.L.O., is typical. An article in the Winter 1977 issue of *Soldier Of Fortune* described "How U.S. Tax Dollars Pay For PLO Terrorism" by being passed through "humanitarian" U.N. agencies. Based on eyewitness reports gathered by Michael Schiff, an investigator who spent eleven days posing as a pro-P.L.O. journalist, the article declared:

> The United Nations Works Relief Agency, which ostensibly cares for Palestinian refugees in Lebanon, has been effectively taken over by the Palestinian Liberation Organization (PLO) in that country and is actively involved in guerrilla causes . . . .
> A major PLO propaganda production and distribution operation is based in UNWRA headquarters in Beirut, and Palestinian guerrilla employees of UNWRA routinely pass along to the Fatah organization [*of the P.L.O.*] reports of Israeli troop movements gathered by United Nations truce observers stationed along the borders.
> Millions of dollars in UNWRA funds, originally contributed by the United States for refugee relief, are diverted to pay for the international agency's activities in support of the PLO.

It seems that a P.L.O. official named Ahmad Jada was assigned to investigator Schiff and readily admitted to being a "full-time employee of the United Nations" while simultaneously serving as "coordinator for the Fatah, the P.L.O., and the United Nations" in Beirut, Lebanon. Jada's department and one other, located in the basement of a building in the U.N. compound, handled the production of P.L.O. propaganda and its distribution throughout the world. When Comrade Jada asked Schiff what pictures he needed to supplement his supposedly pro-P.L.O. story, Schiff replied, "anything that you have that can be good propaganda shots that will make the world stand up." Jada declared, "Oh we have quite a few of those," boasting that U.N. photographers "do all our photography for us." Jada and a colleague also admitted, according to Schiff, that "the only funds they have coming in are the funds allocated by the United States to the United Nations Works Relief Agency." Indeed:

> He [*Schiff*] said he later asked Jada "if the money is being used for this, what money is being used for the refugees?"
> And he said the funds are allocated for the refugees, but they (the Palestinians working in UNWRA headquarters) have complete control over the funds in that building, to do with as they see fit.
> Jada told Schiff that they consider the propaganda operation to be "more important towards the Palestinian cause" than refugee relief.

The U.N. escalated its public display of affection for the P.L.O. in 1974 when Yasir Arafat was invited to address the General Assembly on November thirteenth. It was the first time that a representative of any group lacking official U.N. status had appeared before the Assembly. The next day, Arafat flew to Communist Cuba for a meeting with Fidel Castro. And, on the first anniversary of his U.N. speech (November 13, 1975), Arafat's Al Fatah branch of the P.L.O. "celebrated" by bombing Zion Square in Jerusalem, killing six civilians and injuring forty-two.

According to Hilaire du Berrier, Arafat's speaking engagement at the U.N. was the "break that changed everything for the Palestine Liberation Organization . . . . since then it has been going great guns."

Indeed it has.

On November 8, 1975, the P.L.O. was granted observer status by the U.N. Food and Agriculture Organization.

On November 10, 1975, the General Assembly adopted a Resolution urging that the terrorist P.L.O. be invited to participate in all conferences on the Middle East held under U.N. auspices and asking that steps be taken to secure participation of the P.L.O. in the Geneva Peace Conference on the Middle East. (It was on this same date that the General Assembly adopted its notorious Resolution defining Zionism as "a form of racism and racial discrimination.")

On July 22, 1977, the P.L.O. was granted admission to the U.N. Economic and Social Council's Economic Commission for Western Asia. It was the first time that a non-nation had been granted full membership in a U.N. agency.

In October of 1977 the U.N. Civil Aviation Organization granted observer status to the P.L.O. Although the Palestinians had no airlines, they were nevertheless given the right to have representatives at all meetings where the U.N. discusses moves to assure air security. Incredibly, the U.N.'s excuse for allowing the P.L.O. to participate in such closed meetings was that this terrorist gang's experience with air piracy could be helpful in the search for preventative measures! It is as if the Secret Service were to invite John W. Hinckley Jr. to advise on protecting the President. As Hilaire du Berrier commented at the time, "The United Nations will learn less from the Palestinians on how to prevent skyjacking than the Palestinians and their allies will learn about how to thwart any defensive measures the U.N. proposes."

On October 7, 1978, it was announced that the U.N. Secretariat was launching a $500,000 publicity campaign to promote Palestinian rights and create a moderate image for the P.L.O. in the United States and other Western countries. Scheduled for inclusion in the propaganda package was a film, *Palestinians Do Have Rights*, in which terrorist leader Arafat was to play a leading role and be depicted in an entirely positive light. The film was eventually produced by the U.N. Division of Radio and Visual Services.*

The publicity campaign was timed to reach a peak on November 29, 1978, with an observance of the first "Day of Solidarity with the Palestinian People." The observance, which was sponsored by the P.L.O.-manipulated Special Unit on Palestinian Affairs, concluded with an exhibition sponsored by the P.L.O. The opening was briefly delayed while U.N. officials arranged to remove two especially embarrassing photographs — one showing Secretary-General Waldheim in conversation with terrorist leader Arafat in 1974, and the other depicting armed P.L.O. terrorists.

And, finally, the U.N.-sponsored Mid-Decade Women's Conference, held in Copenhagen between July 14 and 30, 1980, adopted without debate an official paper entitled, "Assistance to Palestinian Women Inside and Outside the Occupied Territories," with such assistance to be channelled through the terrorist P.L.O. Among other things, the P.L.O. was to be authorized to use U.N. funds to "collect and disseminate information and data about the effects of Israeli occupation on the social and economic conditions of the Palestinian women and their struggle for achieving self-determination, right of return, and to establish their independent state in Palestine."

The point, of course, is that the P.L.O. was an almost universally despised congregation of terrorist thugs, best known for perpetrating such tragedies as the slaughter of Israeli athletes during the 1972 Olympics, until it was brought under the U.N.'s wing. Now, thanks primarily to the million-dollar U.N. public relations campaign on its behalf, the P.L.O. has international influence and prestige far surpassing that of many U.N. member-nations.

---

*Congress sought to withhold $190,000 of the American share of the publicity campaign, as well as the $960,000 earmarked for the U.N. Special Unit On Palestinian Rights (which had been established in 1977 over U.S. objections). The Senate supported the cut, but the State Department eventually persuaded Congress to be content with a mere (and meaningless) statement of protest.

ONE OF the most encouraging developments in the new Congress was establishment by the Senate of its new Subcommittee on Security and Terrorism, to be Chaired by Senator Jeremiah Denton (R.-Alabama). Senator Denton has announced that he intends soon to conduct Hearings on matters related to terrorist activities. Information gathered during those Hearings will (with a few classified exceptions) be made available to the public and could prove to be an important educational tool for us all. Naturally the Far Left has already launched a vigorous campaign to sabotage the Subcommittee's efforts.

A similar investigative body is needed in the House. House Resolution 48, which is currently pending before the House Rules Committee, would re-establish the House Committee on Internal Security. This important Resolution merits the support of all who oppose the threat of terrorism.

But what about the United Nations? The Senate Security and Terrorism Subcommittee should definitely include on its agenda a detailed investigation of the extent to which U.S. contributions to the U.N. are in fact financing the terrorists. And the Reagan Administration, as part of its anti-terrorism commitment, should seriously consider withholding further contributions to the U.N. until the matter is clarified — even if it means outright withdrawal from the General Assembly, the Security Council, and those U.N. agencies which can be shown to be aiding and abetting terrorism.

In 1959 the Gallup Poll reported that eighty-seven percent of Americans questioned thought the U.N. was doing a good job. By near the end of last year it was a far different story, as indicated by the following dispatch from the *Salt Lake Tribune* for November 20, 1980:

> The public's rating of the United Nations' performance has declined to a 35-year-low. Currently, only three Americans in 10 (31 percent) feel the U.N. is doing a "good job" in trying to solve the problems it has had to face, while 53 percent feel it is doing a "poor job," . . .
> The Gallup Poll has measured the public's attitudes toward the

U.N. since its formation in 1945 . . . . At no point since then has satisfaction with the overall performance of the world organization been as low as it is today.

Which simply means that the more the American people learn about what the U.N. is actually doing, the less they like it. Beyond doubt, the slogan "Get US out!" (of the United Nations) is an idea whose time has come. ■ ■

Appendix A

Members of the American Institute of International Affairs
(merged in 1921 with the Council on Foreign Relations):

Hamilton Fish Armstrong	Stanley K. Hornbeck
George Barr Baker	Edward M. House
Ray Stannard Baker	Charles P. Howland
Tasker H. Bliss	Manley O. Hudson
Archibald C. Coolidge	Douglas Johnson
F. Trubee Davison	T.B. Kitteredge
Clive Day	Thomas W. Lamont
Martin Egan	Robert H. Lord
Raymond B. Fosdick	George Rublee
Edwin F. Gay	James Brown Scott
Louis H. Gray	Charles Seymour
Jerome Green	Whitney H. Shepardson
Charles H. Haskins	James T. Shotwell
Gerard C. Henderson	Alonzo E. Taylor
Christian A. Herter	Vanderbilt Webb
Herbert Hoover	

Source: Armstrong, Hamilton Fish, *Peace and Counterpeace*
(New York: Harper & Row, 1971), p. 565.

Appendix B

This is a listing of the Officers and Directors of the Council on Foreign Relations for 1980-81. A complete membership list follows on pages 218 to 242.

Officers

David Rockefeller
Chairman of the Board

Gabriel Hauge
Treasurer

Winston Lord
President

John Temple Swing
Vice President and Secretary

Directors

Term expiring 1981
W. Michael Blumenthal
Philip L. Geyelin
James Hoge
Henry A. Kissinger
C. Peter McColough
William D. Rogers
Robert V. Roosa
Marina v.N. Whitman

Lucian W. Pye
David Rockefeller
William D. Ruckelshaus
Martha R. Wallace
Winston Lord, *ex-officio*

Term expiring 1982
Graham T. Allison, Jr.
Richard L. Gelb
Gabriel Hauge
Theodore M. Hesburgh

Term expiring 1983
George S. Franklin
Edward K. Hamilton
Nicholas deB. Katzenbach
Lane Kirkland
Peter G. Peterson
George P. Shultz
Stephen Stamas
Franklin Hall Williams

Honorary Officers

John J. McCloy
Honorary Chairman

Frank Altschul
Honorary Secretary

Directors Emeriti

Frank Altschul
Elliott V. Bell
William A.M. Burden
Arthur H. Dean
Douglas Dillon
William C. Foster
Caryl P. Haskins

Joseph E. Johnson
Grayson Kirk
Henry R. Labouisse
John J. McCloy
Phillip D. Reed
Charles M. Spofford
John H. Williams

A

Aaron, David L.
Abboud, A. Robert
Abegglen, James C.
Abel, Elie
Abelson, Philip Hauge
Abely, Joseph F., Jr.
Abram, Morris B.
Abramowitz, Morton I.
Abrams, Elliott
Abshire, David M.
Achilles, Theodore C.
Adam, Ray C.
Adams, Ruth Salzman
Adamson, David
Agee, William M.
Agnew, Harold M.
Aidinoff, M. Bernard
Akins, James E.
Albert, Judith D.
Albright, Archie E.
Albright, Madeleine
Alderman, Michael H.
Aldrich, George H.
Alexander, Clifford L., Jr.
Alexander, Robert J.
Allan, F. Aley
Allbritton, Joe L.
Allen, Philip E.
Allen, Raymond B.
Alley, James B.
Allison, Graham T.
Allison, Richard C.
Allport, Alexander W.
Alpern, Alan N.
Altman, Roger C.
Altschul, Arthur G.
Altschul, Frank
Andersen, Harold W.
Anderson, John B.
Anderson, Robert
Anderson, Robert B.

Anderson, Robert O.
Angell, James W.
Angulo, Manuel R.
Anschuetz, Norbert L.
Anthoine, Robert
Apter, David E.
Armacost, Michael H.
Armstrong, Anne
Armstrong, DeWitt C., III
Armstrong, John A.
Armstrong, Willis C.
Arnold, Millard W.
Aron, Adam M.
Art, Robert J.
Asher, Robert E.
Aspin, Les
Assousa, George E.
Atherton, Alfred L., Jr.
Atkins, Charles Agee
Attwood, William
Auspitz, Josiah Lee
Averett, Elliott

B

Bader, William B.
Bailey, Charles W.
Baird, Charles F.
Baker, Howard H., Jr.
Baker, James E.
Baker, Pauline H.
Baldrige, Malcolm
Baldwin, Robert E.
Baldwin, Robert H.B.
Bales, Carter F.
Ball, David George
Ball, George W.
Ballou, George T.
Bancroft, Harding F.
Banks, Louis L.
Barber, Charles F.
Barber, Joseph
Barber, Perry O., Jr.

Barger, Thomas C.
Barghoorn, Frederick C.
Barker, Robert R.
Barkin, Solomon
Barlow, William E.
Barnds, William J.
Barnes, Harry G., Jr.
Barnet, Richard J.
Barnett, A. Doak
Barnett, Frank R.
Barnett, Robert W.
Barrand, Harry P., Jr.
Barrett, Edward W.
Barron, Deborah Durfee
Barrows, Leland
Bartholomew, Reginald
Bartlett, Joseph W.
Bartlett, Thomas A.
Bartley, Robert L.
Bass, Robert P., Jr.
Bassow, Whitman
Bastedo, Philip
Batkin, Alan R.
Bator, Francis M.
Bator, Peter A.
Battle, Lucius D.
Bauman, Robert P.
Baumann, Carol Edler
Baxter, Richard R.
Bayne, Edward Ashley
Beam, Jacob D.
Bean, Atherton
Bechtel, S.D.
Becker, E. Lovell
Beckler, David Z.
Beeman, Richard E.
Begley, Louis
Behrman, Jack N.
Beim, David O.
Beinecke, William S.
Bell, Daniel
Bell, David E.
Bell, Holley Mack

Bell, J. Bowyer
Bell, Travers J., Jr.
Bellamy, Carol
Benbow, Terence H.
Bennet, Douglas J., Jr.
Bennett, Donald V.
Bennett, J.F.
Bennett, W. Tapley, Jr.
Benson, Lucy Wilson
Beplat, Tristan E.
Berger, Peter L.
Berger, Suzanne
Bergold, Harry E., Jr.
Bergsten, C. Fred
Berman, Maureen R.
Bernstein, Robert L.
Berry, Sidney B.
Bessie, Simon Michael
Betts, Richard K.
Bialer, Seweryn
Bienen, Henry S.
Bienstock, Abraham L.
Bierley, John C.
Billington, James H.
Binger, James H.
Bingham, Jonathan B.
Birkelund, John P.
Birnbaum, Eugene A.
Bisnow, Mark C.
Bissell, Richard E.
Bissell, Richard M., Jr.
Black, Cyril E.
Black, Edwin F.
Black, Joseph E.
Black, Leon D.
Black, Shirley Temple
Blackmer, Donald L.M.
Blake, Robert O.
Blake, Vaughn R. Downey
Blank, Stephen
Blechman, Barry M.
Blendon, Robert J.
Bliss, Richard M.

Burns, Patrick Owen
Burt, Richard R.
Bush, Donald F.
Bushner, Rolland H.
Bussey, Donald S.
Butcher, Goler Teal
Butcher, Willard C.
Butler, Samuel C.
Butler, William J.
Buttenwieser, Benjamin J.
Byrnes, Robert F.
Byrom, Fletcher

C

Cabot, John M.
Cabot, Louis W.
Cabot, Thomas D.
Cabrañes, José A.
Calder, Alexander, Jr.
Califano, Joseph A., Jr.
Calkins, Hugh
Callander, Robert J.
Calleo, David P.
Campbell, John C.
Camps, Miriam
Canal, Carlos M., Jr.
Canfield, Cass
Canfield, Franklin O.
Carey, Hugh L.
Carey, Jane C.
Carey, John
Carlucci, Frank C.
Carmichael, William D.
Carnesale, Albert
Carroll, J. Speed
Carroll, Mitchell B.
Carson, Charles W., Jr.
Carter, Barry E.
Carter, Edward William
Carter, Hodding, III
Carter, Robert L.
Carter, William D.

Cary, Frank T.
Cary, William L.
Case, Clifford P.
Case, Everett N.
Case, John C.
Casey, William J.
Cater, Douglass
Cates, John M., Jr.
Catto, Henry E., Jr.
Chace, James
Chaikin, Sol Chick
Challenor, Herschelle
Chancellor, John
Chandler, George A.
Chapman, John F.
Charpie, Robert A.
Chase, W. Howard
Chayes, Abram J.
Chayes, Antonia Handler
Cheever, Daniel S.
Chen, Kimball C.
Chenery, Hollis B.
Childs, Marquis W.
Chittenden, George H.
Chollar, Robert G.
Christopher, Robert C.
Christopher, Warren
Chubb, Hendon
Church, Edgar M.
Cisler, Walker L.
Clapp, Priscilla A.
Clark, Bronson P.
Clark, Dick
Clark, Howard L.
Clark, Kenneth B.
Clark, Ralph L.
Clarke, Jack G.
Cleveland, Harlan
Cleveland, Harold van B.
Cleveland, Stanley M.
Clifford, Donald K., Jr.
Cline, Ray S.
Clurman, Richard M.

Day, Arthur R.
Deagle, Edwin A., Jr.
Dean, Arthur H.
Dean, Jonathan
Debevoise, Eli Whitney
Debevoise, Eli Whitney, II
De Borchgrave, Arnaud
Debs, Richard A.
Decter, Midge
De Cubas, José
Dee, Robert F.
Dees, Bowen C.
De Janosi, Peter E.
De Kiewiet, C.W.
De Lima, Oscar A.
De Menil, Lois Pattison
Deming, Frederick L.
DeMuth, Christopher C.
Denison, Robert J.
Dennison, Charles S.
DePalma, Samuel
De Rosso, Alphonse
Destler, I.M.
Deutch, John M.
Deutch, Michael J.
Devine, C.R.
Devine, Thomas J.
DeVries, Henry P.
DeVries, Rimmer
De Windt, E. Mandell
Díaz Alejandro, Carlos F.
Dickey, John Sloan
Dickson, R. Russell, Jr.
Diebold, John
Diebold, William, Jr.
Dietel, William M.
Dillon, Douglas
Dilworth, J. Richardson
Dine, Thomas A.
Dixon, George H.
Dodge, Cleveland E.
Doherty, William C., Jr.
Dolin, Arnold

Domínguez, Jorge I.
Donahue, Donald J.
Donahue, Thomas R.
Donaldson, William H.
Donnell, Ellsworth
Donnell, James C., II
Donnelly, Harold C.
Donovan, Hedley
Doty, Paul M., Jr.
Douce, Wm. C.
Douglas, Paul W.
Douglass, Robert R.
Draper, Theodore
Dreier, John C.
Drell, Sidney D.
Drew, Elizabeth
Drumwright, J.R.
Dubow, Arthur M.
DuBrul, Stephen M.
Duffey, Joseph
Duffy, James H.
Duke, Angier Biddle
Duncan, John C.
Dungan, Ralph A.
Durkee, William P.
Raoul-Duval, Michael
Dyke, Nancy Bearg

E

Eagleburger, Lawrence S.
Earle, Ralph, II
Easum, Donald B.
Eaton, David
Eaton, Frederick M.
Eaton, Leonard J., Jr.
Eberle, William D.
Eckholm, Erik P.
Edelman, Albert I.
Edelman, Gerald M.
Edelstein, Julius C.C.
Edgerton, Wallace B.
Edwards, Howard L.

Edwards, Robert H.
Ehrlich, Thomas
Eilts, Hermann F.
Einaudi, Luigi R.
Einaudi, Mario
Einhorn, Jessica P.
Eliot, Theodore L., Jr.
Elliott, Byron K.
Elliott, Osborn
Elliott, Randle
Ellison, Keith P.
Ellsberg, Daniel
Ellsworth, Robert F.
Elson, Robert T.
Embree, Ainslie T.
Emeny, Brooks
Enders, Thomas Ostrom
Enthoven, Alain
Erb, Guy F.
Erbsen, Claude E.
Erburu, Robert F.
Estabrook, Robert H.
Etzioni, Amitai
Evans, John C.
Evans, John K.
Ewing, William, Jr.
Exter, John

F

Fabian, Larry L.
Fairbank, John King
Fairbanks, Douglas
Falk, Richard A.
Farer, Tom J.
Farmer, Thomas L.
Fascell, Dante B.
Feer, Mark C.
Feiner, Ava S.
Feldman, Mark B.
Feldstein, Martin S.
Fenster, Steven R.
Ferguson, C. Clyde, Jr.

Ferguson, Glenn W.
Ferguson, James L.
Fessenden, Hart
Field, Robert E.
Field, William Osgood, Jr.
Fierce, Milfred C.
Fifield, Russell H.
Finger, Seymour M.
Finkelstein, Lawrence S.
Finley, Murray H.
Finn, James
Finney, Paul B.
Firmage, Edwin B.
Fisher, Adrian S.
Fisher, Pieter A.
Fisher, Richard W.
Fisher, Roger
Fishlow, Albert
Fitzgerald, Edmund B.
FitzGerald, Frances
Fitzgibbons, Harold E.
Flanigan, Peter M.
Fleck, G. Peter
Fogg, Joseph G., III
Forrestal, Michael V.
Foster, William C.
Fousek, Peter
Fowler, Henry H.
Fox, Donald T.
Fox, Joseph C.
Fox, Merritt Baker
Fox, William T.R.
Franck, Thomas M.
Francke, Albert, III
Frank, Charles R., Jr.
Frank, Isaiah
Frank, Richard A.
Frankel, Francine R.
Frankel, Max
Franklin, George S.
Fraser, Donald M.
Frederick, Pauline
Fredericks, J. Wayne

Freeman, Orville L.
Frelinghuysen, Peter H.B.
French, John
Freund, Gerald
Frey, Donald N.
Freytag, Richard A.
Fribourg, Michel
Fried, Edward R.
Friedman, Benjamin M.
Friedman, Irving S.
Friedman, Paul E.
Friele, Berent
Friendly, Henry J.
Fromkin, David
Frye, Alton
Frye, William R.
Fuerbringer, Otto
Fuller, Keith
Funari, John
Funkhouser, E.N., Jr.
Furlaud, Richard M.
Fuzesi, Stephen, Jr.
Fye, Paul M.

G

Gaer, Felice D.
Gallagher, Charles F.
Gallatin, James P.
Ganoe, Charles S.
Gard, Robert G., Jr.
Gardner, Richard N.
Garment, Leonard
Garment, Suzanne Weaver
Garretson, Albert H.
Gart, Murray J.
Garten, Jeffrey E.
Garthoff, Raymond L.
Garvin, Clifton C., Jr.
Garvy, George
Garwin, Richard L.
Gates, Thomas S.
Gati, Charles

Gati, Toby Trister
Geertz, Clifford
Geier, Paul E.
Geiger, Theodore
Gelb, Leslie H.
Gelb, Richard L.
Gell-Mann, Murray
George, Alexander L.
George, W.H. Krome
Geyelin, Henry R.
Geyelin, Philip L.
Giamatti, A. Bartlett
Gibney, Frank B.
Giffen, James H.
Gil, Peter P.
Gilbert, H.N.
Gilbert, Jackson B.
Gilbert, Jarobin, Jr.
Gillespie, S. Hazard
Gilpatric, Roswell L.
Gilpin, Robert
Ginsburg, David
Ginsburg, Ruth Bader
Ginsburgh, Robert N.
Gleysteen, Peter
Globerman, Norma
Glushien, Ruth N.
Godchaux, Frank A., III
Goekjian, Samuel V.
Gogél, Donald Jay
Goheen, Robert F.
Goldberg, Arthur J.
Goldberger, Marvin L.
Golden, William T.
Goldin, Harrison J.
Goldman, Guido
Goldman, Marshall I.
Goldman, Merle
Goldmark, Peter C., Jr.
Goldsborough, James O.
Goldschmid, Mary Tait
Gompert, David C.
Good, Robert C.

Goodby, James E.
Goodman, George J.W.
Goodman, Herbert I.
Goodpaster, Andrew J.
Goodsell, James Nelson
Gordon, Albert H.
Gordon, Lincoln
Gorman, Paul F.
Gornick, Alan L.
Gotbaum, Victor
Gousseland, Pierre
Grace, J. Peter
Graff, Robert D.
Graham, Katharine
Grant, James P.
Grant, Stephen A.
Granville, Maurice F.
Graubard, Stephen R.
Gray, Gordon
Grayson, Bruns H.
Greenberg, Maurice R.
Greenberg, Sanford D.
Greene, James C.
Greene, James R.
Greene, Joseph N., Jr.
Greene, Margaret L.
Greenfield, James L.
Greenfield, Meg
Greenhill, Robert F.
Greenough, William C.
Greenspan, Alan
Greenwald, Joseph A.
Greenwood, Ted
Griffith, Thomas
Griffith, William E.
Grohman, Robert T.
Grose, Peter B.
Gross, Ernest A.
Gross, Patrick W.
Grover, Allen
Groves, Ray J.
Grunwald, Henry A.
Gullion, Edmund A.

Gulliver, Adelaide Cromwell
Gunn, Hartford N., Jr.
Gurganus, William R.
Gutfreund, John H.
Guthman, Edwin O.
Gwin, Catherine B.

H

Haas, Peter E.
Haass, Richard N.
Habib, Philip C.
Hadley, Stephen J.
Haig, Alexander M., Jr.
Haight, G. Winthrop
Halaby, Najeeb E.
Hale, Roger L.
Hale, William E.
Haley, John C.
Hallett, Douglas L.
Hallingby, Paul, Jr.
Halperin, Morton H.
Halsted, Thomas A.
Hamilton, Charles V.
Hamilton, Edward K.
Hamilton, Fowler
Hamilton, Michael P.
Hansen, Roger D.
Hanson, Thor
Harari, Maurice
Harding, Harry
Hardy, Randall W.
Hare, Raymond A.
Hargrove, John L.
Harpel, James W.
Harper, Conrad K.
Harper, Paul C., Jr.
Harriman, W. Averell
Harris, Irving B.
Harris, Joseph E.
Harris, Patricia Roberts
Harrison, Selig S.
Harsch, Joseph C.

Hart, Augustin S.
Hart, Parker T.
Hartley, Fred L.
Hartman, Arthur A.
Haskell, Broderick
Haskell, John H.F., Jr.
Haskins, Caryl P.
Hauge, Gabriel
Hauge, John R.
Hauser, Rita E.
Hauser, William L.
Haviland, H. Field, Jr.
Hawkins, Ashton
Hayes, Alfred
Hayes, Samuel P.
Haynes, Fred
Haynes, Ulric St. C., Jr.
Haywood, Oliver G.
Hazard, John N.
Healy, Harold H., Jr.
Heard, Alexander
Heck, Charles B.
Heckscher, August
Hehir, J. Bryan
Heifetz, Elaine F.
Heintzen, Harry L.
Heinz, H.J., II
Helander, Robert C.
Heldring, Frederick
Hellman, F. Warren
Helms, Richard
Henderson, Julia
Henderson, Lawrence J., Jr.
Henderson, Loy W.
Henderson, William
Henkin, Louis
Hennessy, John M.
Henry, John B.
Herling, John
Herring, Robert R.
Herskovits, Jean
Herter, Christian A., Jr.
Herzfeld, Charles M.

Herzog, Paul M.
Hesburgh, Theodore M.
Hester, James M.
Hewitt, Marilyn Berger
Hewitt, William A.
Heyns, Roger W.
Hickey, William M.
Higgins, Robert F.
Highet, Keith
Hillenbrand, Martin J.
Hilsman, Roger
Hines, Gerald D.
Hinshaw, Randall
Hinton, Deane R.
Hirschman, Albert O.
Hoagland, Jim
Hobby, William P.
Hoch, Frank W.
Hochschild, Harold K.
Hochschild, Walter
Hodgson, James D.
Hoffman, A. Michael
Hoffman, Michael L.
Hoffmann, Stanley
Hoge, James
Hoguet, George R.
Hoguet, Robert L.
Hohenberg, John
Holbrooke, Richard C.
Holland, Jerome H.
Holland, Robert C.
Hollick, Ann L.
Holloway, Anne Forrester
Holmes, Alan R.
Holst, Willem
Holt, Pat M.
Homer, Sidney
Hooks, Benjamin L.
Hoopes, Townsend W.
Hoover, Herbert W., Jr.
Horan, John J.
Hormats, Robert D.
Horn, Garfield H.

Jones, Gilbert E.
Jones, Peter T.
Jones, Reginald H.
Jones, Thomas V.
Jordan, Amos A.
Jordan, Vernon E., Jr.
Jorden, William J.
Josephson, William
Jungers, Frank
Junz, Helen B.

K

Kahan, Jerome H.
Kahin, George McT.
Kahler, Miles
Kahn, Harry
Kahn, Herman
Kaiser, Philip M.
Kaiser, Robert G.
Kaiser, Walter J.
Kalb, Marvin
Kalicki, Jan H.
Kamarck, Andrew M.
Kaminer, Peter H.
Kanter, Arnold
Kaplan, Gilbert E.
Kaplan, Harold
Kaplan, Mark N.
Karalekas, Anne
Karnow, Stanley
Kassof, Allen H.
Katz, Milton
Katzenbach, Nicholas deB.
Kaufman, Henry
Kaufmann, William W.
Kaysen, Carl
Keatley, Anne
Keenan, Edward L.
Keeny, Spurgeon M., Jr.
Kehrl, Howard H.
Kelleher, Catherine M.
Keller, George M.

Kelly, George Armstrong
Kemp, Geoffrey
Kempner, Frederick C.
Kempner, Maximilian W.
Kenen, Peter B.
Keniston, Kenneth
Kennan, George F.
Kennedy, David M.
Kennedy, Roger G.
Kenney, F. Donald
Keohane, Robert O.
Keppel, Francis
Kern, Harry F.
Kester, John G.
Keydel, John F.
Khuri, Nicola N.
Killefer, Tom
Kilpatrick, Robert D.
Kimmitt, Robert M.
King, James E.
King, John A., Jr.
Kintner, William R.
Kirk, Grayson
Kirkland, Lane
Kissinger, Henry A.
Kitchen, Jeffrey C.
Klaerner, Curtis M.
Kleiman, Robert
Klein, David
Klein, Edward
Klotz, Frank G.
Knight, Robert Huntington
Knoppers, Antonie T.
Knowlton, William A.
Knowlton, Winthrop
Kohler, Foy D.
Kolodziej, Edward A.
Koonce, Wayne Allan
Korb, Lawrence J.
Korbonski, Andrzej
Korry, Edward M.
Kotschnig, Walter M.
Kourides, P. Nicholas

Kraar, Louis
Kraemer, Lillian E.
Kraft, Joseph
Kramer, Jane
Krause, Lawrence B.
Kreidler, Robert N.
Kreisberg, Paul H.
Kreps, Juanita M.
Krisher, Bernard
Kristol, Irving
Kruidenier, David
Kubisch, Jack B.
Kurth, James R.

L

Labbok, Miriam H.
Labouisse, Henry R.
Lacy, Alex S.
Lacy, Dan M.
Lake, W. Anthony
Lall, Betty Goetz
Lambrinides, Andrea H.
Lamm, Donald S.
Lamontagne, Raymond A.
Lamson, Roy, Jr.
Landry, Lionel
Langer, Paul F.
Langsam, David E.
Lansner, Kermit
LaPalombara, Joseph
Lapham, Lewis H.
Lardy, Nicholas R.
Larry, R. Heath
Lary, Hal B.
Lau-Kee, Alice Young
Laukhuff, Perry
Laurenson, Edwin Charles
Laventhol, David A.
Lazarus, Ralph
Lazarus, Steven
LeBaron, Eugene
Le Blond, Richard K., II

Leddy, John M.
Lederberg, Joshua
Lederer, Ivo John
Lee, Ernest S.
Lee, James E.
Lee, John M.
Lee, William L.
Leebaert, Derek
Lefever, Ernest
Leghorn, Richard S.
Legvold, Robert H.
Lehman, John R.
Lehman, Orin
Lehrer, Jim
Lehrman, Hal
Lehrman, Lewis E.
Leich, John Foster
Leigh, Monroe
LeMelle, Tilden J.
LeMelle, Wilbert J.
Lemnitzer, Lyman L.
Leonard, James F.
Leonard, James G.
Leslie, John E.
Le Sueur, Lawrence E.
Levine, Irving R.
Levitas, Mitchel
Levy, Marion J., Jr.
Levy, Walter J.
Lewis, Flora
Lewis, John P.
Lewis, John Wilson
Lewis, Samuel W.
Li, Victor H.
Lichtblau, John H.
Lieberman, Henry R.
Lilienthal, David E.
Linder, Harold F.
Lindquist, Warren T.
Lindsay, Franklin A.
Lindsay, George N.
Lindsay, John V.
Linen, James A.

Linowitz, Sol M.
Lipper, Kenneth
Lipscomb, James S.
Lipscomb, Thomas H.
Lipset, Seymour Martin
Lipson, Leon
Lissakers, Karin M.
Little, David
Little, L.K.
Livingston, Robert Gerald
Locke, Edwin A., Jr.
Lockwood, John E.
Lodal, Jan M.
Lodge, George C.
Lodge, Henry Cabot
Loeb, Frances Lehman
Loeb, John L.
Loeb, Marshall
Loft, George
Long, Franklin A.
Longstreet, Victor M.
Loomis, Henry
Loos, A. William
Lord, Charles Edwin
Lord, Winston
Loucks, Harold H.
Lovestone, Jay
Lowe, Eugene Y., Jr.
Lowenfeld, Andreas F.
Lowenstein, James G.
Lowenthal, Abraham F.
Loy, Frank E.
Lubar, Robert A.
Luce, Charles F.
Luck, Edward C.
Luckey, E. Hugh
Ludt, R.E.
Luers, William H.
Luke, David L., III
Lupfer, Timothy T.
Lustick, Ian S.
Luter, Yvonne
Lyet, J. Paul

Lyford, Joseph P.
Lyman, Richard W.
Lynch, Edward S.
Lynn, James T.
Lynn, Laurence E., Jr.
Lyon, E. Wilson
Lyon, Roger A.
Lythcott, George I.

M

McCabe, Thomas B.
McCarthy, John G.
McCarthy, Robert E.
McCloy, John J.
McCloy, John J., II
McColough, C. Peter
McCormack, Elizabeth J.
McCormick, Brooks
McCracken, Paul W.
McDermott, Walsh
McDonald, Alonzo L.
McDonough, William J.
McDougal, Myres S.
McFadden, W. Clark, II
McGee, Gale W.
McGhee, George C.
McGiffert, David E.
McGovern, George S.
McHenry, Donald F.
McKee, James W., Jr.
McKeever, Porter
McKinley, John K.
McKinney, Robert M.
McLean, Sheila Avrin
McLin, Jon B.
McNamara, Robert S.
McNeill, Robert L.
McPherson, Harry C., Jr.
McQuade, Lawrence C.
MacArthur, Douglas, II
MacDonald, Gordon J.
MacEachron, David W.

Mondale, Walter F.
Monson, Judith H.
Montgomery, Parker G.
Moody, William S.
Moore, John Norton
Moore, Jonathan
Moore, Maurice T.
Moore, Paul, Jr.
Moose, Richard M.
Moran, Theodore H.
Morgan, Cecil
Morgan, Henry S.
Morgan, Lee L.
Morgan, Thomas E.
Morgenthau, Hans J.
Morgenthau, Lucinda L. Franks
Morley, James William
Morley, Roger H.
Morrell, Gene P.
Morris, Grinnell
Morris, Max K.
Morrisett, Lloyd N.
Morse, David A.
Morse, Edward L.
Morse, F. Bradford
Morse, Kenneth P.
Moses, Alfred H.
Moyers, Bill
Moynihan, Daniel P.
Mulford, David C.
Mulholland, William D.
Muller, Steven
Munger, Edwin S.
Munroe, George B.
Munroe, Vernon, Jr.
Munyan, Winthrop R.
Murphy, Grayson M-P.
Murray, Douglas P.
Muse, Martha Twitchell
Myers, Anne R.
Myerson, Bess

N

Nachmanoff, Arnold
Nacht, Michael L.
Nagorski, Zygmunt, Jr.
Nason, John W.
Nathan, James A.
Nathan, Robert R.
Neal, Alfred C.
Nelson, Clifford C.
Nelson, Merlin E.
Neustadt, Richard E.
Newburg, André W.G.
Newhouse, John
Newman, Richard T.
Newsom, David D.
Newton, Quigg, Jr.
Ney, Edward N.
Nichols, Rodney W.
Nichols, Thomas S.
Niehuss, John M.
Nielsen, Waldemar A.
Nierenberg, William A.
Nimetz, Matthew
Nitze, Paul H.
Nolte, Richard H.
Nooter, Robert H.
Norman, William S.
Norstad, Lauris
Nossiter, Bernard D.
Notestein, Frank W.
Novak, Michael
Noyes, Charles Phelps
Noyes, W. Albert, Jr.
Nye, Joseph S.

O

Oakes, John B.
Oberdorfer, Don
Odeen, Philip A.
Odom, William E.
O'Donnell, Kevin
Oettinger, Anthony G.
O'Flaherty, J. Daniel
Ogden, Alfred

Ogden, William S.
O'Keefe, Bernard J.
Okimoto, Daniel I.
Oksenberg, Michel
Oliver, Covey T.
Olmstead, Cecil J.
Olson, Lawrence
Olson, William C.
Olvey, Lee D.
O'Malley, Cormac K.H.
O'Neill, Michael J.
Oppenheimer, Franz M.
Ornstein, Norman
Osborn, George K.
Osborne, Richard de J.
Osgood, Robert E.
Osmer, Margaret
Osnos, Peter
Ostrander, F. Taylor, Jr.
Overby, Andrew N.
Owen, Henry
Oxman, Stephen A.
Oxnam, Robert Bromley

P

Packard, George R.
Paffrath, Leslie
Page, Howard W.
Page, John H.
Page, Walter H.
Pais, Abraham
Paley, William S.
Palm, Gregory K.
Palmer, Norman D.
Palmer, Ronald D.
Palmieri, Victor H.
Panofsky, Wolfgang K.H.
Park, Richard L.
Parker, Daniel
Parker, Maynard
Parsky, Gerald L.
Passin, Herbert

Patrick, Hugh T.
Patterson, Charles J.
Patterson, Ellmore C.
Patterson, Gardner
Patterson, Hugh B., Jr.
Patterson, Robert P., Jr.
Pauker, Guy J.
Paul, Roland A.
Payne, Samuel B.
Pearce, William R.
Pearson, John E.
Peay, T. Michael
Pedersen, Richard F.
Pelgrift, Kathryn C.
Pell, Claiborne
Penfield, James K.
Pennoyer, Robert M.
Perera, Guido R.
Peretz, Don
Perkins, James A.
Perkins, Roswell B.
Perle, Richard N.
Perlmutter, Amos
Perry, Hart
Petersen, Donald E.
Petersen, Gustav H.
Petersen, Howard C.
Peterson, Peter G.
Peterson, Rudolph A.
Petschek, Stephen R.
Petty, John R.
Pfaff, William W., III
Pfaltzgraff, Robert L., Jr.
Pfeiffer, Jane Cahill
Pfeiffer, Ralph A., Jr.
Pfeiffer, Steven B.
Phillips, Christopher H.
Phillips, Russell A., Jr.
Phleger, Herman
Picker, Harvey
Picker, Jean
Pickering, Thomas R.
Piel, Gerard

Pierce, William C.
Piercy, George T.
Pierotti, Roland
Pierre, Andrew J.
Pifer, Alan
Pigott, Charles M.
Pilliod, Charles J., Jr.
Pincus, Lionel I.
Pincus, Walter H.
Pino, John A.
Pipes, Daniel
Pipes, Richard E.
Pippitt, Robert M.
Place, John B.M.
Plank, John N.
Platig, E. Raymond
Platt, Jonas M.
Platt, Nicholas
Platten, Donald C.
Plimpton, Calvin H.
Plimpton, Francis T.P.
Podhoretz, Norman
Pogue, L. Welch
Polk, William R.
Pollack, Gerald A.
Polsby, Nelson W.
Pool, Ithiel DeSola
Poor, J. Sheppard
Portes, Richard D.
Posner, Michael H.
Posvar, Wesley W.
Potter, Robert S.
Power, Philip H.
Power, Thomas F., Jr.
Powers, Joshua B.
Powers, Thomas Moore
Pranger, Robert J.
Pratt, Edmund T., Jr.
Press, Frank
Preston, Lewis T.
Prewitt, Kenneth
Price, John R., Jr.
Price, Robert

Pugh, Richard C.
Pulling, Edward
Pursley, Robert E.
Pusey, Nathan M.
Pustay, John S.
Putnam, George E., Jr.
Pye, Lucian W.

Q

Quandt, William B.
Quester, George H.
Quigg, Philip W.
Quigley, Leonard V.

R

Rabb, Maxwell M.
Rabi, Isidor I.
Rabinowitch, Victor
Radway, Laurence I.
Ramsey, Douglas K.
Ranis, Gustav
Rashish, Myer
Rather, Dan
Rathjens, George W.
Rattner, Steven L.
Ravenal, Earl C.
Ravenholt, Albert
Raveson, Thomas J.
Rawson, Merle R.
Raymond, David A.
Raymond, Jack
Read, Benjamin H.
Reed, J.V., Jr.
Reed, Philip D.
Reeves, Jay B.L.
Regan, Donald T.
Rehm, John B.
Reid, Ogden R.
Reid, Whitelaw
Reinhardt, John E.
Reisman, Michael M.

S

Safran, Nadav
Sage, Mildred D.
Said, Edward
Salisbury, Harrison E.
Salomon, Richard E.
Salomon, William R.
Saltzman, Charles E.
Salzman, Herbert
Sample, Steven B.
Samuel, Howard D.
Samuels, Michael A.
Samuels, Nathaniel
Sargeant, Howland H.
Saunders, Harold H.
Sawhill, John C.
Sawyer, John E.
Sawyier, Stephen K.
Scalapino, Robert A.
Scali, John A.
Schacht, Henry B.
Schachter, Oscar
Schaetzel, J. Robert
Schafer, John H.
Schecter, Jerrold
Scheinman, Lawrence
Schell, Orville H., Jr.
Schiff, Frank W.
Schiff, John M.
Schilling, Warner R.
Schlesinger, Arthur, Jr.
Schlosser, Herbert S.
Schmertz, Herbert
Schmoker, John B.
Schneider, Jan
Schneiderman, David
Schneier, Arthur
Schoettle, Enid C.B.
Schorr, Daniel L.
Schubert, Richard F.
Schumer, Charles E.
Schuyler, C.V.R.

Schwab, William B.
Schwartz, Harry
Schwarz, Frederick A.O., Jr.
Schwarz, H. Marshall
Schwebel, Stephen M.
Scott, Harold B.
Scott, Stuart N.
Scoville, Herbert, Jr.
Scowcroft, Brent
Scranton, William W.
Scrimshaw, Nevin S.
Seaborg, Glenn T.
Seabury, Paul
Seagrave, Norman P.
Seamans, Robert C., Jr.
Seawell, William T.
Segal, Sheldon
Seibold, Frederick C., Jr.
Seidman, Herta Lande
Seigenthaler, John L.
Seigle, John W.
Seitz, Frederick
Selin, Ivan
Sellers, Robert V.
Semple, Robert B., Jr.
Sewell, John W.
Sexton, William C.
Seymour, Whitney North
Shapiro, Eli
Shapiro, George M.
Shapiro, Irving S.
Shapiro, Isaac
Shaplen, Robert
Sharp, Daniel A.
Shayne, Herbert M.
Shearer, Warren W.
Sheeline, Paul C.
Sheffield, James R.
Sheinkman, Jacob
Sheldon, Eleanor Bernert
Shelley, Sally Swing
Shelp, Ronald K.
Shelton, Sally A.

Steadman, Richard C.
Stebbins, James H.
Steel, Ronald
Stein, Eric
Stein, Howard
Steinbruner, John D.
Steiner, Daniel
Stepan, Alfred C.
Sterling, Richard W.
Stern, Ernest
Stern, Fritz
Stern, H. Peter
Sternlight, David
Stevens, Charles R.
Stevens, Norton
Stevenson, Adlai E., III
Stevenson, H.L.
Stevenson, John R.
Stewart, Patricia Carry
Stewart, Ruth Ann
Sticht, J. Paul
Stifel, Laurence D.
Stilwell, Richard G.
Stobaugh, Robert B.
Stoessel, Walter J., Jr.
Stoessinger, John G.
Stoga, Alan
Stone, Jeremy J.
Stone, Robert G., Jr.
Stone, Roger D.
Stone, Shepard
Stookey, John Hoyt
Stratton, Julius A.
Straus, Donald B.
Straus, Jack I.
Straus, Oscar S.
Straus, R. Peter
Straus, Ralph I.
Straus, Robert K.
Strauss, Simon D.
Strausz-Hupé, Robert
Strayer, Joseph R.
Stremlau, John J.

Stroud, Joe H.
Sullivan, William H.
Sulzberger, C.L.
Sunderland, Jack B.
Surena, André M.
Surrey, Walter Sterling
Suslow, Leo A.
Sutterlin, James S.
Sutton, Francis X.
Swank, Emory
Swanson, David H.
Swearer, Howard R.
Sweitzer, Brandon W.
Swenson, Eric P.
Swing, John Temple
Swinton, Stanley M.
Symington, W. Stuart
Szanton, Peter L.

T

Taber, George M.
Talbot, Phillips
Talbott, Strobe
Tanham, George K.
Tannenwald, Theodore, Jr.
Tanner, Harold
Tanter, Raymond
Taubman, William
Tavoulareas, William P.
Taylor, Arthur R.
Taylor, George E.
Taylor, Maxwell D.
Taylor, William J., Jr.
Teitelbaum, Michael S.
Tempelsman, Maurice
Tennyson, Leonard B.
Thayer, Robert H.
Theobald, Thomas C.
Thoman, G. Richard
Thomas, Evan
Thomas, Franklin A.
Thomas, Lee B., Jr.

Ward, Martin J.
Warner, Rawleigh, Jr.
Warnke, Paul C.
Washburn, Abbott M.
Watson, Thomas J., Jr.
Watts, Glenn E.
Watts, John H., III
Watts, William
Weaver, George L.P.
Webster, Bethuel M.
Wehrle, Leroy S.
Weidenbaum, Murray L.
Weiksner, George B.
Weinberg, Steven
Weiner, Myron
Welander, Robert O.
Welch, Jasper A., Jr.
Weller, Ralph A.
Wells, Herman B.
Wells, Louis T., Jr.
Wertheim, Mitzi M.
Wessell, Nils Y.
West, J. Robinson
West, Robert LeRoy
Westphal, Albert C.F.
Whalen, Charles W., Jr.
Wharton, Clifton R., Jr.
Wheeler, John K.
Wheeler, John P., III
Wheeler, Richard W.
Whipple, Taggart
Whitaker, Jennifer Seymour
White, Barbara M.
White, Betsy Buttrill
White, Frank X.
White, Robert J.
White, Theodore H.
Whitehead, John C.
Whitehouse, Charles S.
Whiting, Allen S.
Whitman, Marina v. N.
Whitney, John Hay
Whitridge, Arnold

Wickham, John A., Jr.
Wiesner, Jerome B.
Wilbur, Brayton, Jr.
Wilcox, Francis O.
Wilcox, Robert B.
Wildavsky, Aaron
Wilds, Walter W.
Wiley, Richard A.
Wiley, W. Bradford
Wilhelm, Harry E.
Wilkins, Roger W.
Will, George F.
Willes, Mark H.
Willey, Fay
Williams, Franklin Hall
Williams, Haydn
Williams, Joseph H.
Williams, Maurice J.
Willrich, Mason
Wilson, Carroll L.
Wilson, Donald M.
Wilson, John D.
Wimpfheimer, Jacques D.
Winder, R. Bayly
Wingate, Henry S.
Winks, Robin W.
Winslow, Richard S.
Winterer, Philip S.
Wisner, Frank G., II
Witunski, Michael
Wofford, Harris L.
Wohlstetter, Albert
Wohlstetter, Roberta
Wolf, Charles, Jr.
Wolf, Milton
Wolff, Alan Wm.
Wood, Harleston R.
Wood, Richard D.
Woodbridge, Henry S.
Woolf, Harry
Woolsey, R. James
Wortman, Sterling
Wriggins, W. Howard

Appendix C

Members of U.S. Delegation to the San Francisco Conference who were, had been, or would later become members of the Council on Foreign Relations (CFR).

Theodore C. Achilles
James W. Angell
Hamilton Fish Armstrong
Charles E. Bohlen
Isaiah Bowman
Ralph Bunche
John M. Cabot
Mitchell B. Carroll
Andrew W. Cordier
John S. Dickey
John Foster Dulles
James Clement Dunn
Clyde Eagleton
Clark M. Eichelberger
Muir S. Fairchild
Thomas K. Finletter
Artemus Gates
Arthur J. Hepburn
Julius C. Holmes
Philip C. Jessup
Joseph E. Johnson
R. Keith Kane

Foy D. Kohler
John E. Lockwood
Archibald MacLeish
John J. McCloy
Cord Meyer, Jr.
Edward G. Miller, Jr.
Hugh Moore
Leo Pasvolsky
Dewitt C. Poole
William L. Ransom
Nelson A. Rockefeller
James T. Shotwell
Harold E. Stassen
Edward R. Stettinius, Jr.
Adlai E. Stevenson
Arthur Sweetser
James Swihart
Llewellyn E. Thompson
Herman B. Wells
Francis Wilcox
Charles W. Yost

Appendix D

Members of Congress who signed "A Declaration of INTERdependence" (Asterisks indicate those who repudiated their connection with
the Declaration after the list of names was made public):

SENATE

James Abourezk (D.-SD)	Charles Mc. Mathias (R.-MD)
Edward W. Brooke (R.-MA)	Lee Metcalf (D.-MT)
Dick Clark (D.-IA)	Walter F. Mondale (D.-MN)
Alan Cranston (D.-CA)	Gaylord Nelson (D.-WI)
Frank Church (D.-ID)	Robert Packwood (R.-OR)
Jacob K. Javits (R.-NY)	James B. Pearson (R.-KS)
Mike Gravel (D.-AK)	Claiborne Pell (D.-RI)
Philip Hart (D.-MI)	William Proxmire (D.-WI)
Vance Hartke (D.-IN)	Abraham A. Ribicoff (D.-CN)
Mark Hatfield (R.-OR)	Richard S. Schweiker (R.-PA)*
Hubert H. Humphrey (D.-MN)	Hugh D. Scott (R.-PA)
Daniel K. Inouye (D.-HI)	John Sparkman (D.-AL)
Gale W. McGee (D.-WY)	Adlai E. Stevenson, III (D.-IL)
George McGovern (D.-SD)	John V. Tunney (D.-CA)
Thomas J. McIntyre (D.-NH)	Milton R. Young (R.-ND)*
Mike Mansfield (D.-MT)	Harrison A. Williams, Jr. (D.-NJ)

HOUSE OF REPRESENTATIVES

Carl Albert (D.-OK)	Edward G. Biester, Jr. (R.-PA)
Mark Andrews (R.-ND)*	Jonathan B. Bingham (D.-NY)
John B. Anderson (R.-IL)	Edward P. Boland (D.-MA)
Les Aspin (D.-WI)	Richard Bolling (D.-MO)
Herman Badillo (D.-NY)	John Brademas (D.-IN)
William A. Barrett (D.-PA)	George E. Brown, Jr. (D.-CA)
Berkley Bedell (D.-IA)	William M. Brodhead (D.-MI)

Yvonne B. Burke (D.-CA)

Goodloe E. Byron (D.-MD)*

Robert Carr (D.-MI)

Cardiss Collins (D.-IL)

Silvio O. Conte (R.-MA)

John J. Conyers, Jr. (D.-MI)

James C. Corman (D.-CA)

George E. Danielson (D.-CA)

Ronald V. Dellums (D.-CA)

Robert F. Drinan (D.-MA)

Robert B. Duncan (D.-OR)

Robert W. Edgar (D.-PA)

Don Edwards (D.-CA)

Joshua Eilberg (D.-PA)

Millicent H. Fenwick (R.-NJ)

Daniel J. Flood (D.-PA)*

James J. Florio (D.-NJ)

William D. Ford (D.-MI)

Edwin B. Forsythe (R.-NJ)

Donald M. Fraser (D.-MN)

Sam M. Gibbons (D.-FL)

William J. Green (D.-PA)

Gilbert Gude (R.-MD)

Thomas R. Harkin (D.-IA)

Michael Harrington (D.-MA)

Augustus F. Hawkins (D.-CA)

Henry Helstoki (D.-NJ)

Frank Horton (R.-NY)

Robert E. Jones (D.-AL)

Barbara Jordan (D.-TX)

Martha Keys (D.-KS)

Robert Leggett (D.-CA)

Norman F. Lent (R.-NY)

Clarence D. Long (D.-MD)

Torbert H. Macdonald (D.-MA)

Paul N. McCloskey, Jr. (R.-CA)

Matthew F. McHugh (D.-NY)

Spark Matsunaga (D.-HI)

Lloyd Meeds (D.-WA)

Ralph H. Metcalf (D.-IL)

Helen D. Meyner (D.-NJ)

Edward Mezvinsky (D.-IA)

Abner J. Mikva (D.-IL)

Norman Y. Mineta (D.-CA)

Patsy Mink (D.-HI)

William S. Moorhead (D.-PA)

John E. Moss (D.-CA)

Thomas E. Morgan (D.-PA)

John M. Murphy (D.-NY)*

Robert N.C. Nix (D.-PA)

Richard Nolan (D.-MN)

Richard Ottinger (D.-NY)

Claude D. Pepper (D.-FL)

Charles B. Rangel (D.-NY)

Thomas M. Rees (D.-CA)

Henry S. Reuss (D.-WI)

Frederick W. Richmond (D.-NY)

Peter W. Rodino, Jr. (D.-NJ)

Fred B. Rooney (D.-PA)

Charles Rose (D.-NC)*

Edward Roybal (D.-CA)

Leo J. Ryan (D.-CA)

Fernand J. St. Germain (D.-RI)

Herman T. Schneebeli (R.-PA)

Patricia Schroeder (D.-CO)

John F. Seiberling, Jr. (D.-OH)

Paul Simon (D.-IL)

Fortney H. Stark (D.-CA)

Louis Stokes (D.-OH)

James W. Symington (D.-MO)

Frank Thompson, Jr. (D.-NJ)

Paul E. Tsongas (D.-MA)

Morris K. Udall (D.-AZ)

Lionel van Deerlin (D.-CA)

Richard F. Vander Veen (D.-MI)

Charles A. Vanik (D.-OH)

Bob Wilson (R.-CA)*

Clement Zablocki (D.-WI)*

Appendix E

WHAT'S WRONG WITH DEMOCRACY?
(A Clarification)

Here and there throughout this book will be found slighting references to "democracy," as if there were something wrong with the concept of "democracy" as a form of government.

There is.

Fifty years ago the explanation that follows would have been unnecessary, since the organized drive to mislead Americans into believing that the United States is a "democracy" was barely underway. Today, however, a clarification is required lest critics of "democracy" be branded unpatriotic, disloyal, or worse. A few years ago, the leader of a prominent patriotic society accurately described "democracy" as a "deceptive phrase, a weapon of demagoguery, and a perennial fraud."[1] A national magazine subsequently ran a nasty profile which began by urging readers to "Turn the page for the story of the man who believes 'democracy is . . . a fraud.' "[2] The obvious intent was to smear the individual with an implication of disloyalty to our form of government. Yet, our government was never intended by its Founders to be a "democracy."

Democracy is rule by the majority. A republic is rule by law even when that law precludes the majority from having its way. Under a true republic the rights of individuals and minorities are protected against the tyranny of the majority by a written code of laws, often called a Constitution. Thus, our Bill of Rights, when respected, makes it possible for us to worship as we please, or speak as we please, as long as we do not harm or hinder others in exercising the same rights. This is so even if we are the only ones who are practicing a particular faith or expounding a particular point of view; legally, even a majority of the Congress cannot interfere with such rights.

You may recall our earlier reference to Congressman John Rousselot's observation that the best example of "democracy" is a lynch mob, since there is only one man against it. When a dozen riders on horseback capture the suspected cattle rustler, and the "vote" comes out twelve to one against the suspect, the democratic thing to do is hang him then and there. But when the principles of a republic prevail, Marshall Matt Dillon rides up and *lays down the law.* He tells the mob, "You can't hang him unless he's proven guilty after a fair trial." So the suspect is transported to jail, a trial is held before a jury of his peers, and the jury decides the question of his guilt or innocence based on the evidence gleaned from both the defense and the prosecution. In the meantime, the suspect is not to be held for excessive bail or compelled to testify against himself — regardless of what the majority of townsmen might desire.

If the United States was founded as a democracy, then why doesn't that word appear even once in the Declaration of Independence, the Constitution, the Bill of Rights, the Pledge of Allegiance to the Flag, or the Constitutions of any of the fifty states? In contrast, the United States Constitution guarantees each state a *Republican* form of government, and it is to the *Republic* for which our Flag stands that we pledge our allegiance.

In 1928, the U.S. War Department used a training manual for the Armed Forces which included this startling definition of democracy:

> Government of the masses.
> Authority derived through mass meeting or any other form of "direct" expression.
> Results in mobocracy.
> Attitude toward property is communistic — negating property rights.
> Attitude toward law is that the will of the majority shall regulate, whether it be based upon deliberation or governed by passion, prejudice and impulse, without restraint or regard to consequences.[3]

In contrast, that same training manual included the definition of republic found in historian Harry Attwood's book, *Our Republic*:

> A *republic* is a form of government under a constitution which provides for the election of (1) an *executive* and (2) a *legislative* body, who, working together in a representative capacity, have all the power of appointment, all power of legislation, all power to raise revenues and appropriate expenditures, and are required to create (3) a *judiciary* to pass upon the justice and legality of their governmental acts and to recognize (4) certain inherent *individual* rights.
> Take away any one or more of those four elements and you are drifting into autocracy. Add one or more to those four elements and you are drifting into democracy.[4]

The executive, legislative, and judicial branches referred to in the training manual comprise yet another distinguishing characteristic of a true republic: *a system of checks and balances*. If Congress passes a law that is subsequently vetoed by the President, it may then override the President's veto by a two-thirds vote of both Houses; the Supreme Court can strike down the law as unconstitutional; the Congress can impeach and remove from office the Supreme Court Justices or the President; and the President may sign a treaty that the Senate refuses to ratify. This system of checks and balances is an invaluable protection against dictatorship, preventing any one branch of government from obtaining too much power. It is also very *un*democratic!

Former Senator Margaret Chase Smith (R.-Maine) once summarized the crucial differences between a republic and a democracy in these words:

> The basic distinction between democracy and republic is in the degree of majority rule. Majority rule is unrestricted in a democracy while it is restricted in a republic. "The Bill of Rights" part of our Constitution places definite limitations on the power of the representatives of the people. They are denied the power to abridge our freedom of speech, right of assembly, press, trial by jury, against unreasonable searches and seizures, and other individual rights — regardless of how much the majority might be opposed to such individual rights. Under a pure or true democracy, there is no protection of such individual rights against the rule of the majority.
>
> Democracy actually means unrestricted majority rule that our Constitution so carefully prohibits. . . .
>
> A republic is a truly representative government. It provides representation for the minority as well as the majority. It places individual freedom and rights above majority rule. If we were really a political democracy, instead of the republic we are, the will of the majority would habitually ride roughshod over the will of the minority. A republic creates and develops tolerance that acts as a bulwark against tyranny by the majority.[5]

The United States was founded as a republic — not a democracy — for very sound reasons, and our future as a free nation largely depends on the extent to which we can keep it that way.

Footnotes

Foreword

1. Senate Foreign Relations Committee, *The United States And The United Nations* (Hearings), May 7-8, 14-15, 21-22, and June 4, 1975, p. 6 (statement of former UN Ambassador Henry Cabot Lodge, May 7th).
2. Charles Malik, *Man In The Struggle For Peace* (New York: Harper & Row, 1963), p. 97.
3. Speech at Drake University; reprinted, *Congressional Record*, November 24, 1970, p. E9874.
4. *Human Events*, November 27, 1971, p. 2.
5. Cited by Lodge, Senate Foreign Relations Committee, op. cit., p. 6.
6. *Human Events*, January 10, 1976, p. 2.
7. *Salt Lake Tribune*, November 20, 1980, p. 6A.
8. Lodge, op. cit., p. 6.
9. *Parade*, February 9, 1975, p. 4.
10. Charles H. Percy, *The United Nations*, Report to the Senate Foreign Relations Committee, March 14, 1975, p. 23.
11. Senate Foreign Relations Committee, op. cit., p. 299 (May 22nd).
12. *Congressional Record*, November 10, 1975, p. S19520.
13. Address prepared for delivery to the Governor's Conference on the United Nations, Milwaukee, Wisconsin, May 12, 1976; reprinted, *Congressional Record*, June 15, 1976, p. S9325.
14. On July 13, 1978, 82 members of the House of Representatives actually voted to oust Young. On one occasion or another during his career, Young had claimed that U.S. jails hold hundreds of thousands of political prisoners; that Cuban troops brought "stability" to Angola; that former presidents Richard Nixon and Gerald Ford (as well as the Swedes and the British)

were racists; that anti-Communist Rhodesian Prime Minister Ian Smith had massacred missionaries who were actually slaughtered by the Marxist terrorists who eventually succeeded Smith; and that he would probably support the destruction of Western Civilization if he were to become convinced that it would "liberate" the rest of the world. On July 26, 1979, Young met clandestinely with an official of the terrorist Palestine Liberation Organization, later lied to his superiors about what transpired, then resigned on August 15th. The next day he asserted that it would be in "the best interest of our nation" to recognize the Communist Vietnamese government "at once" and lift the trade embargo against Red Cuba "immediately." (See *The Review Of The News*, September 6, 1978, p. 35 and August 29, 1979, p. 3.)
15. *Arizona Republic*, October 9, 1975, p. A-6.
16. Article, *V.F.W. Magazine*, June, 1971; reprinted, *Congressional Record*, June 15, 1971, p. E5901.

Chapter One

1. Cecil V. Crabb, Jr., *American Foreign Policy In The Nuclear Age*, Second Edition (New York: Harper & Row, 1965), p. 394.
2. George Sylvester Viereck, *The Strangest Friendship in History* (New York: Liveright, Inc., 1932), p. 249.
3. *Ibid.*, pp. 53-54
4. Francis X. Gannon, *Biographical Dictionary of the Left* (Boston: Western Islands, 1969), Volume I, p. 54.
5. Alan Stang, *The Actor* (Boston: Western Islands, 1968), p. 19.
6. *Ibid.*
7. Gannon, op. cit., pp. 54-55.
8. *The Federalist Papers*, Essay No. 8

254

The United Nations Conspiracy

(New York: The Modern Library, no date), p. 42.
9. Hamilton Fish Armstrong, *Peace And Counterpeace* (New York: Harper & Row, 1971), p. 565.
10. Phyllis Schlafly and Chester Ward, *Kissinger on the Couch* (New Rochelle, N.Y.: Arlington House, 1975), pp. 150-151.
11. *Ibid.*, p. 151.
12. H.A. Washington (Editor), *The Works of Thomas Jefferson* (Townsend Mac Coun., 1884), Volume 1, p. 130; as quoted in Jerrald L. Newquist (Compiler), *Prophets, Principles and National Survival* (Salt Lake City: Publisher's Press, 1964), p. 145.
13. John W. Davis, *The Council On Foreign Relations: A Record of Twenty-Five Years, 1921-1946* (New York: Council on Foreign Relations, 1947), pp. 15-17.
14. Department of State, *Report to the President on the Results of the San Francisco Conference,* Publication 2349, June 26, 1945, p. 20.
15. *Time*, May 18, 1953.
16. John Foster Dulles, *War or Peace* (New York: The Macmillan Company, 1950), p. 33.
17. Dean Acheson, *Present At The Creation* (New York: W.W. Norton & Company, Inc., 1969), p. 149.
18. Quoted in James F. Byrnes, *Speaking Frankly* (New York: Harper & Brothers Publishers, 1947), p. 41.
19. *Ibid.*
20. *Ibid.*
21. Robert E. Sherwood, *Roosevelt and Hopkins*, Revised Edition (New York: Grosset & Dunlap, 1950), p. 876.
22. John T. Flynn, *The Roosevelt Myth*, Revised Edition (New York: The Devin-Adair Company, 1956), p. 390.
23. Secretary Stettinius's speech was broadcast by the Columbia Broadcasting System network and reprinted, *Department of State Bulletin*, April 8,

1945, and *Congressional Record,* October 21, 1971, p. E11155.

Chapter Two
1. Statement at press conference, UN headquarters in New York, December 21, 1962; reprinted, *Department of State Bulletin*, January 28, 1963, and as Department of State Publication 7505, released March, 1963, p. 5.
2. Leland Goodrich (contributor), *The United Nations; Twenty Years* (New York: The United Nations Association of the United States of America, 1965), p. 77.
3. Dean Acheson, *Present At The Creation* (New York: W.W. Norton & Company, 1969), p. 334.
4. *Washington Daily News*, August 16, 1948, p. 27.
5. Quoted in Francis X. Gannon, *Biographical Dictionary of the Left* (Boston: Western Islands, 1969), Volume I, p. 229.
6. *Ibid.*
7. Acheson, *op. cit.*, pp. 469-470.
8. Alexander Uhl, *The US and the UN: Partners for Peace* (Washington: Public Affairs Institute, 1962), p. 3.
9. United States Committee for the United Nations, *Facts for Fallacies: Answers to Current Questions about the United Nations*, Revised Edition, March, 1963, p. 4.
10. House Committee on Un-American Activities, *Hearings Regarding Communist Espionage in the United States*, 1948, p. 657.
11. *Foreign Affairs*, October, 1950, pp. 76-77.
12. G. Edward Griffin, *The Fearful Master* (Boston: Western Islands, 1964), p. 110.
13. *Ibid.*, p. 111.
14. *LID News Bulletin*, April, 1947, pp. 2-4; as quoted in Philip Crane, *The Democrat's Dilemma* (Chicago: Henry Regnery Company, 1964), p. 352.
15. Trygve Lie, *In The Cause Of Peace*

(New York: The Macmillan Company, 1954), pp. 8, 9.
16. George E. Taylor and Ben Cashman, *The New United Nations: A Reappraisal of United States Policies* (Washington: American Enterprise Institute for Public Policy Research, June, 1965), pp. 57-58; see also: Lie, *op. cit.*, p. 26.
17. *Foreign Affairs*, op. cit., p. 69.
18. *Ibid.*, p. 73.
19. *Ibid.*, pp. 67-68.
20. Lie, *op. cit.*, p. 171.
21. *Ibid.*
22. *Foreign Affairs*, op. cit., p. 77.
23. Taylor and Cashman, *op. cit.*, pp. 57-58.
24. *New York Daily News*, October 14, 1965.
25. *Human Events*, January 22, 1955, p. 1.
26. *New York Times*, December 4, 1972.
27. Norris McWhirter and Ross McWhirter, *Guinnes Book Of World Records* (New York: Sterling Publishing Co., 1976 edition), p. 397.
28. Senate Internal Security Subcommittee, *The Human Cost of Communism in China* (Study), August 12, 1971, p. 16.
29. Griffin, *op. cit.*, p. 114.
30. Taylor and Cashman, *op. cit.*, p. 60.
31. *46 Angry Men* (Belmont, Mass.: American Opinion, 1962).
32. Senate Internal Security Subcommittee, *The Bang-Jensen Case* (Report), September 14, 1961, p. 61.
33. Griffin, *op. cit.*, p. 115.
34. Senate Internal Security Subcommittee, *The Bang-Jensen Case, op. cit.*, p. 61.
35. *Family Weekly*, August 18, 1963, p. 4.
36. Taylor and Cashman, *op. cit.*, p. 65.
37. *Washington Post*, July 28, 1966, p. A21.

38. *Toward Peace and Democracy* (Burmese Ministry of Information, 1949), as quoted in Griffin, *op. cit.*, p. 117.
39. *Washington Post Book World*, May 8, 1966, p. 3.
40. *Washington Post*, December 2, 1966, p. A-1.
41. *Human Events*, March 15, 1969, p. 14.
42. Excerpted, *New York Times*, September 19, 1966; quoted, *The Review of the News*, October 5, 1966, p. 17.
43. *Washington Post*, November 12, 1966.
44. *Ibid.*, April 2, 1967.
45. *Ibid.*, July 31, 1967.
46. *Ibid.*
47. *Salt Lake Tribune*, May 27, 1964, p. 10A.
48. *Los Angeles Times*, April 7, 1970.
49. John Barron, *KGB: The Secret Work of Soviet Secret Agents* (New York: Reader's Digest Press, 1974), p. 19.
50. *Ibid.*
51. *New York Times*, December 22, 1971.
52. *Ibid.*
53. *The Review Of The News*, January 26, 1972, p. 25.
54. Speech reprinted, *Congressional Record*, May 8, 1975, p. S7718.
55. *Vista*, April, 1973, p. 45.
56. *Ibid.*
57. *Ibid.*
58. *Ibid.*, p. 26.
59. Gannon, *op. cit.*, p. 224.
60. *New York Times*, December 22, 1971.
61. *Ibid.*, February 11, 1972.
62. *Ibid.*, (editorial), August 10, 1972.
63. *Peking Review* (published in Red China), January 23, 1976, p. 41.
64. *The Inter Dependent* (successor to *Vista* as official publication of the UNA-USA), April, 1975, p. 5.
65. *Washington Post*, April 5, 1975, p. A5.

66. Press conference at UN headquarters in New York, January 14, 1975, UN press release SG/SM/2139, p. 17.

Chapter Three

1. Department of State, *Report to the President on the Results of the San Francisco Conference*, Publication 2349, June 26, 1945, p. 11.
2. *National Review*, May 4, 1965, p. 355.
3. *Foreign Affairs*, October, 1945, p. 19.
4. *Ibid.*, July, 1955, pp. 463-464.
5. *Ibid.*, p. 464.
6. Charles Malik, *Man In The Struggle For Peace* (New York: Harper & Row, 1963), pp. 124-125.
7. J. Reuben Clark, Jr., unpublished cursory analysis of the UN Charter, pp. 9, 10, 13. (Author has copy.)
8. *Ibid.*, p. 25.
9. Address published as *The United Nations: A Hope or a Menace* (1952), p. 23.
10. Clarence K. Streit, *Freedom Against Itself* (New York: Harper & Brothers, 1954), p. 106.
11. Malik, *op. cit.*, p. 64.
12. *Fortune*, November, 1975; reprinted, *Congressional Record*, November 11, 1975, p. S19708.
13. *Ibid.*
14. Reprinted, *U.S. News & World Report*, August 20, 1962, p. 84.
15. *King Henry IV (Part Two)* by William Shakespeare, in *The Works of William Shakespeare (Complete)* (Roslyn, N.Y.: Black's Readers Service, 1972), p. 524.
16. Leland M. Goodrich and Edvard Hambro, *Charter of the United Nations: Commentary and Documents*, Second and Revised Edition (Boston: World Peace Foundation, 1949), p. 3.
17. Malik, *op. cit.*, p. 66.
18. Lincoln P. Bloomfield, testimony, Subcommittee on International Organizations of the House Committee on International Relations, *The United States In The United Nations*,

February 10-11, 1976, p. 12. Professor Bloomfield's statement was given February 10th.
19. Stuart Chase, *The Road We Are Traveling: 1914-1942* (New York: The Twentieth Century Fund, 1942), p. 25.
20. *Vista*, April, 1973, p. 23.
21. Statement to the Joint Congressional Committee on the Investigation of the Pearl Harbor Attack, March 21, 1946, as quoted in George Morgenstern, *Pearl Harbor* (New York: Devin-Adair Company, 1947), p. 309.
22. *Ibid.*, p. 292.
23. Wendell Willkie, *One World* (New York: Simon and Schuster, 1943), p. 171.
24. Vernon Duckworth-Barker, *Breakthrough to Tomorrow: The Story of International Co-operation for Development Through the United Nations* (United Nations, N.Y.: United Nations Centre for Economic and Social Information, 1970), p. 6.
25. Quoted, *Los Angeles Times*, April 7, 1970.
26. *Foreign Affairs*, September, 1923, p. 48.
27. *Ibid.*, January, 1949, p. 185.
28. Subcommittee on Future Foreign Policy Research and Development of the House International Relations Committee, *Reassessment of U.S. Foreign Policy* (Hearings), July 15, 22-24, 1975, p. 132.
29. *UNESCO Courier*, November, 1970, p. 23.
30. Clark M. Eichelberger, *UN: The First Fifteen Years* (New York: Harper & Brothers, 1960), p. 5.
31. *Washington Star*, October 24, 1975, p. A15.
32. Clark, *op. cit.*, p. 4.
33. *Foreign Affairs*, January, 1957, pp. 185-186.
34. "Introduction to the Report of the Secretary General on the Work of the Organization — August, 1973," reprinted, *Congressional Record*, Sep-

tember 11, 1973, p. S16249.
35. Senate Foreign Relations Committee, *The United States and the United Nations* (Hearings), May 7–8, 14–15, 21–22 and June 4, 1975, p. 129 (May 14th).
36. Senate Foreign Relations Committee, *The Charter of the United Nations* (Hearings), July 9–13, 1945, p. 215 (July 9th).
37. *Intellect*, April, 1975, p. 430.
38. *Ibid.*
39. *Fortune, op. cit.*, p. S19708.
40. Cecil V. Crabb, Jr., *American Foreign Policy In The Nuclear Age*, Second Edition (New York: Harper & Row, 1965), p. 413.
41. G. Edward Griffin, *The Fearful Master* (Boston: Western Islands, 1964), p. 229.
42. Goodrich and Hambro, *op. cit.*, p. 38.
43. *Congressional Record*, June 13, 1974, p. S10543.
44. *Socialist International Information*, November, 1970, as quoted in Rose L. Martin, *The Selling of America* (Santa Monica, Calif.: Fidelis Publishers, 1973), p. 17.
45. *Ibid.*, p. 34.
46. Karl Marx, *Critique of the Gotha Program* (1875), as quoted in John Bartlett, *Familiar Quotations*, Fourteenth Edition (Boston: Little, Brown & Company, 1968), p. 687.
47. *The Federalist Papers* (New York: The Modern Library, no date), Essay Seven, p. 39.
48. Quoted in Department of State, *UNESCO Leaders Speak* (Washington: U.S. Government Printing Office, 1949), p. 4.
49. Malik, *op. cit.*, p. 101.
50. Harlan Cleveland (contributor), *The United Nations: Twenty Years* (New York: The United Nations Association of the United States of America, 1965), p. 144.
51. Senate Foreign Relations Committee, *The United States and the United Nations, op. cit.*, p. 94.
52. *Ibid.*

Chapter 4
1. Department of State, *Report to the President on the Results of the San Francisco Conference*, Publication 2349, June 26, 1945, p. 41.
2. Quoted, *Foreign Affairs*, January, 1954, p. 214.
3. Quoted, "Aggression, According To U.N.," by John F. McManus, syndicated column (pre-publication copy), July 18, 1974.
4. Annex to "Resolution Adopted By The General Assembly [*on the report of the Sixth Committee (A/9890)*] 3314. Definition of Aggression," January 14, 1975, p. 2.
5. *Ibid.*

Chapter 5
1. Department of State, *United States Participation in the United Nations: Report by the President to the Congress for the Year 1951*, Publication Number 4583, released July, 1952, p. 49.
2. Sir Leslie Munro, *United Nations: Hope For A Divided World* (New York: Holt, Rinehart and Winston, 1960), p. 47.
3. Christian Herter, *Toward An Atlantic Community* (New York: Harper & Row, 1963), p. 62.
4. *Congressional Record*, June 30, 1965, p. 14844.
5. Nikita S. Khrushchev, *Khrushchev Remembers* (Boston: Little, Brown & Company, 1970), pp. 367–369.
6. *Ibid.*, p. 370.
7. *Foreign Affairs*, October, 1950, p. 67.
8. *Ibid.*, October, 1951, p. 8.
9. *Ibid.*, April, 1952, p. 351.
10. Department of Defense (Office of Public Information) release Number 465-54, May 15, 1954, p. 1.
11. *Ibid.*

12. *Ibid.*, p. 5.
13. *Ibid.*
14. *Ibid.*
15. Douglas MacArthur, *Reminiscences* (New York: McGraw-Hill Book Company, 1964), p. 365.
16. Harry S Truman, *Memoirs* (Garden City, N.Y.: Doubleday & Company, 1956), Volume II, p. 339.
17. MacArthur, *op. cit.*, p. 331.
18. MacArthur, *op. cit.*, p. 359.
19. Senate Internal Security Subcommittee, *Institute of Pacific Relations* (Hearings), Part 13, April 8, 1952, p. 4537.
20. *Ibid.*, p. 4536.
21. *Ibid.*
22. Senate Internal Security Subcommittee, *Interlocking Subversion in Government Departments* (Hearings), Part 24, September 29, 1954, p. 2032.
23. House Committee on Un-American Activities, *World Communist Movement: Selective Chronology, 1818–1957*, Volume III (1951–1953), p. 670.
24. Mark Clark, *From the Danube to the Yalu* (New York: Harper & Brothers, 1954), p. 11.
25. MacArthur, *op. cit.*, pp. 374-375.
26. *Ibid.*, p. 375.
27. Senate Internal Security Subcommittee, *Interlocking Subversion in Government Departments*, *op. cit.*, p. 2033.
28. *Washington Post*, October 8, 1967, p. A22.
29. Clark, *op. cit.*, p. 1.

Chapter 6

1. UN document A/RES/2024 (XX).
2. UN document S/RES/216 (1965)/ Rev. 1.
3. UN document S/RES/217 (1965).
4. Based on findings of Charles Burton Marshall, Professor of International Politics at Johns Hopkins School of Advanced International Studies, as reported in special supplement edition of *Rhodesian Viewpoint* entered into the *Congressional Record*, March 10, 1970, p. S3311.
5. Representative John Rarick (D.-Louisiana), *Congressional Record*, March 12, 1970, p. H1768.
6. UN document S/RES/232 (1966).
7. Section 8, paragraph 3.
8. *Weekly Compilation of Presidential Documents*, January 9, 1967, pp. 9–10.
9. *Ibid.*, August 5, 1968, pp. 1170–1171.
10. *Private Boycotts Vs. The National Interest*, Department of State Publication 8117, released August, 1966, pp. 18, 19.
11. Testimony before joint hearing of the House Subcommittee on Africa and the Subcommittee on International Organizations and Movements, October 17, 1973; cited, *Congressional Record*, October 18, 1973, p. H9280.
12. Representative Glenard Lipscomb (R.-California), *Congressional Record*, October 17, 1966, p. 26088.
13. *Reader's Digest*, July, 1966, p. 84.
14. *U.S. News & World Report*, March 22, 1971, p. 8.
15. *Congressional Record*, June 14, 1973, p. S11222.
16. *Congressional Record*, December 13, 1973, p. S22834.
17. Colloquy reprinted, *Congressional Record*, March 20, 1974, p. S3983.
18. *Weekly Compilation of Presidential Documents*, March 21, 1977, p. 402.
19. *46 Angry Men* (Belmont, Mass. American Opinion, 1962), pp. 23, 62, etc.

Chapter 7

1. *Congressional Record*, June 23, 1964, p. 14291.
2. Department of State, *You and the United Nations*, Publication Number 5887 (1955), as quoted in Cecil V. Crabb Jr., *American Foreign Policy in the Nuclear Age* (New York: Harper & Row, 1965), p. 416.

3. Quoted, United States Committee for the United Nations, *The United Nations in Action* (folder), August, 1963, p. 4.
4. *U.S. News & World Report*, September 27, 1976, p. 34.
5. Quigg Newton and James B. Pearson, *The U.S. and the U.N.: An Urgent Need for an Increased U.S. Commitment*, Report to the Senate Committee on Foreign Relations, September, 1973, p. 6.
6. Earl Browder, *Victory and After* (New York: International Publishers, 1942), p. 110.
7. Department of State, *Foreign Relations of the United States: The Soviet Union, 1933-1939* (Washington: U.S. Government Printing Office, 1952), p. 227; as quoted in Anthony Kubek, *How The Far East Was Lost* (Chicago: Henry Regnery Company, 1963), p. xiv.
8. Bella V. Dodd, *School of Darkness* (New York: The Devin-Adair Company, 1954), p. 179.
9. *Political Affairs*, April, 1945, pp. 289-300.
10. Francis O. Wilcox, *Congress, the Executive, and Foreign Policy* (New York: Harper & Row, 1971), p. 115.
11. United World Federalists, *No Longer A Dream* (booklet, 1965); excerpted, *Congressional Record*, June 25, 1965, p. 14269.
12. Corliss Lamont, *Soviet Foreign Policy*, Second Edition (New York: Philosophical Library, Inc., 1955), pp. 300-301.
13. Quoted, Department of State, *The Kremlin Speaks*, Publication Number 4264, released October, 1951, p. 35.
14. *Ibid.*
15. Quoted, Richard N. Gardner, *In Pursuit of World Order* (New York: Frederick A. Praeger, 1964), p. 47.
16. *Daily Worker*, December 21, 1954, p. 5.

17. *Constitution of the Communist Party, U.S.A.* (New York: New Century Publishers, April, 1957), pp. 4, 5.
18. Quoted, Gardner, *op. cit.*, p. 60.
19. *People's World* (editorial), October 7, 1961.
20. *The Worker*, January 21, 1962, p. 6.
21. *People's World*, January 23, 1965, p. 7.
22. Moscow radio broadcast, June 27, 1965, as quoted in *Los Angeles Herald American* editorial, July 29, 1965; editorial reprinted, *Congressional Record*, August 4, 1965, p. A4317.
23. *Political Affairs*, April, 1973, p. 39.
24. *U.S. News & World Report*, September 24, 1962, p. 21.
25. *U.S. News & World Report* (interview), November 26, 1954, p. 88.
26. Quoted, Department of State, *United Nations: Guardian of Peace*, Publication Number 7225, released September, 1961, p. 24.
27. United Press International report, *Deseret News* (Salt Lake City, Utah), December 25, 1961.
28. Reprint of speech, B.Y.U. *Speeches of the Year* series, p. 7.
29. *Deseret News*, June 13, 1964, p. A1.
30. *Salt Lake Tribune*, November 8, 1964, p. 12A.
31. *U.S. News & World Report*, December 12, 1952, p. 32.
32. *Washington Post*, November 3, 1971, p. B11.
33. Quoted, John Barron, *KGB: The Secret Work of Soviet Secret Agents* (New York: Reader's Digest Press, 1974), p. 354.
34. *Ibid.*, p. 20.
35. *The Freeman*, March, 1955, p. 340.
36. Trygve Lie, *In The Cause Of Peace* (New York: The Macmillan Company, 1954), p. 45.
37. Louis Dolivet, *The United Nations* (New York: Farrar, Straus and Company, 1946), p. 29.

38. Lie., op. cit., p. 45–46.
39. Ibid., p. 46.

Chapter 8

1. Department of State, United States Participation in the United Nations: Report by the President to the Congress for the Year 1951, Publication Number 4583, released July, 1952, p. iv.
2. U.S. News & World Report (Interview), November 26, 1954, p. 92.
3. Department of State, You and the United Nations, Publication Number 7442, released December, 1962 (revised), pp. 54–55.
4. Charles Malik, Man In The Struggle For Peace (New York: Harper & Row, 1963), p. 78.
5. Robert S. Benjamin, Foreword, The United Nations: Twenty Years (New York: The United Nations Association of the United States of America, 1965), p. 5.
6. Senate Foreign Relations Committee, The United States and the United Nations (Hearings), May 7–8, 14–15, 21–22 and June 4, 1975, p. 59 (May 8th).
7. Foreign Affairs, April, 1961, pp. 403–404.
8. Washington Post, November 26, 1974, p. C7.
9. Henry A. Kissinger, Nuclear Weapons and Foreign Policy (New York: Harper & Brothers, 1957), pp. 332, 333.
10. Ibid., p. 333.
11. Foreign Affairs, April, 1967, p. 431.
12. Foreign Affairs, July, 1949, pp. 622–623.
13. Ibid., p. 621.
14. Ibid., p. 623.
15. Quoted in Nathan H. Mager and Jacques Katel (Editors), Conquest Without War (New York: Pocket Books, Inc., 1961), p. 185.
16. Hugh Gaitskell, The Challenge of Coexistence (Cambridge: Harvard University Press, 1957), p. 29.

17. Clark M. Eichelberger, UN: The First Fifteen Years (New York: Harper & Brothers, 1960), pp. 29–30.
18. Quoted by Francis O. Wilcox (Assistant Secretary of State for International Organization Affairs), speech to the American Association for the United Nations, September 15, 1957; reprinted as Department of State Publication 6553, released November, 1957, pp. 5–6.
19. Foreign Affairs, April, 1967, p. 431. (Article by Professor Hans Morgenthau.)

Chapter 9

1. U.S. News & World Report, November 30, 1964, p. 40.
2. December 22, 1963, p. 2 of printed transcript.
3. Congressional Record, June 23, 1964, p. 14291.
4. Department of State, The United States and the United Nations: Reflections on the 17th General Assembly, Publication Number 7436, released October, 1962, p. 19.
5. Text reprinted, Department of State Bulletin, November 9, 1964, p. 690.
6. Text reprinted, Ibid., pp. 687–688.
7. Ibid., November 16, 1964, p. 699.
8. Washington Post, July 1, 1965, p. F7.
9. Department of State Bulletin, September 13, 1965, pp. 455–456.
10. Washington Star, August 17, 1965; reprinted, Congressional Record, August 17, 1965, p. 19879.
11. Stoessinger, John (contributor), The United Nations: Twenty Years (New York: The United Nations Association of the United States of America, 1963), pp. 80–81.
12. Washington Star, August 17, 1965, p. A7.
13. Washington Post, October 13, 1965, p. A25.
14. Saturday Review World, March

23, 1974; reprinted, *Congressional Record*, April 23, 1974, p. S6096.

Chapter 10

1. Advertising Council, *Challenge to Americans* (booklet), 1962, as quoted in Francis X. Gannon, *Biographical Dictionary of the Left* (Boston: Western Islands, 1971), Volume II, p. 6.
2. Richard E. Stebbins, *The United States in World Affairs, 1949* (New York: Harper & Brothers, 1950), p. 278.
3. Adlai E. Stevenson, statement to press conference, December 21, 1962; reprinted as Department of State Publication 7505, released March, 1973, p. 14.
4. Harry S Truman, quoted in "An Open Letter to the American People," in Emery Reves, *The Anatomy of Peace* (New York: Harper & Brothers, 1945), dust cover.
5. J. William Fulbright (testimony), Senate Foreign Relations Committee, *The United States and the United Nations* (Hearings), May 7-8, 14-15, 21-22 and June 4, 1975, p. 55 (May 8th).
6. Frank E. Holman (article), *The Freeman*, March, 1955, p. 360.
7. *The Federalist Papers* (New York: The Modern Library, no date), Essay Two, pp. 8-9.
8. *Foreign Affairs*, January, 1969, p. 364.
9. *Washington Post*, April 24, 1974, p. A26.
10. Robert A. Taft, *A Foreign Policy For Americans* (New York: Doubleday & Company, 1951), p. 44.
11. Leland M. Goodrich and Edvard Hambro, *Charter of the United Nations* (Boston: World Peace Foundation, 1949), p. 89.
12. *The American Citizens Handbook*, United Nations edition (Washington: National Education Association, 1946), p. 232.

13. Clark M. Eichelberger, *The United Nations Charter: What Was Done At San Francisco*, booklet (New York: American Association for the United Nations, July, 1945), p. 4.
14. Goodrich and Hambro, *op. cit.*, p. 20.
15. Reves, *op. cit.*, p. 285.
16. Alexander Uhl, *The US and The UN: Partners for Peace* (Washington: Public Affairs Institute, 1962), p. 29.
17. Department of Health, Education, and Welfare (Office of Education), *Teaching About the United Nations in the United States: January 1, 1960, through December 31, 1963*, Report of the United States of America to the United Nations Economic and Social Council (OE-14038-63, Bulletin 1964, No. 25), p. 107.
18. Richard N. Gardner, *In Pursuit of World Order* (New York: Frederick A. Praeger, 1964), p. 241.
19. *Weekly Compilation of Presidential Documents*, December 13, 1971, p. 1632.
20. *Ibid.*, December 9, 1974, p. 1521.
21. *Ibid.*, December 12, 1977, p. 1838.
22. Quoted in John Foster Dulles, *War or Peace* (New York: The Macmillan Company, 1950), p. 203.
23. *The Inter Dependent*, July-August, 1975, p. 120.
24. *The Freeman*, December, 1975, p. 721.
25. Goodrich and Hambro, *op. cit.*, p. 97.
26. Edgar Snow, *Stalin Must Have Peace* (New York: Random House, 1947), p. 41.
27. Charles Malik, *Man In The Struggle For Peace* (New York: Harper & Row, 1963), p. 89.
28. *Universal Declaration of Human Rights*, final authorized text, United Nations Office of Public Information, September, 1966, p. 8.
29. United Nations Office of Public Information, Publication Number

OPI/422 — 03306, February, 1973, p. 9.
30. *Ibid.*, p. 11.
31. United Nations Office of Public Information, Publication Number OPI/542 — 75-38308, February, 1975, p. 5.
32. *Ibid.*, p. 6.
33. *Ibid.*, p. 10.
34. Subcommittee on International Organizations of the House Committee on International Relations, *The United States In The United Nations* (Hearings), February 10–11, 1976, p. 39.
35. The Convention as printed in *UN Monthly Chronicle*, January, 1966, p. 7 (reprint).
36. *Foreign Affairs*, April, 1967, p. 423.
37. Text of Convention reprinted, *Congressional Record*, January 28, 1974, pp. S560–561.
38. Testimony reprinted, *Congressional Record*, April 10, 1973, p. S6964.
39. John Barron and Anthony Paul, "Murder of a Gentle Land," *Reader's Digest*, February, 1977, pp. 227ff.
40. *Congressional Record*, May 25, 1970, p. S7732.
41. Dan Smoot, "The Trap," *American Opinion*, March, 1973, p. 33.
42. Petition was photographically reproduced, *Ibid.*, p. 29.
43. Department of State, *United States Participation in the United Nations: Report by the President to the Congress for the year 1951* (Washington: U.S. Government Printing Office, 1952), p. 196.
44. This and subsequent excerpts taken from the Covenant as printed in *UN Monthly Chronicle*, February, 1967, pp. 41–51.
45. *The International "Bill of Human Rights": A Brief History of the International Covenants on Human Rights (and Optional Protocol)*, background paper, United Nations Office of Public Information, June, 1976, pp. 2–3.

46. *Ibid.*, p. 5.
47. The Covenant as printed in *UN Monthly Chronicle*, February, 1967, pp. 58–59.
48. *New York Times*, September 29, 1973.

Chapter 11

1. Senate Foreign Relations Committee, *The Charter of the United Nations* (hearings), Senate Foreign Relations Committee, July 9–13, 1945, p. 533.
2. *Ibid.*, pp. 511, 513.
3. *Ibid.*, p. 520.
4. *Ibid.*, p. 524.
5. *Ibid.*, p. 515.
6. *U.S. News & World Report*, January 19, 1976, p. 25.
7. Senate Foreign Relations Committee, *op. cit.*, p. 613.
8. *Ibid.*
9. *Foreign Affairs*, April, 1952, p. 357.
10. *U.S. News & World Report* (Interview), November 26, 1954, p. 92.
11. *Congressional Record*, June 23, 1964, pp. 14288–14289.
12. Dean Acheson, *Present At The Creation* (New York: W.W. Norton & Company, Inc., 1969), p. 160.
13. Gale McGee (D.-Wyoming) and James B. Pearson (R.-Kansas), *The U.S. And The U.N.: An Urgent Need For An Increased U.S. Commitment*, report to the Senate Committee on Foreign Relations, September, 1973, p. 2.
14. Abraham Yeselson and Anthony Gaglione, "The Use of The United Nations In World Politics," *Intellect Magazine*, April, 1975, p. 430.
15. *New York Times Magazine* (article), January 14, 1962; reprinted, *Congressional Record*, January 16, 1962, p. A203.
16. John Foster Dulles, *War or Peace* (New York: The Macmillan Company, 1950), p. 204.
17. *Foreign Affairs*, April, 1961, p. 393.
18. Clark Eichelberger, *UN: The First*

Footnotes

Fifteen Years (New York: Harper & Brothers, 1960), p. 100.
19. United Nations Office of Public Information, *United Nations General Assembly,* Publication OPI/163-64-03210 (4th Edition), March, 1964, p. 2.
20. Hugh Gaitskell, *The Challenge of Coexistence* (Cambridge: Harvard University Press, 1957), p. 21.
21. Cecil Crabb, *American Foreign Policy In The Nuclear Age,* Second Edition (New York: Harper & Row, 1965), p. 402.
22. *The Inter Dependent,* July-August, 1975, p. 62.
23. Richard N. Gardner, *In Pursuit of World Order* (New York: Frederick A. Praeger, Inc., 1964), p. 9.
24. *Ibid.,* p. 12.

Chapter 12

1. LeLand M. Goodrich, and Edvard Hambro, *Charter of the United Nations: Commentary and Documents* (Boston: World Peace Foundation, 1949), pp. 22 23.
2. James J. Wadsworth, *The Glass House: The United Nations In Action* (New York: Frederick A. Praeger, 1966), p. 123.
3. William Carr, *One World In The Making* (Boston: Ginn and Company, 1946), p. 45.
4. *American Bar Association Journal,* April, 1949 (35 ABAJ 285).
5. Department of State, *Foreign Affairs Policy* (Foreword), Publication Number 3972, released September, 1950.
6. Amelia C. Leiss (Editor), *Apartheid And United Nations Collective Measures: An Analysis* (New York: Carnegie Endowment for International Peace, March, 1965), p. 159.
7. Clarence Manion, *The Conservative American* (New York: The Devin-Adair Company, 1964), p. 145.
8. *Human Events,* September 9, 1972, p. 20.
9. *Salt Lake Tribune,* September 7,

1978, p. A3.
10. Goodrich and Hambro, *op. cit.,* p. 120.
11. Senate Committee on Foreign Relations, *Review of the U.N. Charter — A Collection of Documents,* January 7, 1954, pp. 108-109.
12. G. Edward Griffin, *The Fearful Master* (Boston: Western Islands, 1964), p. 188.
13. *Foreign Affairs,* April, 1974, p. 556 ff.
14. *Foreign Affairs,* July, 1970, p. 676.

Chapter 13

1. Clarence Streit, *Union Now* (short version) (New York: Harper & Brothers, 1940), pp. 182-183.
2. Quoted, *Washington Star-News,* January 6, 1973, p. A5.
3. Willard Clopton, "Washington's Honesty Is Upheld Again," *Washington Post,* September 21, 1965, p. B1.
4. Ronald G. Shafer, "Presidents and Pot, Or Were Washington and Jefferson Stoned?" *Wall Street Journal,* October 20, 1971, p. 1.
5. *National Review,* January 5, 1973, p. 6.
6. Ezra Taft Benson, *Title of Liberty* (Salt Lake City: Deseret Book Company, 1964), p. 201.
7. Renata Adler, "War Movie Arrives at the Warner Theater," *New York Times,* June 20, 1968; reprinted, *Congressional Record,* June 26, 1968, p. S7817.
8. Clive Barnes, "'Hair' — It's Fresh and Frank — Likable Rock Musical Moves to Broadway," *New York Times,* May 1, 1968; reprinted, *Congressional Record,* June 26, 1968, p. S7817.
9. *Republican Congressional Committee Newsletter,* June 15, 1962, p. 2.
10. *Look,* December 1, 1970, p. 19 ff. (article by Leonard A. Stevens).
11. Associated Press dispatch, *Salt Lake Tribune,* August 17, 1977, p. 2A.

12. William F. Buckley, Jr., "Getting Involved Can Be Perplexing," *Washington Evening Star*, June 24, 1970, p. A-18.
13. *Washington Post*, December 17, 1971, p. A32.
14. *Washington Evening Star*, December 29, 1971, p. C3.
15. *Washington Evening Star and Daily News*, January 16, 1973, p. D3.
16. *Washington Post*, January 17, 1973, p. C6.
17. *Life*, September 13, 1968, p. 20.
18. *Senior Scholastic*, October 6, 1969, p. 11.
19. *Saturday Review*, June 25, 1966, pp. 45 ff.
20. *Newsweek*, December 2, 1968, pp. 86, 89.
21. *Reader's Digest*, December, 1968, pp. 179-180 (a condensation of *Life* article, footnote 17 *supra*.
22. *My Weekly Reader*, February 28, 1968, p. 3.
23. *This Week*, February 9, 1969, pp. 2, 14–15.
24. *Scholastic Teacher*, November 22, 1968, p. 7.
25. *Christian Century*, October 23, 1968, pp. 1327–1328.
26. "Walter Cronkite Reporting," September 8, 1972, transcript supplied by CBS.
27. "The World Tonight," September 13, 1972, transcript supplied by CBS.
28. *The Review Of The News*, September 27, 1972, p. 16.
29. Quoted, *The Dan Smoot Report*, September 3, 1962, p. 281.
30. *Ibid.*
31. Resolution (with signatures) photographically reproduced, *Butler County (Ohio) American*, September 21, 1968, p. 4.
32. *Ibid.*
33. Text supplied by World Affairs Council of Philadelphia.
34. Lafayette Day exercises, New York City, September 6, 1918; as quoted in Albert Bushnell Hart and Herbert Ronald Ferleger (Editors), *The Theodore Roosevelt Cyclopedia* (Roosevelt Memorial Association, 1941), p. 415.
35. *Great Ideas Today, 1971* (Chicago: Encyclopedia Britannica, Inc.), p. 85.

Chapter 14

1. Department of State, *Report to the President on the Results of the San Francisco Conference*, Publication 2349, June 26, 1945, p. 18.
2. The statement, which had appeared in the press earlier, was printed on the dust jacket of Emery Reves, *The Anatomy of Peace* (New York: Harper & Brothers, 1945). It was signed by Justice Owen J. Roberts; Senator J.W. Fulbright (D.-Arkansas); Senator Claude Pepper (D.-Florida); Senator Elbert D. Thomas (D.-Utah); Rt. Rev. Henry St. Geo Tucker; Rev. Edward A. Conway, S.J.; Dr. Louis Finkelstein; Mortimer J. Adler; Charles G. Bolte; Gardner Cowles, Jr.; Albert Einstein; Dorothy Canfield Fisher; Albert D. Lasker; Thomas Mann; Lieutenant Cord Meyer, U.S.M.C.R.; Christopher Morley; Carl Van Doren; Mark Van Doren; Walter F. Wanger; and Robert J. Watt.
3. *The United Nations* (booklet), Headline Series No. 59 (New York: Foreign Policy Association, September-October, 1946), pp. 43–44.
4. Dwight D. Eisenhower, *Crusade In Europe* (New York: Doubleday & Company, Inc., 1948), p. 459.
5. Quoted, Department of State, *UNESCO Leaders Speak* (1949), p. 1.
6. John Foster Dulles, *War or Peace* (New York: The Macmillan Company, 1950), p. 40.
7. *Saturday Review*, March 23, 1953.
8. Clark Eichelberger, *U.N.: The First Ten Years* (New York: Harper & Brothers, 1955), p. 89.
9. United States Committee for the

United Nations, *Facts for Fallacies: Answers to Current Questions about the United Nations*, Revised Edition, March, 1963, p. 5.
10. *Great Ideas Today, 1971* (Chicago: Encyclopedia Britannica, Inc.), p. 87.
11. *Ibid.*
12. *Foreign Affairs*, April, 1952, pp. 349–350.

Chapter 15

1. *Fortune*, November, 1975; reprinted, *Congressional Record*, November 11, 1975, p. S19710.
2. Testimony, Subcommittee on Future Foreign Policy Research and Development of the House Committee on International Relations, *Reassessment of U.S. Foreign Policy* (Hearings), July 15, 22–24, 1975, p. 60 (July 22nd).
3. Testimony, Subcommittee on International Organizations of the House Committee on International Relations, *The United States In The United Nations* (Hearings), February 10–11, 1976, pp. 4–5 (February 10th).
4. *New America* (article), November 30, 1974; reprinted, *Congressional Record*, January 27, 1975, p. E184.
5. *Congressional Record*, August 1, 1975, p. S14951.
6. Clarence K. Streit, *Union Now* (short edition) (New York: Harper & Brothers, 1940), p. 93.
7. *Ibid.*, p. 96.
8. Congressional testimony, February 10, 1976. See footnote 3 *supra*, p. 10.
9. *New York Times Magazine* (speech text), May 4, 1975; reprinted, *Congressional Record*, June 9, 1975, p. S10068.
10. *Foreign Affairs*, July, 1953, p. 602.
11. *Yale Review*, Summer, 1957; quoted in *Strengthening Free World Security: NATO And Atlantic Cooperation, The United States And World Government*, Senate Committee on Foreign Relations, July 26, 1960, p. 51.
12. John Pittman, "Arena of Class

Struggle: The United Nations," *Political Affairs* (theoretical journal of the Communist Party, U.S.A.), April, 1973, p. 37.
13. *Washington Post*, November 27, 1976, p. A13.

Chapter 16

1. Quoted in Henry A. Kissinger, *Nuclear Weapons and Foreign Policy* (New York: Harper & Brothers, 1957), p. 337.
2. Quoted, Department of State, *United Nations: Guardian of Peace*, Publication 7225, released September, 1961, p. 20.
3. *U.S. News & World Report*, July 22, 1960, p. 8.
4. *U.S. News & World Report*, December 19, 1960, pp. 16–17.
5. Statement reprinted in Gale McGee (D.-Wyoming) and James Pearson (R.-Kansas), *The U.S. and the U.N.: An Urgent Need for An Increased U.S. Commitment*, report to the Senate Committee on Foreign Relations, September, 1973, p. 27.
6. *Ibid.*, p. 32.
7. *Meet The Press* (NBC radio and television), September 14, 1975, p. 3 of transcript.
8. *Face The Nation* (CBS radio and television), October 26, 1975, p. 14 of transcript.
9. *U.S. News & World Report*, December 1, 1975, p. 10.
10. "Conversations With Eric Sevareid," CBS Television Network broadcast, May 30, 1976, p. 3 of transcript.
11. *Great Ideas Today Yearbook, 1971* (Chicago: Encyclopedia Britannica, Inc.), p. 83.

Chapter 17

1. *U.S. News & World Report*, August 29, 1977, p. 61.
2. United Nations General Assembly, *Introduction to the Report of the Secretary-General on the Work of the Organization* (provisional version), docu-

ment A/8401/Add.l, September 17, 1971, p. 35.

3. *Wall Street Journal,* August 27, 1974; reprinted, *Congressional Record,* September 19, 1974, p. E5897.

4. *Ibid.*

5. Item from the *Richmond News Leader* (date not given), quoted in *Human Events,* February 12, 1972, p. 15.

6. Letter to the author from Louis E. Frechtling, Director of the State Department's Office of International Administration, September 11, 1970.

Chapter 18

1. *Foreign Policy Decision Making: The New Dimensions,* report of a National Policy Panel established by the United Nations Association of the USA in cooperation with the Carnegie Endowment for International Peace, May, 1973, p. 45.

2. "NGO — The Special Ingredient," by Herman W. Steinkraus, President of the United Nations Association of the USA, in *The United Nations: Twenty Years* (New York: The United Nations Association of the USA, 1965), p. 95.

3. *Washington Post,* March 4, 1976, p. D5.

4. *Washington Star,* March 3, 1976, p. A8

5. *Congressional Record,* June 19, 1961, p. 10690.

6. *Congressional Record,* December 27, 1967, p. A6409.

7. Quoted, "UNICEF Official Disguises Facts in Letter to The News," by M. Stanton Evans, Editor, *Indianapolis News,* January 26, 1962. The official referred to in the headline was not Mr. Pate, but rather C. Lloyd Bailey, Executive Director of the U.S. Committee for UNICEF, who had denied in a letter to Mr. Evans that UNICEF money had been used for any purpose other than "to aid needy children and mothers in over 100 countries."

8. *New York Times,* April 16, 1974; reprinted, *Congressional Record,* April 25, 1974, p. E2521.

9. See statement by Martin F. Herz, Deputy Assistant Secretary of State for International Organization Affairs, in *Foreign Assistance and Related Agencies Appropriations for 1974* (hearings), Subcommittee on Foreign Operations and Related Agencies of the House Committee on Appropriations, Part 2, July 12, 1973, p. 1309.

10. *Human Events,* June 7, 1975, p. 9.

11. *Ibid.*

12. *Ibid.*

13. *National Stamp News,* May 20, 1972, pp. 1, 3.

Chapter 19

1. U.S. Committee for UNICEF *Bulletin,* November 5, 1959.

2. *Redbook,* October, 1967, p. 25.

3. *Dennis The Menace Pocket Full Of Fun (Xmas Xtra),* No. 14, published by the Hallden Division of Fawcett Publications Inc., Sparta, Illinois, October, 1972, pp. 32–40.

4. Photocopies of all quoted documents are in the author's files.

Chapter 20

1. Quoted, *Salt Lake Tribune,* April 20, 1963, p. 23.

Chapter 21

1. Trygve Lie, *In The Cause Of Peace* (New York: The Macmillan Company, 1954), pp. 58–59, 60.

2. Leland M. Goodrich and Edvard Hambro, *Charter of the United Nations: Commentary and Documents,* Second and Revised Edition (Boston: World Peace Foundation, 1949), p. 54.

3. *Foreign Affairs,* October, 1950, p. 71.

4. Louis Dolivet, *The United Nations* (New York: Farrar, Straus and Company, 1946), p. 24.

5. Senate Internal Security Subcommittee, *United Nations Headquarters Site Status of Agreement Resolutions*, March 15, 1967.
6. *Ibid.*, p. 14.
7. *Congressional Record*, December 13, 1967, p. S18587.
8. *Congressional Record*, December 11, 1967, p. S18347.

Chapter 22
1. Senate Committee on Foreign Relations, *The Charter of the United Nations*, July 9–13, 1945, pp. 232-233. (Testimony of Dr. Pasvolsky, July 9, 1945.)
2. Department of State, *Report to the President on the Results of the San Francisco Conference*, Publication 2349, June 26, 1945, p. 48.
3. Senate Committee on Foreign Relations, *op. cit.*, p. 234.
4. *Ibid.*, p. 235.
5. *Ibid.*, p. 346. (Testimony of Green H. Hackworth, July 10, 1945.)
6. *List of Treaties and Other International Agreements Between the United States of America and the Union of Soviet Socialist Republics, With Indications of Those Which It Is Considered the Soviet Union Has Violated*, prepared by the Assistant Legal Advisor for Treaty Affairs, Department of State; reprinted, *Congressional Record*, September 24, 1963, p. 16906.

Chapter 23
1. *The Inter Dependent*, June, 1976, p. 2.
2. Quoted in Robert Welch, *The Blue Book of The John Birch Society*, Eighteenth Printing (Boston: Western Islands, 1961), p. 150.
3. Robert White and H.L. Imel, *American Government: Democracy At Work* (New York: D. Van Nostrand Company, Inc., 1961), p. 516.
4. *Human Events*, November 13, 1971, p. 10.
5. *Report Of The Third News Media*

Seminar At The United Nations, sponsored by the Stanley Foundation, December 1–3, 1971; excerpted, *Congressional Record*, July 21, 1972, p. E6971.
6. Quoted, *The Inter Dependent*, July-August, 1975, p. 27.
7. James J. Wadsworth, *The Glass House: The United Nations In Action* (New York: Frederick A. Praeger, 1966), p. 97.
8. *The Inter Dependent*, May, 1976, p. 5.
9. I.P. Tsamerian and S.L. Ronin, *Equality of Rights Between Races and Nationalities in the USSR* (UNESCO, 1962), pp. 11, 12, 13, 37.
10. *The United Nations: Twenty Years* (New York: The United Nations Association of the USA, 1965), p. 106.
11. Quoted by former Senator J.W. Fulbright (D.-Arkansas), testimony, Senate Foreign Relations Committee, May 8, 1975; see *The United States And The United Nations* (hearings), Senate Foreign Relations Committee, May 7-8, 14-15, 21-22 and June 4, 1975, p. 56.
12. Quoted by Brian Urquhart, Under Secretary General of the United Nations for Special Political Affairs, at the first Annual Awards Dinner of The Ralph Bunche Institute, May 22, 1974; see *Congressional Record*, July 11, 1974, p. S12231.
13. *Washington Post*, November 27, 1975, p. K22.
14. *Congressional Record*, July 28, 1945; reprinted, *Congressional Record*, October 18, 1972, p. E8848.
15. *Congressional Record*, October 26, 1971, p. S16764.
16. Transcript (PR 370) supplied by the Bureau of Public Affairs, Office of Media Services, Department of State, p. 8.
17. Letter to Bishop Mandell Creighton, April 5, 1887, as quoted in John Bartlett, *Familiar Quotations* (Emily Morison Beck, Editor), Fourteenth

Edition (Boston: Little, Brown & Company, 1968), p. 750.

18. "The Harbinger" (short story) from *The Voice of the City* in *The Complete Works of O. Henry* (New York: Doubleday & Company, Inc., 1953), Volume II, p. 1277.

Appendix E

1. Robert Welch. *The Blue Book of The John Birch Society* (Boston: Western Islands, 1959), sixteenth printing, p. 153.

2. *Look*, September 26, 1961, p. 23 ff.

3. War Department Training Manual No. 2000-25, November 30, 1928, p. 91.

4. *Ibid.* (with minor typographical errors) and Harry Attwood, *Our Republic* (Massachusetts: Destiny Publishers, 1918), pp. 28-29.

5. Margaret Chase Smith, "Our Republic — Bulwark Against the Tyranny of Majorities," undated statement reprinted as No. 60 in the *Spotlight for the Nation* Series distributed by the Committee for Constitutional Government, Inc., New York City.

Index

Index